BEING MAASAI,
BECOMING INDIGENOUS

BEING MAASAI, BECOMING INDIGENOUS

Postcolonial Politics in a Neoliberal World

DOROTHY L. HODGSON

INDIANA UNIVERSITY PRESS
BLOOMINGTON · INDIANAPOLIS

This book is a publication of

Indiana University Press
601 North Morton Street
Bloomington, Indiana 47404-3797 USA

iupress.indiana.edu

Telephone orders	800-842-6796
Fax orders	812-855-7931
Orders by e-mail	iuporder@indiana.edu

♾ The paper used in this publication meets the
minimum requirements of the American
National Standard for Information Sciences—
Permanence of Paper for Printed Library
Materials, ANSI Z39.48-1992.

Manufactured in the United States of
America

Library of Congress Cataloging-in-
Publication Data

Hodgson, Dorothy Louise.
Being Maasai, becoming indigenous :
postcolonial politics in a neoliberal world /
Dorothy L. Hodgson.
    p. cm.
  Includes bibliographical references and index
  ISBN 978-0-253-35620-8 (cloth : alk.
paper) — ISBN 978-0-253-22305-0 (pbk. :
alk. paper) 1. Maasai (African people)—
Tanzania—Politics and government. 2.
Indigenous peoples—Africa—Politics and
government. 3. Indigenous peoples—
Tanzania—Politics and government. 4.
Identity politics—Africa. 5. Identity
politics—Tanzania. 6. Non-governmental
organizations—Political aspects—Africa. 7.
Non-governmental organizations—Political
aspects—Tanzania. 8. Africa—Social
conditions—1960- 9. Tanzania—Social
conditions—1964- 10. Neoliberalism—
Africa—Social aspects. 11. Neoliberalism—
Tanzania—Social aspects. I. Title.
  DT443.3.M37H628 2011
  323.1196'5—dc22
                      2010047854

1 2 3 4 5 16 15 14 13 12 11

In memory and celebration of my son
Tobias "Toby" Lund Schroeder
2001–2005

Contents

Preface

Toward the end of 1987, as I was preparing to leave Tanzania after three years of working in community development for the local Catholic Diocese (now Archdiocese) of Arusha, I was invited to lunch by Lepilall ole Molloimet. At the time, Lepilall was in his second five-year term as the member of Parliament for Monduli District, one of the so-called pastoralist districts comprised of predominantly (but not exclusively) Maasai people. I was completing my second year as coordinator of the Arusha Diocesan Development Office (ADDO), the organization responsible for coordinating and implementing community development and food relief efforts for the local Catholic Diocese of Arusha. We used participatory problem-posing methods to encourage dialogue, critical awareness, and self-defined development among communities. Since the boundaries of the Diocese of Arusha encompassed the entire former "Masai District" (which was initially the "Masai Reserve"), much if not most of our outreach, education, and development work occurred with Maasai. I had therefore come to know Lepilall through our work in Monduli District, as we asked for (and received) his constant help in navigating the bureaucratic thickets of the Tanzanian government and one-party state for permissions, delivery of materials and supplies, secondment of personnel, and more.

We met in the lush garden of the Equator Hotel, a formerly glamorous hotel in the center of downtown Arusha that was somewhat rundown by 1987. Over a lunch of grilled goat meat and beer, Lepilall discussed his dream:

> I want to start an NGO [nongovernmental organization] that is run by Maasai to serve Maasai people and interests. We have been well served by ADDO, and we have learned a great deal about how to do development. We very much respect the work that you have done. But it is now time that Maasai take responsibility for themselves. Several of us been talking about forming our own NGO and we would like your help. Could you perhaps review our constitution

and funding proposals, and help us raise money from donors? We'd like for you to serve as an informal advisor of sorts as we get ourselves started.[1]

After a lengthy conversation, I agreed to help. In the end, however, they asked me to do very little, since I soon returned to the United States and it was still difficult to communicate between Tanzania and the United States at the time.

By the time I returned to Tanzania in 1991 to begin two years of research on gender and social change among Maasai for my dissertation, several NGOs had been started by Maasai, and more were being organized every day. I knew most of the organizers and leaders from my three years of work with ADDO (before I became coordinator, I spent a year as the women's development fieldworker and project proposal writer) and three years in residence (including one year of part-time teaching) at Oldonyo Sambu Junior Seminary, one of the few institutions at the time to offer a secondary-school education to Maasai boys. The leaders of these fledgling NGOs—my friends, former colleagues, and students—invited me to attend various workshops and meetings, to review constitutions and funding proposals, and to introduce them to my donor contacts. My ability to help was severely limited by the logistics and demands of my research, which required prolonged periods in remote areas, but I did what I could during my almost weekly overnight visits to Arusha for supplies, hot showers, and clean water.

I followed the progress and rapid proliferation of these NGOs during subsequent research trips, and included a brief discussion of their emergence in my first book, *Once Intrepid Warriors* (Hodgson 2001a). By the summer of 2000, however, the trickle had become a flood: I counted more than one hundred NGOs and CBOs (community-based organizations) that had been started by Maasai and other pastoralists in northern Tanzania. Many had organized themselves by positioning themselves as "indigenous people," in order, in part, to engage with the increasingly powerful international indigenous rights movement. By most measures, they had achieved tremendous success, attracting millions of dollars from international donors and becoming prominent actors at the United Nations and other international fora.

But my participation in a major workshop in June 2000 to discuss the future of PINGOs Forum, the "umbrella group" that was supposed to help nur-

1. This is a paraphrase of our conversation, based on notes that I wrote that evening.

ture and coordinate these NGOs and CBOs, suggested that all was not well; their work was marred by jealousy, competition, allegations of corruption, frustration, discrimination, financial mismanagement, and mistrust. Despite, or perhaps because of, their success at gaining international visibility and recognition for their struggles, their relations with the Tanzanian government seemed increasingly hostile. I began to wonder about the potential and pitfalls of these organizations, their social dynamics, and the structural tensions evident in their relationships with donors, the Tanzanian government, their constituencies, and themselves. Most importantly, I was curious as to whether, and if so how, these organizations had contributed to the ongoing struggles of Maasai men and women for political recognition, economic resources, and social and cultural rights that I had analyzed for the colonial and early postcolonial period. And so the idea for this book was born.

By the time I returned to Tanzania in July 2005 for a year of research on the NGOs and CBOs, the terms of engagement had changed significantly. Most of these organizations, especially the two umbrella organizations, had consciously repositioned themselves in three ways: from basing their political claims on discourses of indigeneity to discourses of livelihoods; from engaging in international advocacy to national advocacy; and from calling themselves NGOs and CBOs to civil society organizations (CSOs). How and why Maasai activists positioned and then repositioned themselves in these ways to pursue their interlocked struggles for representation, recognition, resources, and rights is the historical and ethnographic subject of this book. But although the focus is on the case of Maasai, the themes explored in this book—of the possibilities for political action in a world shaped so powerfully by the legacies of colonialism and the contemporary realities of neoliberal social, political, and economic policies—reflect broader trends and tensions in the Global South.

As always, my debts are huge and my thanks enormous to the many people and organizations who have supported my research and writing. I am deeply grateful to the numerous Maasai activists, leaders, and community members who have shared their lives, experiences, and perspectives with me over the past twenty-five years. Since our days working together at ADDO, Alais ole Morindat has been a stalwart friend, an inspiring leader, and a key interlocutor. He has influenced the direction and conclusions of this study in ways he might not even realize. The leaders of the three key main organizations that I was affiliated with, Moses Sangale (TAPHGO), Edward Porokwa (PINGOs Forum), and Ndinini Kimesera Sikar (MWEDO), and their staffs welcomed and facilitated my constant presence in their offices, workshops, and meetings. Perhaps one of the greatest pleasures in conducting research for this project was my reunion with many of my former students from Oldonyo Sambu, who now lead and work for the NGOs. They include Francis ole Ikayo, the late Rafael Mako, William ole Seki, William ole Nasha, and Edward Porokwa. I am grateful to these and other Maasai activists and leaders, including Naomi Kipuri, Benedict Nangoro, Saruni Ndelelya, Maanda Ngoitiko, the late Saruni ole Ngulay, Esupat Ngulupa, Lazaro Moringe Parkipuny, Loserian Sangale, and Peter Toima, for their willingness to include me in their critical reflections and debates and to provide me with copies of relevant documents. My research in Tanzania and at the United Nations also benefited from the advice and insights of Eamon Brehony, Ced Hesse, Jens Dahl, Rie Odgaard, Michael Odhiambo, Liz Singleton, Andrew Williams, and the libraries and archives of the Tanzania Natural Resources Forum, Sand County Foundation, and MS Training Center for Development Cooperation.

Many other friends in Tanzania provided friendship, emotional sustenance, laughter, good food, warm hospitality, and logistical support for me and my family, especially during our year of research in Tanzania in 2005–2006. My gratitude, love, and thanks to Jo Driessen and Judith Jackson, Linda and Mark Jacobson, Leo Fortes, Marjorie Mbilinyi, Trish McCauley and Kees Terhell, Saning'o Milliary, Pat Patten, Robin and Thad Peterson, Daudi and Trude Peterson, Lisa and Mike Peterson, Trish McCauley, Fini and Paul Strebel, and Barbara and Rod Stutzman.

Initial research for this project in the winter of 1996–97 and the summer of 2000 was funded by a Richard Carley Hunt Postdoctoral Fellowship from the Wenner-Gren Foundation, an Anne U. White Award from the Association of American Geographers (in collaboration with Richard Schroeder), and a Faculty Research Grant from the Research Council of Rutgers University. Early drafts of several sections of the book (in the form of two articles in *American Anthropologist*) were completed while I was a Fellow at the Center for Advanced Study in the Behavioral Sciences in 2001–2002, supported by Grant #29800639 from the Andrew W. Mellon Foundation and a Competitive Fellowship Leave from Rutgers University. I developed many of my early ideas through vibrant interdisciplinary weekly seminars as a Faculty Fellow at the Institute for Research on Women (2002–2003, on the theme of

"Reconfiguring Gender and Class: Identities, Rights and Social Movements," led by Dorothy Sue Cobble) and the Center for Critical Analysis of Contemporary Culture (2003–2004, on the theme of "Citizenship," led by Linda Bosniak) at Rutgers. In 2005–2006, I returned with my family for a year of research in Tanzania with the support of a John Simon Guggenheim Memorial Foundation Fellowship, a Fulbright-Hays Faculty Research Abroad Award, and an American Council of Learned Societies Faculty Fellowship. A National Endowment for the Humanities Fellowship and Competitive Fellowship Leave award from Rutgers enabled me to spend 2006–2007 analyzing my data and writing several chapters of this book. I am indebted to the Tanzanian Commission for Science and Technology for permission to undertake this research, and to Professor Simeon Mesaki for serving as my local research contact. I benefited from research assistance in Tanzania by Morani Poyoni, Esupat Ngulupa, and Moses Lengaa, and at Rutgers from Belinda Blinkoff and Lana Sacks.

Tania Li, Ronald Niezen, Elliot Fratkin, and two anonymous reviewers for the press read and commented on the entire manuscript. I am especially grateful to them for their thoughtful suggestions, as well as to the numerous colleagues and friends who read parts of the manuscript as either book chapters or articles or just listened to and commented on my ideas. They include Laura Ahearn, Misty Bastian, Charles Briggs, Vigdis Broch-Due, Manuela Carneiro da Cunha, Barbara Cooper, Clifton Crais, Jens Dahl, Ben Gardner, Laurie Graham, Daniel Goldstein, Cindi Katz, Temma Kaplan, Bruce Knauft, Cory Kratz, Tania Li, Fran Mascia-Lees, Adeline Masquelier, Andrea Muehlbach, Rod Neumann, Glenn Penny, Joanne Rappaport, Sidsel Saugestad, Rick Schroeder, Pamela Scully, Judy Walkowitz, Brad Weiss, Pnina Werbner, and Dick Werbner. Sections of the book were presented in talks at Yale University, Emory University, the University of Notre Dame, Columbia University, Princeton University, University of Dar es Salaam, Rutgers University, Hamilton College, Florida International University, George Washington University, University of Chicago/Northwestern University, Brigham Young University, Clark University, University of Washington, University of California-Berkeley, and the University of California-Davis; conferences hosted by the University of Bergen, University of Minnesota, Stockholm University, Tallinn University, University of Iowa, University of Michigan, University of Texas-Austin; and meetings of the Berkshire Conference on the History of Women, the New York Area History Workshop, the American Anthropological Association, the African Studies Association, and the Symposium on Contemporary Perspectives in Anthropology. I am grateful to participants at all of these venues for their comments, questions, and critiques as well as to colleagues, staff, and students in the Department of Anthropology, the Institute for Research on Women, and the Center for African Studies for their intellectual engagements, logistical support, and collegial interactions.

As with most academics, the solitary focus of research and writing is possible for me only with the emotional and social sustenance of my friends and family. During the long course of this project, I relied on them even more than usual when my youngest son, Toby, died suddenly of severe bacterial pneumonia on December 3, 2005, in Tanzania at the age of four and three-quarters (as he would have calculated his age). My husband, Rick, our son Luke, and I were quickly wrapped in the love and strength of friends, family, colleagues, and even strangers in Tanzania, the United States, and elsewhere as we faced the sudden, tragic loss of Toby. Many have already been named, and in the blur of the time I am sure I have forgotten some—but special thanks to Marjorie Mbilinyi, Pat Patten, Robin Peterson, Thad Peterson, Christy Clark, Fini Strebel, Rod Stutzman, and Barbara Stutzman in Tanzania; Laura Ahearn, Barbara Cooper, Seth Kaper-Dale, Cindi Katz, Marc Manganaro, Kevin St. James, and the staff of the RLDCC in the United States. I am grateful to the "Tri-wenches" for keeping my body going when my spirit was down, and to the friendship, good humor, and wise counsel of Laura Ahearn, Rick Black, Ethel Brooks, Gerri Callahan, Barbara Cooper, Becca Etz, Janet Finn, Daniel Goldstein, Temma Kaplan, Cindi Katz, Patricia Kuhn, Fran Mascia-Lees, Sheryl McCurdy, Donna Nolan, Liz Roberts, Pam Scully, Anne Sherber, Barbara Stutzman, Debbie Sussman, and Scott Sussman.

My extended family, especially my parents Sigrid and Hutch, have always given me that rarest of gifts—unconditional love. My brother Ed's honesty, warmth, and irreverent sense of humor have buoyed my spirits and kept me laughing, as have the delightful personalities and antics of my nieces and nephews. I have shared a life of love, scholarship, politics, and now sadness with my husband, Rick. His feminist convictions to be a fully engaged parent and partner have never been mere rhetoric; instead, they are realized on a daily basis in the often overwhelming juggling of domestic duties, parenting commitments, and academic careers. Thank you. And Luke—our remarkable son who amazes us every day with his resilience, empathy, brilliance, kindness, musical talent, humor, and athletic abilities—you are the sunshine of our days.

This book is dedicated to the memory of our other son, Tobias ("Toby") Lund Schroeder, who will always be remembered for his fierce love, his fearless curiosity, his goofy sense of humor, and his much-coveted "Toby hugs."

I am grateful to the following publishers for permission to publish selections, usually revised, from the following: "Cosmopolitics, Neoliberalism, and the State: The Indigenous Rights Movement in Africa," in *Anthropology and the New Cosmopolitanism: Rooted, Feminist and Vernacular Perspectives*, ed. Pnina Werbner (Association for Social Anthropology Monographs, Oxford: Berg, 2008), 215–30, with the permission of the Association for Social Anthropology; "Becoming Indigenous in Africa," *African Studies Review* 52, no. 3 (2009): 1–32, with the permission of the African Studies Association; "Introduction: Comparative Perspectives on the Indigenous Rights Movement in Africa and the Americas," *American Anthropologist* 104, no. 4 (2002): 1037–49, and "Precarious Alliances: The Cultural Politics and Structural Predicaments of the Indigenous Rights Movement in Tanzania," *American Anthropologist* 104, no. 4 (2002): 1086–97, with the permission of the American Anthropological Association; and "Critical Interventions: Dilemmas of Accountability in Contemporary Ethnographic Research," *Identities* 6, nos. 2/3 (1999): 201–24, with the permission of Taylor & Francis.

Key Organizations and Documents

Maasai and Pastoralist NGOs/CBOs/CSOs

BULGADA	Barabaig for "dry lands"
CORDS	Community Research and Development Services
CRT	Ujamaa Community Resource Trust
Ilaramatak Lolkonorei	Orkonerei Integrated Pastoralist Survival Programme
Inyuat e Maa	Maa Pastoralists Development Organization, Maa Advancement Association
Inyuat e Moipo	Moipo Integrated People's Organization
KIDO	Kisongo Integrated Development Organization
KINNAPA	Kimana, Ndaleta, Namelok and Partimbo Association
KIPOC	Korongoro Integrated People Oriented to Conservation
KIPOC—Barabaig	Barabaig branch of KIPOC
LADO	Loliondo Area Development Organization
LCDO	Longido Community Development Organization
LOSADEI	Loliondo and Sale Development Initiatives
MAA	Maasai Advancement Association
MINGO	Maa Indigenous Non-Governmental Organization
MWEDO	Maasai Women Development Organization

NGOPADEO	Ngorongoro Pastoralist Development Organization
NGOEPO	Ngorongoro Environmental Peoples Organization
NHPO	Ngorongoro Highlands Pastoralist Organisation
NIA	Ngorongoro Indigenous Association
OSEREMI	Oloirien Secondary Education Route and Eradication of Maasai Illiteracy
PANET	Pastoralist Network of Tanzania
PINGOs Forum	Pastoralists Indigenous Non-Governmental Organization
PWC	Pastoralist Women's Council
TAPHGO	Tanzania Pastoralists and Hunter Gatherers Organization

Other Organizations

AC Working Group	African Commission Working Group on Indigenous Populations/Communities
ADDO	Arusha Diocesan Development Office
African Caucus	informal caucus of African delegates that meets regularly at the UN
African Commission	African Commission on Human and Peoples' Rights
African Union	established in 1999 by leaders of African states to replace the Organization of African Unity
AIWO	African Indigenous Women's Organization
AWF	African Wildlife Foundation
DANIDA	Danish International Development Agency (Denmark)
ECOSOC	UN Economic and Social Council
FTPP	Forest, Trees and People Programme
HIVOS	Humanist Institute for Development Cooperation (The Netherlands)
IFAD	International Fund for Agricultural Development
IIED	International Institute for Environment and Development (U.K.)
ILO	International Labour Organization

Indigenous Caucus	informal caucus of indigenous peoples that meets regularly at the UN
IPACC	Indigenous Peoples of Africa Coordinating Committee
IUCN	International Union for the Conservation of Nature
IWGIA	International Work Group on Indigenous Affairs (Denmark)
NORAD	Norwegian Agency for Development (Norway)
OIPA	Organization for Indigenous Peoples of Africa
SIDA	Swedish International Development Agency
TAMUT	an Amazigh NGO (Morocco)
UN HRC	UN Human Rights Council
UN Permanent Forum	UN Permanent Forum on Indigenous Issues
UN Working Group	UN Working Group in Indigenous Populations
USAID	United States Agency for International Development

Documents

African Charter on Human and People's Rights (ratified by the African Union in 1987)

Arusha Resolutions (adopted in 1999 by delegates to the Conference on Indigenous Peoples in Eastern, Central, and Southern Africa)

Declaration on the Rights of Indigenous Peoples (adopted by the UN General Assembly in 2007)

The Indigenous and Tribal Peoples Convention 169 (adopted by ILO in 1989 to replace earlier 1957 Convention)

Miscellaneous Abbreviations

GRO	grassroots organization
MDGs	Millennium Development Goals
MP	member of Parliament
NCAA	Ngorongoro Conservation Area Authority
NGO	nongovernmental organization
PRS	poverty reduction strategy
SAP	structural adjustment policy

BEING MAASAI,
BECOMING INDIGENOUS

INTRODUCTION

Positionings—The Cultural Politics of Representation,
Recognition, Resources, and Rights

Long-marginalized peoples in Africa and elsewhere today confront a radically restructured political field with new opportunities and constraints for political action. Decades after independence and the end of apartheid, most postcolonial states have now withdrawn from their exuberant developmentalist aspirations, coaxed and coerced by the demands of international capital, the United States and its allies, and multinational financial institutions such as the World Bank to reduce funding for social services, privatize formerly state-controlled functions and industries, establish strict private-property regimes, and ensure "free" markets and "free" trade for multinational corporations. Ideologies of *ujamaa* (familyhood), economic nationalism, protectionism, communal patrimony, and collective well-being have been replaced by the neoliberal ideal of the entrepreneurial individual who has internalized the values of profit maximization, self-motivation, and desire for self-advancement and whose personal ambition and accumulation is enabled by a minimalist state, myriad economic "opportunities," and porous national borders.[1] According to John Gledhill (2004:342), "the deep logic of neoliberalization [is] the transformation of life itself into a marketable commodity and the imperative for us all to market ourselves." As a result of the pervasiveness of this "neoliberal governmentality" (Ferguson and Gupta 2002), political and economic oppression often seem more diffuse and dispersed, a confusing and constantly changing constellation of actors, institutions, and practices. In response, there has been a renewed flourishing of "civil society," as disenfranchised peoples have joined together to protest the increased economic stratification, resource alienation, and social upheaval that have resulted from the imposition of neoliberal political-economic regimes. Many of these civil society organizations have challenged state claims of "vertical encompassment" (Ferguson and Gupta 2002) by joining transnational networks and movements and seeking justice from international institutions such as the United Nations.

The current historical conjuncture poses an array of theoretical challenges: Do states matter anymore, or, following scholars such as Arjun Appadurai (1996), is it more appropriate to characterize the world as composed of free-flowing transnational processes and "scapes" (mediascapes, technoscapes, and so forth) in which the influence of the state is declining if not defunct? Should we celebrate the emancipatory possibilities of transnational activism and advocacy, or does it have limits? How do activists and civil society organizations navigate the twisted terrain of community-state-transnational relations to demand recognition, rights, and resources? Most fundamentally, what are the possibilities for effective political action in a world shaped by the legacies of colonialism and the contemporary policies and practices of neoliberalism?

One important transnational movement that has emerged over the past few decades as a powerful site of political protest and mobilization for historically marginalized groups is the indigenous peoples' movement. Indigenous activists and organizations have a long history in the Americas (Gray 1997; Ramos 1998; Warren 1998; Warren and Jackson 2002, Jackson and Warren 2005, de la Peña 2005), Australia (Povinelli 1993, 2002; Merlan 2005), New Zealand, and other former settler colonies where their status as "first peoples"—in the face of conquest, imperialism, colonialism, and capitalism—is generally uncontested. For years, indigenous inhabitants in these regions participated in various collective actions to redress past wrongs and to protect and promote present and future rights. In recent decades, however, these scattered disenfranchised groups have recognized the similarities in their historical experiences and structural positions within their respective nation-states and coalesced into a broad-based, transnational social movement.[2] As a result, they have reframed formerly "domestic" disputes into international claims for recognition and rights and transformed the status of indigenous peoples from peripheral minority groups with little political recognition or power vis-à-vis their nation-states to transnational activists with formidable international lobbies and leverage. Like the formation of transnational campaigns for environmental protections, human rights, women's rights, and so forth,[3] the formation of a viable, visible, and effective indigenous rights movement has been facilitated by an array of "transnational connections" (Hannerz 1996): the increased (although still uneven) access to and affordability of the Internet and other communication and transportation technologies; the transnational production, consumption, and circulation of popular media images; and, especially, the exchange of ideas, experiences, and strategies afforded by international meetings and networks.[4]

In Africa, by contrast, where the term "indigenous" was adopted more recently as a tool for social and political mobilization, the contemporary lack of a dominant colonial population converged with long histories of conquest, assimilation, migration, and movement to make the criteria for claiming indigeneity far murkier. Nonetheless, as a result of the expanding presence and resonance of this movement in Africa (and Asia), many anthropologists, including myself, watched the people with whom we worked for years reframe their long-term collective identities based on criteria such as ethnicity or livelihood to embrace a new identity as "indigenous" (e.g., Brosius 1999c; Hodgson 2001a; Jackson 1991, 1995, 1999; Li 2000; Turner 1991).[5] Given the challenges of being recognized as "indigenous" by African nation-states, how and why did certain historically marginalized people in Africa decided to become "indigenous"? What was the appeal to African activists of linking their agendas and organizations to the transnational networks and discourses of indigenous rights? What strategies, arguments, and alliances did they use to articulate and advance their claims? How did these claims to indigenous identity, in both concept and practice, play out in the context of economic liberalization, transnational capitalism, political democratization, and renewed donor investments and interest in the development of "civil society"? What were the achievements, challenges, and costs of using the category of indigenous as a platform for localized economic and political action? Although the concept entails a particular cultural and ethnic politics, what kinds of gender and class politics has it not only entailed but produced? How and why have the spatial, social, cultural, and political dynamics of the movement changed over time? Finally, how did the involvement of African activists reshape the practices and politics of the transnational indigenous rights movement?

This book addresses these questions through an ethnohistorical case study of the historical and contemporary dynamics of the involvement with and eventual disengagement from the indigenous rights movement by Maasai from Tanzania. The book first examines the emergence and embrace of transnational advocacy, in the form of the indigenous rights movement, by African activists, especially Maasai activists, in the 1990s. It analyzes the complex, overlapping politics of representation involved as some Maasai, through the creation of nongovernmental organizations (NGOs), positioned themselves to engage with transnational networks, international donors, and multinational organizations such as the United Nations to seek recognition and rights from the Tanzanian nation-state. It traces the history of the emergence of the term "indigenous" in Maasai discourses; the ways the concept was imagined, understood, and used by Maasai activists, communities, donors, and states; and the opportunities and obstacles it posed for their ongoing struggles for recognition, resources, and rights. The book then explores the recent shift, in the 2000s, by Maasai activists from discourses of indigeneity to discourses of livelihoods, from international to national advocacy, and from calling themselves NGOs to civil society organizations (CSOs).

This book proposes and elaborates the concept of "positionings" to explore the dynamic contours and content of postcolonial political struggle in a neoliberal world. Through my analysis of the political positionings and repositionings of Maasai activists and organizations, I seek to inform, challenge, and complicate ongoing theoretical and political debates about the contours of political agency, the struggles of civil society and transnational social movements, the experience of neoliberalism, and the enduring political salience of the state. In contrast to Appadurai and others, I argue that we must take seriously the mediating role of the state in shaping political positionings and possibilities for civil society to engage with transnational advocacy networks and movements. This is especially true now, at the height of the neoliberal "reforms" advocated by multilateral lending institutions and international capital, which cannot circumvent states but must be implemented through them—in the revision of state laws, policies, procedures, and priorities. The ability of nongovernmental organizations and civil society organizations to position themselves to obtain international recognition and support for their demands has become both increasingly possible and problematic as states in Africa, as elsewhere, have been radically transformed by neoliberal political, economic, and social policies. The continuing power of states to influence the content and form of civil society politics exposes the "structural predicaments" produced by the convergence of neoliberalism and identity politics and thus some of the limits of transnational advocacy.

Positionings

So what do I mean by "positionings," and why do I find it an analytically useful concept? A number of anthropologists have explored the complex cultural politics of identity, images, and representation involved when groups intentionally manipulate, project, and homogenize their public images and identities to accord with "Western" stereotypes in order to seek recognition and demand rights as "indigenous" peoples (Conklin 1997; Conklin and Graham 1995; Turner 1991).[6] Some scholars, drawing on the "invention of tradition" literature (Hobsbawm and Ranger 1983), have debated the usefulness of such concepts as "authenticity" to characterize or condemn these indigenous strategies of representation.[7] Others have explored the tensions between scholarly and political uses of essentialism and social constructions in such strategies (Bowen 2000; Field 1999; Jackson 1999). Much of the debate has been passionate and even contentious as, to paraphrase Jean Jackson (1989), anthropologists have struggled over whether there is a way to talk about making culture without making enemies. Recent work on representation, however, has moved beyond debates about authenticity, essentialism, and social constructionism to examine the historical, social, political, and economic contexts shaping how and why certain groups decide to project and promote particular images of themselves as, for example, indigenous, environmentalist, or feminist.[8]

In a 2000 article, Canadian anthropologist Tania Li drew on and elaborated Stuart Hall's concepts of "articulation" and "positioning" to analyze indigenous politics in Indonesia. As she wrote:

> A group's self-identification as tribal or indigenous is not natural or inevitable, but neither is it simply invented, adopted or imposed. It is rather a *positioning* which draws upon historically sedimented practices, landscapes and repertoires of meaning, and emerges through particular patterns of engagement and struggle. The conjunctures at which (some) people come to identify themselves as indigenous, realigning the ways they connect to the nation, the government and their own, unique tribal place, are the contingent products of agency and the cultural and political work of articulation. (Li 2000:151)

Moreover, this positioning takes place within complex, potent, shifting fields of power, including not just the nation-state, but international NGOs, the United Nations, and transnational advocacy networks. As such, a historical understanding of how such representations and positionings have been constrained and enabled by colonial legacies, capitalist incursions, "development" interventions, and other modernist discourses, practices, and institutions is crucial.

Such representations, or positionings, are central to seeking and gaining political recognition by their respective nation-states as "indigenous peoples" (cf. Taylor 1994; Povinelli 2002). As Li (2001a:652), invoking Johannes Fabian, elaborates, recognition is at once an "act of cognition," an "act of memory," and an "act of acknowledgement." Demanding such recognition involves learning the relevant legal and bureaucratic categories and processes, lobbying at various levels and sites of government, appealing to the popular media, seeking international support, and molding their images, identities, and agendas accordingly: "Those who demand that their rights be acknowledged must fill the places of recognition that others provide, using dominant languages and demanding a voice in bureaucratic and other power-saturated encounters, even as they seek to stretch, reshape, or even invert the meanings implied" (Li 2001a:653). The politics of recognition is closely tied to the politics of political representation,

> of who represents and speaks for whom, in particular how far minorities are entitled to be represented by themselves. . . . [R]ecognition and representation go hand in hand; claims and struggles over one carry forward with those of the other; and both effect and are effected, in turn, by the most familiar politics of all, the redistributive politics of who gets what benefits and resources from whom, and perhaps most importantly in . . . democracies . . . from the agencies of the state. (Werbner 2002:119)

Of course the paradox is that indigenous groups must demand recognition from the very nation-states that have historically treated them as second-class citizens (if citizens at all) by ignoring their rights, exploiting their resources, and disparaging their cultures and identities (cf. Li 2001a:653; Ramos 1998; Saugestad 2001; Solway 2002).

But gaining such recognition is the first step toward demanding rights and protecting resources. A key impetus for the emergence of indigenous activism on its current scale has been, as in the Maasai case, the sustained threats to indigenous land, territories, and resources by colonial and postcolonial state interventions, capitalist industry, and other incursions. The brutal and sometimes quite violent abuse of the rights of indigenous peoples by corrupt and greedy states and industry is well documented—Ken Saro-Wiwa, Shell Oil, and the Ogoni conflict in Nigeria serving perhaps as just one ghastly reminder (see, e.g., Watts 2000). But the overlap between indigenous rights and environmental agendas has been complex and contradictory.[9] Indigenous peoples have often suffered greatly *because* of certain environmental interventions in the name of conservation and tourism: they have been forcibly relocated to make room for game parks and buffer zones, prohibited from accessing and using customary resources to protect forest reserves, and so forth (Zerner 2000; Hodgson 2001a; Brockington 2002; West et al. 2006). Nonetheless, in recent years some Western environmentalists (and some indigenous activists) have linked issues of biological diversity to cultural diversity and promoted particular images of indigenous peoples, practices, and knowledge to justify and publicize their campaigns (see, e.g., Brosius 1997a, 1997b; Conklin 1997, 2002; Conklin and Graham 1995; Dove 2006). In effect, the relationship between culture and nature has been inverted as representations of indigenous peoples have been transformed from being the "destroyers" of nature to the "protectors" of biodiversity and practitioners of environmental "sustainability." The resulting alliances between some indigenous groups and certain environmental organizations (who, of course, are quite diverse in their agendas, strategies, and goals) have ranged from mutually beneficial to patronizing, debilitating, and tense (cf. Turner 1999).

Finally, many indigenous groups are demanding rights that extend beyond their territorial resources. These demands hinge on the right to self-determination and include the right to determine their own development and to control and protect their cultural knowledge and performances, material remains, languages, indigenous knowledge, and biogenetic material. Development, as much recent scholarship makes clear, is an ambiguous term used to justify an array of interventions and agendas (Hodgson 2001a; Escobar 1995; Ferguson 1990). Indigenous peoples often hold alternative ideas about their "development," visions of progress and prosperity that may clash with the dominant modernization and economic productivity paradigms of most nation-states and international donors.[10] Moreover, the pursuit of their ideals and goals is predicated not just on protecting their territories and resource base, but on controlling the education and socialization of their children, improving their health and social welfare, ensuring the continuity of their languages, and protecting and maintaining their cultural knowledge and institutions. The issue of legal protection of and economic compensation for the collection, appropriation, or use of their intellectual property—whether cultural knowledge, material remains, or biogenetic resources—is the subject of lively and contentious international debate.[11] The emergence of transnational indigenous rights coalitions and networks has enabled indigenous peoples to better assert and lobby for their own interests and demands in these deliberations.

Of course, state institutions, transnational organizations, and NGOs engage in positionings as well. During the past few decades, there have been radical changes in the priorities and practices of multilateral institutions and other development donors. As part of the neoliberal "reforms" of the 1990s, most shifted resources away from nation-states in favor of "local" NGOs and community-based organizations that were presumed to be more effective in reaching the "grassroots" (Bebbington and Riddell 1997; Edwards and Hulme 1992, 1995; Fowler 1995). States were accused of being corrupt, bloated, inefficient, and ineffective service providers, unwilling (and, perhaps, structurally unable) to listen to and engage the diverse concerns of their citizens. In contrast, "grassroots" NGOs were lauded as the "magic bullet" (Edwards and Hulme 1995), an alternative "bottom-up" model of development capable of mobilizing and empowering local people to improve their lives.

Moreover, NGOs aligned with the indigenous rights movement in Africa and elsewhere seem to have captivated the special attention of donors, whether because of the historical guilt of some donors over their country's colonial history; the exotic, if temporary, media appeal of indigenous activists; or the complex and contradictory overlap of indigenous rights and environmental agendas. Whatever their allure, the tremendous expansion of donor resources channeled to NGOs, especially those identified with indigenous causes, in the interests of "strengthening civil society" facilitated the growth of the movement, but also increased its dependence on donor aid and, thus, vulnerability to donor demands and agendas (Bratton 1989; Comaroff and Comaroff 1999). But by the late 2000s, as part of a realignment of donor-state relations, there seemed to be a trend toward channeling donor funds away from NGOs to "basket-funds" to be controlled and redistributed to state and non-state development organizations by the state.

The concept of positionings therefore encompasses and signals the interlocking struggles over representation, recognition, resources, and rights that are central to any form of political action, especially in the "postcolony." As Achille Mbembe observes,

> The postcolony is made up not of one coherent "public space," nor is it determined by any single organizing principle. It is rather a plurality of "spheres" and arenas, each having its own separate logic yet nonetheless liable to be entangled with other logics when operating in certain specific contexts: hence the postcolonial "subject" has had to learn to continuously bargain [*marchander*] and improvise. Faced with this . . . the postcolonial "subject" mobilizes not just a single "identity," but several fluid identities which, by their very nature, must be constantly "revised" in order to achieve maximum instrumentality and efficacy as and when required. (Mbembe 1992a; cited in Werbner 1996:1)

Positionings, therefore, incorporate and index agency, structure, meaning, and power; they demonstrate the articulation of political economy and cultural domains of meaning, signification, and representation. Positionings are thus, by definition, inherently relational. Individuals and groups position themselves for and against certain ideas, issues, institutions, and identities. As a result, any one positioning has consequences for other relationships, for other positionings, often at distinct political scales. As such, I think that the plural form, "positionings," in contrast to Li and Hall's singular "positioning," suggests more clearly the multiple, at times possibly contradictory, and always dynamic and shifting possibilities and locations.

Politics in Postcolonial Africa

In Africa, the possibilities for and obstacles to the realization of such political positionings and repositionings for marginalized groups such as Maasai depend, in part, on the historical legacies of colonialism. Despite centuries of political formations and formulations prior to contact, the key terms of political struggle in contemporary Africa are deeply colonial products: *the state* as the dominant organizing principle for governance, law, economics, and social welfare; *the nation* as a modernist ideal embraced and pursued by postcolonial African leaders; *citizenship* as the privileged mode of belonging; *ethnicity* as a primary form of collective identification and mobilization; *property* as the legally sanctioned framework through which to understand, access, and use resources such as land; *development* (and, by implication, *productivity* and *profit*) as the self-legitimating goal of African leaders; and *modernity* as the aspiration of both leaders and people. Of course, given the startling diversity of the continent—in terms of environments, peoples, histories, resources, beliefs, livelihoods, languages, and colonial and postcolonial experiences—the manifestations, meanings, and effects of these legacies are various, complex, and contingent.

Recent work on the contours and content of politics in present-day Africa has illuminated the power, processes, and problems of these legacies. The most relevant studies for my arguments and analysis take a historical perspective to understanding the continuities (and differences) between colonial and postcolonial political forms and struggles, or explore ethnographically the everyday realities of life, especially political life, in postcolonial Africa. In other words, those scholars interested in *process*, or "how the trajectories of a colonizing Europe and a colonized Africa and Asia shaped each other over time" (Cooper 2005:3–4), and *practice,* or how these processes shaped and were shaped by the actions, meanings, imaginations, and relationships of people "on the ground." Key works include explorations of the cultural politics of identity formation and expression, especially the tensions between ethnic, national, and other forms of belonging (e.g. Mamdani 1996; Werbner and Ranger 1996; Englund and Nyamnjoh 2004; Englund 2006); the sometimes fraught and always incomplete efforts at nation building through the implementation of language policies, development of national symbols, revision of school curricula, and production of popular culture (e.g. Askew 2002; Coe 2005; Simpson 2008); the historical precedents, inherent power dynamics, and enduring ambivalence of "development" projects and programs (e.g., Ferguson 1990; Schroeder 1999; Hodgson 2001a) and "expectations of modernity" (e.g., Ferguson 1999; Comaroff and Comaroff 1993; Hodgson 2001b); the impact of new economic regimes of privatization, commoditization, consumption, and productivity (e.g., Burke 1996; Weiss 2003); the possibilities and perils of civil society (e.g., Comaroff and Comaroff 1999); and the shifting ideas, practices, and relationships of gender, generation, and class that shape and are shaped by these changes (e.g., Hodgson 2001a, 2005; Lindsay and Miescher 2003).

With the imposition of neoliberal regimes, African states have been variously characterized as corrupt, inefficient, or ineffective, caught between the demands of the World Bank, the International Monetary Fund, and powerful states such as the United States for the decentralization of state power to localities, privatization of state services and resources, and retrenchment of personnel in the name of "efficiency" and "good governance"; the insistence of international capital for open access to strategic resources such as oil, land, and coltan; and the needs of their citizens for health, education, political freedom, and economic security. James Ferguson has called the current power of the World Bank and IMF in shaping the governance of African states "scientific capitalism," which refers to the dominance of economic and technical assertions and justifications for policy imperatives that mask moral and political concerns (Ferguson 2006:78). One consequence of the willful refusal of these international financial organizations (and their sponsoring states) to consider the moral and political implications of these policies, especially the sometimes brutal actions of their African political allies, is that some African political leaders have used their positions as gatekeepers to appropriate (or "eat") the national patrimony in the form of profits from mineral sales, bribes to conduct business, and so forth, a situation that Jean-François Bayart (1993) aptly termed "the politics of the belly." Achille Mbembe, one of the most provocative theorists of "the African postcolony," has referred to the excesses and greed of these leaders and the state institutions they have created to serve their own interests as "the banality of power" (Mbembe 1992b, 2001; see also Mbembe 1992a). Although Tanzania, as discussed in chapter 2, is certainly not as notorious as states such as Congo or Zimbabwe for the brutality and corruption of its rule or rulers, the alignment of capital and the state in the quest for privatization, productivity, and profit has produced documented instances of corruption, greed, and violence.

One response to this seemingly impossible situation has been what Arundhati Roy (2004), among others, has called the "NGO-ization" of politics and resistance. For reasons discussed above, the spread of neoliberal economic, political, and social policies throughout Africa and the rest of the Global South was accompanied by the rapid proliferation of NGOs. The NGO, as an institutional form, became not only the dominant structure for the design and implementation of development projects, but also, in many places, the key structure for the mobilization and expression of political advocacy and activism. Thus, as in the case of the international indigenous rights movement, NGOs have increasingly become the "building blocks" of many social movements, the expected formation through which to organize and engage in local, national, and transnational advocacy.[12] After initial enthusiasm by donors and activists over the political potential of NGOs, growing numbers of scholars such as Roy have become increasingly pessimistic about not just the possibilities for NGOs to "do good" (Fisher 1997), but their impact on political change. Roy, among others, argues that most (but not all) NGOs "defuse political anger" rather than helping people channel their sense of oppression into collective actions for social change:

> Eventually—on a smaller scale, but more insidiously—the capital available to NGOs plays the same role in alternative politics as the speculative capital that flows in and out of the economies of poor countries. It begins to dictate the agenda. It turns confrontation into negotiation. It depoliticizes resistance. It interferes with local peoples' movements that have traditionally been self-reliant. NGOs have funds that can employ local people who might otherwise be activists in resistance movements, but now can feel they are doing some immediate, creative good (and earning a living while they're at it). . . . The NGO-ization of politics threatens to turn resistance into a well-mannered, reasonable, salaried, 9-to-5 job. With a few perks thrown in. (Roy 2004:45–46)

But as William Fisher noted over ten years ago, the literature on NGOs "is based more on faith than fact": "There are relatively few detailed studies of what is happening in particular places or within specific organizations, few analyses of the impact of NGO practices on relations of power among individuals, communities and the state, and little attention to the discourse within which NGOs are presented as the solution to problems of welfare service delivery, development, and democratization" (Fisher 1997:441). Although there have been a spate of thoughtful ethnographic studies of NGOs in Africa (and elsewhere) since Fisher's assertion,[13] many scholars still analyze NGOs in the abstract, either romanticizing them as a universal panacea to impoverishment and oppression or, more commonly now, demonizing their leaders as pawns of international donor agendas (e.g., Kuper 2003), unreflective opportunists (e.g., Igoe 2006), and even the "new compradors" (Hearn 2007).[14]

In contrast to the current sport of "NGO-bashing," (Lister 2004:1, cited in Hearn 2007:1097), I offer a more nuanced analysis that explores (rather than assumes) their motivations, imaginings, and reflections in order to understand how the dynamics of agency, structure, and power at once enable and limit their political agency in a world shaped ever more forcefully by "neoliberal governmentality" (Mbembe 2001; Ferguson and Gupta 2002; Solway 2002; Gupta and Sharma 2006; Hodgson and Brooks 2007; Yarrow 2008). Moreover, rather than provide a comprehensive ethnographic study of just one NGO, I analyze the broader NGO landscape in northern Tanzania, situating detailed analyses of specific NGOs and activists in terms of their relations to each other, the communities they represent, state institutions, and transnational organizations. Finally, I do so historically, in order to trace the factors behind the emergence of NGOs, the dynamics of their successes and failures, and the shifting meanings, intentions, perspectives, and practices of individuals and institutions as they position and reposition themselves in the face of changing opportunities, challenges, and experiences.

Modes of Anthropological Engagement

A related question is the positioning or positionings of anthropology and anthropologists to such topics, as many of us increasingly engage issues and domains once left to political scientists, economists, and other social scientists who claim to study the "big picture." Like Bruce Knauft, Anna Tsing, Sally

Engle Merry, and others, I have been contemplating the possibilities, contributions, and challenges for doing an "ethnography of the global," an "anthropology in the middle" that tries to map and understand the connections, "frictions," and "awkward encounters" between the so-called local and global, and in so doing, provides alternative perspectives, explanations, and even theories about the content, form, and nature of these processes, encounters, and articulations. I also join other anthropologists, such as Veena Das (Das and Poole 2004) and Akhil Gupta (1998; see also Gupta and Sharma 2006), who are trying to understand states in terms of how they have changed (rather than assuming they have just "declined"), as well as how to study them ethnographically.

But the engagement of anthropologists with these movements raises not just theoretical questions, but political, ethical, and methodological questions about our own positionings as well—are we academics, advocates, and/or activists? Ethnography may provide important insights into indigenous movements, but what does it mean to study, much less critique, such avowedly political movements? Are we accountable in distinct ways to the people we study and with whom we work because of their "indigenous" status or because they participate in such movements? What is the relationship among analysis, activism, and advocacy?

Not surprisingly, there is little agreement among anthropologists about the answers to these questions. Most would agree, however, that in the current postcolonial era, anthropologists are (or should be) "hyperconscious [about their] strategies of research, writing and activism" (Field 1999:198). Much has already been written about the politics of anthropological research in a postcolonial world,[15] the politics of ethnographic authority and representation in our writing,[16] and the well-documented complicity of anthropological findings, concepts, and theories with imperial and colonial projects of conquest, rule, and regulation.[17] Thus, the recognition of expanded indigenous rights in the UN Declaration on the Rights of Indigenous Peoples and expectations of protection and accountability in the revised anthropological Code of Ethics (American Anthropological Association 2009) underscore the already established need for self-conscious political, ethical, and methodological reflection on what we study, how we study it, and how we publish and disseminate our findings in all fields of anthropology, not just the sociocultural field. What some may have once considered mundane research activities—talking to people, collecting botanical samples, and so forth—have become highly politicized in the present context.

Nonetheless, as Peter Brosius argued in a special issue of *Identities* (1999d), anthropologists who study environmental, indigenous, or other "emancipatory" social movements occupy a distinctly "precarious position":

> The danger exists that our accounts and critiques may be appropriated by the opponents of these movements and deployed against them. In a world of online library databases and internet search engines, where text and images can be instantly circulated and received across global information networks, there is no longer any such thing as a distanced academic critique safely ensconced in an obscure academic journal. We are now participants—mostly uninvited—in the production of identities, or in the legitimation of identities being produced by others. To the degree that these movements represent an attempt to create new meanings and identities—which in turn have the potential to produce new configurations of power—such a role cannot remain unacknowledged. (1999b:180–81)

In other words, given the centrality of particular claims about culture and history to assertions of indigenous identity, how do the proponents and opponents of indigenous movements use the theories and findings of anthropology to assert or contest certain claims? Such concerns are directly linked to the kinds of ethnographic accounts produced by anthropologists, the "intimate inside portraits [that] reveal the inner working of such movements—their strategies, disagreements, uncertainties, perceived strengths, and weaknesses, all the things that comprise their hidden transcripts" (Brosius 1999c:370). As a result, some anthropologists are wary of critiquing, however constructively, the ideas, practices, and agendas of these movements for fear of undermining their political support and agendas. For example, few anthropologists have been willing to investigate the social inequalities, such as gender discrimination, that have been masked or even reinforced by certain forms of indigenous activism (but cf. Hodgson 1999d; Muratorio 1998; Stephen 1997, 2005). Indigenous women themselves, however, have begun to challenge such "strategic silences" about their marginalization within the movement (see, e.g., Vinding 1998; Stephen 1997; Van Achterberg 1998; Speed et al. 2006).

There are, therefore, a range of overlapping positions, from advocacy and collaboration, to dialogue and discussion, to scholarly detachment. Some anthropologists, such as the late David Maybury-Lewis, have been relentless advocates for indigenous rights, working through nonprofit organizations such as Cultural Survival, IWGIA, and Survival International to facilitate and finance indigenous networking and advocacy. Others, such as

Les Field, argue for a position that combines scholarship and collaboration. Field describes himself as "an academic who works within the metropolitan academy as a theorist critical of conventional and particularly colonial-derived categories and also collaborates with an indigenous community and its intellectuals in their various projects, attempting to negotiate and reconcile these very different kinds of work" (Field 1999:195).

In contrast, I characterize my position as an "interlocutor" rather than "collaborator," that is, as a scholar who shares her ideas and work with Maasai activists and organizations in ongoing, constructive, and, perhaps, even occasionally contentious dialogues and debates in an effort to inform and shape their policies and practices, without directly aligning myself with one group or faction of the movement (cf. Jackson 1999). Like Gupta and Ferguson (1997a:30), I see our "political task not as 'sharing' knowledge with those who lack it but as forging links between different knowledges that are possible from different locations and tracing lines of possible alliance and common purpose between them." As such, our "interlocutors" may be many and varied, including not just indigenous activists but the constituencies, institutions, organizations, and people with which we, and they, engage and interact. During the course of this project, for example, I continually shared my ideas, perspectives, and critiques, as well as copies of my published and unpublished work, with the leaders and members of all of the organizations that I worked with and studied. Moreover, at the end of my research year, I organized a workshop for the leaders of the umbrella organizations and a few other NGOs in which I presented my preliminary conclusions and critiques as both an effort at transparency and a catalyst for their own reflection on their political and personal projects and practices.

A few anthropologists caution even more distance, given the implication of anthropological ideas of "culture" and "indigenous" in promoting, through reterritorialization efforts, not just "hierarchies of belonging" but also ethnic cleansing:

> Ethnic cleansing describes the process through which people who consider themselves indigenous or (ab)original violently reclaim territories taken from them by people they consider outsiders. Ethnic cleansing disrupts the prominent image of indigenous people as victims of violence perpetrated by vicious regimes, corporation, or settlers intent on grabbing their land. It forces academics and activists who have analyzed and, indeed, promoted "resistance" and "empowerment" by indigenous people to confront the violently embodied

outcomes which can ensue, even while they hold the hope of peaceful resolution. (Li 2002:361)

Other positions exist as well that complicate any easy divide between scholarly and political, or even indigenous and academic, engagement (cf. Field
1999). Nevertheless, all anthropologists who study indigenous movements
confront the tensions between political and scholarly uses of essentialist and
constructivist concepts of identity (Albert 1997). We are also likely to shift
positions in our careers as a result of changing political, personal, or intellectual concerns and dynamics (e.g., Ramos 1998).

All of these positions engage in varying ways the question of "how community diversity complicates anthropological collaborations" (Sturm
1999:206). Whatever their need to project and promote essentialist images of
themselves, indigenous peoples, like peoples everywhere, are differentiated
by gender, generation, education, religion, class, and a variety of other factors. These social differences may also reflect political differences in approach and strategy to the question of indigenous identities and rights and
may even be institutionalized in competing political factions, parties, or
organizations. The question, therefore, is whose interests do we choose to
represent? With which faction or organization do we choose to collaborate?
To whom are we accountable? As I have argued elsewhere,

> an ethical and political stance that holds that we are equally accountable to all
> people masks the sometimes quite stark differences in economic, political and
> cultural power that exist among these peoples. In my case, to speak of equal
> accountability to "all people," serves, like the category "indigenous," to obscure
> the relationship of power between Maasai men and women, other Tanzanian
> people, the international NGOs, and myself. (Hodgson 1999d:213)

In some cases, there seem to be clear divisions not only within and among
indigenous groups but also between the leaders and their supposed constituencies (Jackson 1999; Li 2001b).

There are no easy answers to any of these questions. As the contributors
to Brosius (1999d), among others, make clear, these are questions that each
of us must ask ourselves and answer in the context of our specific research
situations. In my case, my long personal history of relationships with Maasai
men and women, many of whom are now the leaders of the NGOs that are
the subject of this study, has provided me unique access and insight, but also
has made me very cautious and reflexive about such ethical and political is-

sues as naming, confidentiality, and the potential consequences of my talks and publications.[18] To minimize risks, however unforeseeable, to the people and organizations I worked with and studied, I have therefore adopted a fairly conservative and protective approach by limiting naming of any kind. I do name major pastoralist organizations and prominent activists and political leaders who are easily identifiable and whose documents, publications, or activities I relied on to construct a history of the movement. But I mask the identification of activists, community members, and organizations (including those named elsewhere) when citing interview excerpts or comments that could be interpreted as critiquing the government, donor organizations, or specific individuals and organizations. I believe that the practice of "delinking" names from critiques allowed me to present crucial evidence to support my arguments while protecting my "sources" from the risk of retribution and me from accusations of betrayal. Moreover, I hope that the time lag between my active research and the publication of this book will further limit any unwelcome repercussions for the activists and organizations who agreed to participate in my study.

Nodal Ethnography

Finally, how does one conduct an ethnography of positionings? How to conduct research on such a widespread, multi-sited, and ever-changing phenomenon as the shifting relations among NGOs, the state, donors, constituencies, and transnational social movements? In some ways, I have been studying the movement all along, through my long-term, longitudinal research on and with Maasai since 1985, as a participant-observer, interlocutor, former teacher, development worker, and friend. All of my research to date had been "multi-sited," most of it based on a comparative study of three Maasai communities with different histories of development, missionary evangelization, and so forth. But multi-sited research seemed an insufficient design for this project, as it presumed the existence of distinct geographic "sites" and did not specify the connections among those "sites." My colleague at Rutgers, Louisa Schein, has proposed the phrase "itinerant ethnography" (Schein 2000:26) to capture the roving and fortuitous nature of her research on the cultural politics of gender, ethnicity, and nationalism among Hmong/ Miao in China and the United States, but this also seemed inadequate, given the assumption that most of the research was impromptu and unplanned. I have come, instead, to describe my research methodology as what I call "nodal ethnography."

Initially, my research focused on the "major nodes"—the key players and the key sites. After almost fifteen years of following the work of several Maasai NGOs on an ad hoc basis as part of other research projects, I spent over a year (July 2005 to June 2006, and October 2006) in Tanzania researching and working primarily with three organizations. Two of these, Pastoralist Indigenous Non-Governmental Organization Forum (PINGOs Forum, or just PINGOs) and Tanzania Pastoralists and Hunter Gatherers Organization (TAPHGO), were the "umbrella groups" or coordinating councils set up to advise, assist, and coordinate advocacy for their member organizations—Maasai and non-Maasai nongovernmental organizations (NGOs) and community-based organizations (CBOs). PINGOs and TAPHGO were "key players" in that they interacted with and brought together representatives from their membership organizations on a regular basis and served as primary "gatekeepers" with donors, transnational advocacy organizations, and, often, the national-level institutions of the Tanzanian state (such as Parliament, the ministries, and the Office of the Prime Minister). The third organization, Maasai Women's Development Organization (MWEDO), was one of only two NGOs created to address the concerns of Maasai women, and thus an interesting comparative case through which to understand the gendered politics of the "NGO-ization" of development, advocacy, and indigenous rights. With their agreement, I circulated on a regular basis among the head offices of each organization (all of which were located in Arusha, a large regional town in northern Tanzania), interviewing and chatting with the staff and leaders, reading files and documents, participating in meetings and workshops, accompanying them on community visits, and tracking their activities. My questions probed their personal background; the history of their involvement with NGOs; the history, objectives, structure, achievements, and challenges of their NGO; their perspectives on cultural, social, and economic change; their development priorities; their relationship with the Tanzania government, donors, advocacy groups, and international institutions such as the UN; and their opinions of the costs and benefits of using "indigenous rights" as a political platform. In exchange for their time and assistance, I read and edited English-language project proposals, project reports, newsletters, Web sites, and other materials. I also, when asked, provided advice and ideas about proposed projects and feedback on workshop sessions. Finally, I met regularly with the leaders of the organizations to share, as an "interlocutor," my insights, questions, and critiques about their work from my ongoing research, prompting dialogue, debate, and sometimes disagreement.

In addition to these NGO offices, the other major nodes/key sites of my research were the annual meetings of the UN Permanent Forum on Indigenous Issues in New York (which I attended in 2003, 2004, 2005, 2007, 2008, and 2009) and the UN Working Group on Indigenous Populations in Geneva (2004) and the workshops sponsored by the umbrella groups. At the UN meetings, I observed and participated in formal sessions, informal caucus meetings, social events, and other activities in order to study how the Maasai delegations (and other African delegations) acted, interacted, and represented themselves and their key issues with donors and other activists in these different venues. I was especially attentive to dynamics of gender, age, ethnicity, language, and class. I also interviewed Maasai delegates, other African delegates, and donor representatives informally and more formally (using a semi-structured interview format) to investigate their agendas, perspectives, experiences, backgrounds, and assumptions. These interviews and conversations were conducted in Swahili, English, French, and Maa, depending on the context and participants, and all translations to English in the book are my own.

I applied a similar research strategy to the umbrella-group workshops, which brought together dozens of representatives from pastoralist and hunter-gatherer NGOs and CBOs from throughout northern Tanzania and so were a major node of interaction and insight. Thus, in addition to observing and participating in the formal sessions of the workshops (as part of the regular round of preliminary introductions, I always introduced myself to all of the workshop participants as a researcher studying the organizations) and the informal conversations at breaks and meals, I conducted opportunistic interviews and conversations with representatives about their own organizations, as well as their perspectives on and experiences of the umbrella organizations, the idea of indigenous peoples, the current situation of their constituencies, the policies and practices of the Tanzanian government, relationships with donors, and more. Throughout, in order to ensure breadth and depth of perspectives, I spoke to men and women, elite and non-elite, Maasai and non-Maasai, and representatives of organizations from different geographical areas. Most of these interviews were in Swahili, although a few were in English or Maa.

I then traced the links—of funding, ideas, people, affiliations, and so forth—of these major nodes—the key actors and sites—with more "minor nodes": the other groups, institutions, people, places, and so forth. I selected certain minor nodes for more in-depth ethnographic study (participant observation, interviews, document reviews, project visits). One set of minor nodes was the array of Maasai NGOs and CBOs—from well-established organizations to foundlings—working in all of the pastoralist districts. Where possible, I visited their offices and projects, interviewed leaders and staff, studied their documents, spoke to community members they claimed to represent, and traced the history of their activities. A second set of minor nodes was the representatives of donor and advocacy groups who supported and worked with the Maasai NGOs. As opportunities presented themselves (such as donor visits, regional workshops, and the UN meetings), I interviewed these representatives about their background, the history and objectives of their organization, the details of their involvement with Maasai NGOs, and their perspectives on the future of Maasai and the indigenous rights movement. In addition, I studied relevant documents, Web sites, and reports to trace their interactions and agendas. A third set of minor nodes was government officials. Here, because of the political sensitivity of the NGOs and especially the concept of indigenous rights, I was more circumspect than I initially intended. Rather than conduct formal interviews, I took advantage of opportunities to chat with different officials about the NGOs; listened carefully to their speeches, comments, and conversations; read their reports and statements; and drew from media accounts to trace their perspectives and practices.

The final set of minor nodes was the communities themselves that the NGOs and umbrella organizations claimed to represent and work with. While I term them "minor nodes" because of their dispersed locations and thus the diffuse nature of my research with them (in contrast to long-term ethnographic research in one site), they were very central to my theoretical questions about the work of NGOs. I conducted a broad survey of the present situation and concerns of different Maasai communities by traveling through all five of the so-called pastoralist districts to observe conditions of daily life (which I was able to compare, in most cases, with my visits and travels from almost twenty-five years ago during my three years of community development work in Tanzania) and to conduct opportunistic and snowball interviews with individuals and groups of men and women of different ages about the changes in their lives, what they perceived as problems, and whether, and if so how, the government, churches, and pastoralist NGOs had helped them address these problems. I also interviewed twelve members from each of my three long-term research communities in Monduli District (stratified, as above, by age and gender) to build on my rich longitudinal research about their changing situations, experiences, and perspectives.

In sum, the methodology of nodal ethnography enabled me to identify, map, and evaluate the web of articulated relationships among both major and minor actors, institutions, and places, at various political scales (local, regional, national, transnational). I was able to concentrate my research efforts on the most intense sites of interaction (the major nodes), use them to identify, track, and study other interested parties (minor nodes), and trace the always-shifting nature and content of relationships and connections among them across different times and spaces.

Conclusion

This book explores the rise and fall of the involvement of Maasai from Tanzania with the international indigenous peoples' movement in order to explore the possibilities for and limitations of political action in world shaped forcefully by the legacies of colonialism and the pressures of neoliberal political and economic regimes. Chapter 1 reviews the history of how and why certain African groups, primarily pastoralists and hunter-gatherers such as Maasai, became involved in the international indigenous rights movement, focusing on their struggles for recognition at the United Nations and on the African continent, internal tensions over political representation among African delegates, and their experiences of and perspectives about becoming and being "indigenous" activists at the United Nations. Chapter 2 shifts the analytical lens from the United Nations and Africa to Tanzania and Maasai. After a brief historical overview of shifting state economic and political policies, I analyze the emergence of Maasai and pastoralist NGOs in Tanzania and compare the strategies and agendas of two primary NGOS vis-à-vis indigenous rights and state politics in order to evaluate the impact of the formation of NGOs and their involvement in the indigenous rights movement for the ongoing struggles of Maasai for political recognition, protection of their resource base, and rights as pastoralist citizens. Chapter 3 assesses the social dynamics and structural dilemmas of these NGOs, including the politics of gender, generational, and class relationships among and between NGO leaders and the communities they claimed to represent; their sometimes "precarious alliances" with donors and each other; and the efforts of NGO representatives themselves to address these challenges at a key moment of introspection and transition. One eventual result of their collective deliberations was a decision in the early 2000s to disengage from active involvement in the international indigenous rights movement and re-position themselves in a way to more effectively inform the policies and practices of the Tanzanian state. Chapter 4 analyzes the causes, effects, and effectiveness of this repositioning from international to national advocacy, from framing their struggles in the language of "indigenous rights" to that of "pastoralist livelihoods," and from calling themselves NGOs to civil society organizations (CSOs), in part through a detailed analysis of their efforts in 2005 and 2006 to shape the new livestock policy proposed by the Tanzanian government. Chapter 5 explores perhaps the most important question of all: after almost twenty years of activity, advocacy, and activism by Maasai NGOs, what have been the effects, if any, of their projects and programs on the everyday lives and livelihoods of Maasai men, women, and children? Through a broad survey and interviews and conversations with Maasai from different regions of Tanzania, I analyze the key changes and challenges in their lives over the past twenty years and present their experi-ences with and perspectives on these changes and the role of the govern-ment, religious organizations. and NGOs in helping them to cope. Finally, in the concluding chapter I review the arguments and insights of the previ-ous chapters to ponder what the way forward in these troubled times might be for Maasai, as well as other marginalized peoples.

Together, these chapters explore some of the inherent ironies and para-doxes of political action in a postcolonial world: of educated Africans de-fending their rights and resources by relying on colonial stereotypes and international agencies; of the absurdity of demanding justice from the pri-mary perpetrators of injustices, nation-states; and of the challenges of col-lective organization and action in the wake of such colonial legacies as na-tional boundaries, dominant languages, disparate resources, and uneven infrastructure. As such, the book draws from and contributes to ongoing debates about the cultural politics of new social movements (e.g., Escobar 1992; Escobar and Alvarez 1992; Gupta 1992; Edelman 2001), the conse-quences of transnational advocacy for national politics (Keck and Sikkink

1998), cultural difference, and citizenship (Alonso 1994; Werbner 2002), the struggles of nongovernmental organizations (Fisher 1997; Fowler 1995; Igoe and Kelsall 2005), the cultural politics of human-rights discourses and practices (An-Na'im 2002; Bowen 2000; Mamdani 2000; Niezen 2003, 2004, 2009), the strengths and constraints of identity politics (Calhoun 1994; Brubaker and Cooper 2000; Dean and Levi 2003; Wilmsen and McAllister 1996), and the contours and content of the political struggles of postcolonial peoples in a neoliberal world (Mbembe 2001; Ferguson and Gupta 2002; Gupta and Sharma 2006; Hodgson and Brooks 2007).

1

BECOMING INDIGENOUS IN AFRICA

On August 3rd, 1989, Moringe ole Parkipuny, long-time Maasai activist and former member of the Tanzanian Parliament, addressed the sixth session of the United Nations Working Group on Indigenous Populations (UN Working Group) in Geneva, Switzerland. After noting that this was a "historic moment," since he and a Hadza man from Tanzania were the "first representatives of any community in Africa that have been able to attend this very important forum," he described in vivid terms the contemporary situation in Africa: "The environment for human rights in Africa is severely polluted by the ramifications of colonialism and neo-colonial social and economic relationships in which we are compelled to pursue our development and our sovereignty in a global system replete with injustices and exploitation" (Parkipuny 1989). He discussed the relative recentness of political independence for most African countries; the difficulties of overcoming colonial legacies of unequal rights, resources, and access to political power; and the "might of Western economic hegemony." But, he warned, the intense efforts by many African nation-states to build national solidarity through the production of national identities "have thrown wide open the floor for prejudices against the fundamental rights and social values of those peoples with cultures that are distinctly different from those of the mainstream national population. Such prejudices have crystallized in many African countries into blatant cultural intolerance, domination and persistent violations of the fundamental rights of minorities" (Parkipuny 1989). In East Africa, he claimed, two of the most "vulnerable minority peoples" were hunter-gatherers and pastoralists:

> These minorities suffer from common problems which characterize the plight of indigenous peoples throughout the world. The most fundamental rights to maintain our specific cultural identity and the land that constitutes the foundation of our existence as a people are not respected by the state and fellow citizens who belong to the mainstream population. In our societies the land and natural re-

sources are the means of livelihood, the media of cultural and spiritual integrity for the entire community as opposed to individual appropriation.

As a result, "our cultures and way of life are viewed as outmoded, inimical to national pride and a hindrance to progress. What is more, access to education and other basic services are minimal relative to the mainstream of the population of the countries to which we are citizens in common with other people" (Parkipuny 1989).

As Parkipuny claimed, this speech did indeed mark a historic moment in local, national, and international affairs; it was the first public assertion by a Maasai leader that Maasai, and indeed, certain other historically marginalized groups in Africa, were part of the transnational community of indigenous peoples. Moreover, the forum for this pronouncement, the UN Working Group, indicated a new willingness of that body to entertain claims that African groups such as Maasai shared common histories, grievances, and structural positions within their nation-states with long-recognized "first peoples" from white settler colonies in the Americas, New Zealand, Australia, and elsewhere. As such, long-accepted definitions of "indigenous" were being challenged, with pressure to expand their meanings to encompass new categories of similarly disenfranchised peoples.

Over the next twenty years, Maasai, Kung San, Batwa, and other African groups became actively involved in the international indigenous peoples' movement with the support of transnational advocacy groups. They also formed regional and continental networks to pressure African states to recognize the presence and rights of indigenous peoples within their borders, to support and coordinate the activities of African NGOs within the UN process, and, more specifically, to promote ratification of the UN Declaration on the Rights of Indigenous Peoples (Declaration). Although they quickly achieved international recognition and visibility for their struggles, they encountered deep hostility from most African nation-states, who claimed that all of their citizens were indigenous, argued that indigenous rights fomented "tribalism," and challenged any discussion of collective rights or restitution. As I was told (sometimes quite forcefully) every time I presented my research in Tanzania, "we are all indigenous in Africa."

Given the hostility of their nation-states and fellow citizens, how and why did certain historically marginalized people in Africa decide to become "indigenous"? This chapter traces the history of the engagement of African groups with the international indigenous peoples' movement; how the concept of "indigenous" has been imagined, understood, and used by African activists, donors, advocates, and states; and the experience and impact of the participation of African groups in the movement.[1] As suggested by the comment "we are all indigenous in Africa," the key struggle for African activists has been to translate their hard-won international recognition as indigenous peoples into national recognition. As described in detail below and in subsequent chapters, not only did this tension shape the dynamics of their participation in the movement, but it also demonstrated the ongoing significance of states in shaping the contours and content of transnational advocacy.

The Spread of the Indigenous Peoples Movement in Africa

The involvement of various African groups with the indigenous peoples' movement is the product of the historical convergence of several factors: visionary leaders such as Parkipuny who saw the connections and were able to reframe long-standing claims to land rights and cultural self-determination in the language of indigenous rights; shifts in donor agendas from financing huge state-run development programs to supporting the initiatives of "grassoots" organizations (Edwards and Hulme 1992; Hulme and Edwards 1997); the new political possibilities and economic exigencies produced by the neoliberal restructuring of states and economies under pressure from the World Bank, IMF, and other global institutions (Gledhill 2004; Harvey 2005); the seeming failure of prior forms of political struggle to produce effective results (e.g., Hodgson 2001a); and chance encounters and connections.

Exploring how Parkipuny came to speak before the UN Working Group offers insights into these complex articulations. Parkipuny was born in Nayobi, a Maasai village on the edge of the Rift Wall in Tanzania, and sent to school when his grandfather was forced by colonial officers to "contribute" one son for schooling. Although his grandfather urged him to purposefully fail the exam to qualify for middle school, Parkipuny refused: "I already had a sense of how Maasai were being treated. I decided I must go on."[2] He completed secondary school and eventually received his BA and then MA in development studies from the University of Dar es Salaam. His MA thesis was a critique of the huge, ten-year, $20 million USAID Masai Range Project that was taking place at the time, a "development" project designed to increase the productivity and offtake of Maasai livestock for the benefit of the national economy (Parkipuny 1975; see also Hodgson 1999b, 2001a).

As we sat one night in September of 2005 over a dinner of roasted goat meat and beer in a bar in Arusha, Tanzania, he explained how and why he had decided to link up with the indigenous rights movement. In 1977, he was hired by the Tanzanian government to work for the Masai Range project. But USAID balked, given his harsh critiques of the project in both his thesis and published newspaper editorials. As a compromise, they sent him on a study tour of the United States to visit "proper ranches":

> I traveled to Washington, D.C., Oregon, California, Arizona, and more to visit extension schools, ranches, and so forth. But I became fed up; it was too monotonous. So at the airport one day, I met a Navaho from Windrock. We talked some and he invited me to visit. I said, "Let's go!" So I stayed with them for two weeks, and then with the Hopi for two weeks. It was my first introduction to the indigenous world. I was struck by the similarities of our problems. I looked at Windrock, the poor state of the roads and reservations, it was just like the cattle trails in Maasailand. *But this was in the United States!*

For Parkipuny, as for many African activists, this epiphany was transformative. Seeing the similarities between the contemporary situation and historical struggles of Maasai and that of Native Americans enabled Parkipuny to think beyond the specifics of Maasai circumstances to a deeper understanding of the exploitative relationships between nation-states and certain kinds of people, relationships that had been produced and exacerbated by colonialism, nation building, and economic modernization (cf. Niezen 2003, Maybury-Lewis 2002). He quickly realized that the Maasai experience of land alienation, forced settlement, deep disparities in the provision of social services such as education and health, cultural disparagement, and, at times, forced assimilation first by the colonial and then by the postcolonial state were not unique, but part of a global pattern (Parkipuny 1979).

Eventually, in search of a political space to advocate for justice, Parkipuny ran for and was elected to serve as a member of the Tanzanian Parliament in 1980. As he explained, "At the time, it was the only door open under the one-party system to voice outcry. There were no civil society organizations at the time. You had to work through the party." During his ten years as a member of Parliament (MP), he fought tirelessly, especially against the rising tide of illegal land alienation by the government, speaking in Parliament, filing court case after court case against the government, pleading with political leaders, and rallying Maasai. As his reputation as a formidable intellectual and political leader of Maasai grew, so did the number of his enemies inside and outside of Parliament. "They all kept their distance from me. And when I would go to Parliament and voice problems, nothing would happen, there was no action."

I first met Parkipuny in 1986 in my capacity as coordinator of the Arusha Diocesan Development Team (ADDO), when I was visiting the town of Loliondo, the headquarters of Ngorongoro District, which was the district he represented as MP. ADDO was refurbishing one of the town's water systems, and Parkipuny had been helping us to negotiate the bureaucratic thicket of permits, procurement of supplies, and so forth in a time of rationing, "black" markets, restrictions on foreign currency, and general economic distress. He was a tall, slim man, dressed in a navy suit, with a warm manner, piercing gaze, and effortless English. I was immediately struck by his intensity, remarkable intelligence, and political-economic savvy. Our conversation quickly shifted from the mundane details of the water project to the politics of the World Bank, U.S. imperialism, and the marginalization of Maasai. By that time, Parkipuny was clearly weary of the constant political struggles and accusations he was experiencing as MP, yet continued to challenge what he perceived as the many injustices perpetrated on Maasai by the Tanzanian state.

Despite, or perhaps because of, his political battles with representatives of the Tanzanian state, Parkipuny continued to nurture and develop his transnational connections, including communicating, through a mutual friend, with Jens Dahl, an anthropologist who was a board member (and later director) of the International Work Group for Indigenous Affairs (IWGIA). In 1983, Parkipuny toured Europe and Canada to publicize the plight of Maasai. During his travels, he visited the offices of IWGIA in Copenhagen, where he was interviewed for their newsletter (IWGIA 1983). As the title of the article ("Wildlife Have More Rights than Maasai") suggests, Parkipuny described the predicament of Maasai living in the Ngorongoro Conservation Area in Tanzania, where wildlife conservation policies premised on separating wildlife from humans were undermining Maasai rights to land, endangering their livelihoods, and possibly promoting the further eviction of Maasai from Ngorongoro. As he argued, "to separate Maasai, their cattle and wildlife would be a disaster both ethically and ecologically" (IWGIA 1983:183). In response, IWGIA commissioned a research report on the situation of Maasai in Ngorongoro by Swedish anthropologist Kaj Århem (1985a, see also 1985b). Impressed by Parkipuny's mission and message, Dahl invited Parkipuny to Canada to present on a panel he had organized on indigenous peoples and human rights[3] and later sponsored (through IWGIA) Parkipuny's participation in the 1989 UN Working Group.[4] Although Dahl recognized the possible political repercussions for any African who addressed the UN Working Group, he believed that "Parkipuny was the perfect person, since as a Member of Parliament he had much less risk of being arrested when he returned to Tanzania."[5] By 1989, Parkipuny was feeling embattled by Tanzanian politics and ready to "get out of this place." Through the support of friends and a progressive advocacy network in the United States, "I traveled to Europe, the U.S., as far as Berkeley!" Before his speech in Geneva, he met with Native Americans in New Mexico and Canada to further his comparative understanding of indigenous issues. Parkipuny returned to the UN Working Group several more times,[6] but his last trip was in 1991, after he had decided not to run again for MP: "finally I decided that I can't keep coming [to the UN], I have to stay home and concentrate on grass-roots organizing."

IWGIA, a transnational advocacy network of human rights activists and researchers based in Denmark, was instrumental in encouraging certain African groups to link their struggles to the indigenous rights movement, promoting the participation of Africans such as Parkipuny at the relevant UN meetings, and expanding the working definition of "indigenous" to embrace their positions and claims.[7] In 1990 in an article in the annual *IWGIA Yearbook*, Espen Wæhle, an IWGIA board member, argued for the applicability of the concept of "indigenous" "in a structural sense" to certain African groups (Wæhle 1990). Echoing Parkipuny's speech to the UN Working Group, he described three key parallels between African political struggles and those of recognized indigenous peoples: "1) the assertion of group rights which parallels ethnic/indigenous assertion of rights elsewhere; 2) the grave situation of human rights in many parts of Africa (also in the sense of collective group rights); and 3) African concerns for self-development and self-determination" (Wæhle 1990:147). With the support of IWGIA, Wæhle then co-organized an international "Conference on Indigenous Peoples in Africa" in Denmark in 1993, which included representatives from select African groups. Most of the papers in the published conference proceedings (Veber et al. 1993) focused on specific peoples with possible claims to indigeneity: "Pastoralists of Eastern Africa," "Bushmen of Southern Africa," "Pygmies of Central Africa," and "The Tuareg Pastoralists of Northwestern Africa."

As the UN Year of the World's Indigenous People (1993) was followed by the UN Decade of the World's Indigenous People (1995–2004), IWGIA expanded its efforts to promote the involvement of African groups (especially representatives of the four groups listed above) in the international indigenous rights movement. They sponsored national, regional, and international workshops to encourage awareness and discussion of the applicability of the concept;[8] publicized the debates and initiatives in their annual *Yearbook* and quarterly periodical, *Indigenous Affairs;* financed and nurtured the participation of African activists at the annual meetings of the UN Working Group, the UN Permanent Forum on Indigenous Issues (UN Permanent Forum), and relevant UN World Summits; and funded the capacity-building, land-rights, and human-rights programs of some African NGOs (Dahl 2009).[9] Many of the activists whom I interviewed attributed their awareness of the indigenous peoples' movement and their involvement with the UN to a 1999 conference co-sponsored by IWGIA and PINGOs (a network of organizations representing pastoralists and hunter-gatherers in Tanzania; see chapter 2) in Tanzania (the "Conference on Indigenous Peoples in Eastern, Central and Southern Africa") and a three-week follow-up training course on indigenous rights and international legal frameworks in September 1999 that was sponsored by PINGOs and funded by the European Union and the Saami Council (from Norway).[10] IWGIA's logic in promoting the participation of Africans and others in the movement was straightforward; IWGIA was convinced that participation in UN meetings offered unique opportunities for indigenous peoples to convey their situation and compel the international community and national governments to fully live up to their obligations to respect and protect human rights in order to secure the cultural and physical survival of indigenous peoples (Dahl 2009). Other international transnational advocacy groups also supported the expansion of the indigenous rights movement in Africa through workshops, funding, and publicity, although their motivations differed and sometimes conflicted. These organizations included the International Institute for Environment and Development (United Kingdom),[11] Survival International (United Kingdom), Minority Rights International (United Kingdom), and Cultural Survival (United

States), and their agendas ranged from ecological sustainability to cultural preservation to ensuring the right of indigenous peoples to control their own "development." Most, like IWGIA, genuinely saw themselves as helping indigenous peoples confront and overcome long histories of injustice and dispossession perpetrated by their nation-states, but a few organizations seem to hijack indigenous struggles for rights and recognition to support their own agendas.

"Making Place": Africans at the United Nations

During preparations for the Year of Indigenous Peoples (1993), Africa was not even considered as an appropriate site for activities.[12] But after Parkipuny's speech in 1989, increasing numbers of African activists and NGOs began to attend the UN Working Group with the support of IWGIA and other organizations, "making place" (Muehlebach 2001) for themselves at the United Nations.[13] Although only one African NGO participated in 1993, by 2002 attendance had increased to more than twenty-six African NGOs, including Batwa representatives from Rwanda, Amazigh from Morocco, Tuareg from Algeria, and Dorobo, Ogiek, and Maasai from Kenya.[14] Some African NGOs, such as the Maa Development Association, and certain African activists participated steadily over the years, while other groups and individuals came and went. Observers from African states such as Senegal, Nigeria, and South Africa occasionally attended as well.[15]

The UN Working Group was established in 1982 by the UN Economic and Social Council (ECOSOC) on the recommendation of the Sub-Commission on Prevention of Discrimination and Protection of Minorities (the Sub-Commission, renamed the Sub-Commission on the Promotion and Protection of Human Rights in 1999) in response to the demands of increasingly organized and vocal indigenous rights activists.[16] The original mandates of the UN Working Group were to:

  (a) Review developments pertaining to the promotion and protection of human rights and fundamental freedoms of indigenous peoples . . .
  (b) Give special attention to the evolution of standards concerning the rights of indigenous peoples, taking account of both the similarities and the differences in the situations and aspirations of indigenous peoples throughout the world.[17]

The UN Working Group was composed of five independent experts from the Sub-Commission, who were elected to represent what the UN considered the five geographic regions of the world at the time (Africa, Asia, Latin America, Eastern Europe, Europe [including the United States, Australia, and New Zealand]). The experts, none of whom were indigenous, were elected for two-year terms, although many, such as Erica-Irene A. Daes and Miguel Alfonso Martínez, served multiple terms over the years. Every year, from 1982 through 2006 (except in 1986 because of a UN funding crisis), the UN Working Group met for a week of public meetings, and then filed a report of its deliberations with the Sub-Commission.

The establishment of the UN Working Group was a crucial moment in international indigenous politics, providing a space and platform for indigenous activists to voice their concerns, network among themselves, and lobby for increased attention to indigenous affairs by the United Nations, and through the United Nations, member states. From the beginning, pressure from indigenous activists shaped the rules of procedure adopted by the UN Working Group in 1982, which allowed any interested person to address the UN Working Group and submit information, instead of just representatives from the few indigenous organizations that had "consultative status" with ECOSOC.[18] The flexible and inclusive structure of the UN Working Group made it unique in the UN, and attracted a diverse array of indigenous activists from across the world, representatives of advocacy groups such as IWGIA that supported their endeavors, UN specialized agencies, NGOs, state "observers," researchers, and in fact anyone who wanted to attend. As the word spread, attendance grew, from 30 participants at the first meeting in 1982 to 615 participants (275 NGOs) in 1992, to a peak of 1,076 participants (270 NGOs) in 2002.[19]

Among other notable achievements, the UN Working Group successfully recommended that the UN proclaim first a Year of the World's Indigenous People (1993), then a Decade of the World's Indigenous People (1995–2004), and eventually a second Decade of the World's Indigenous People (2005–2014) in order to focus attention on the situation and struggles of indigenous people. The UN Working Group also sponsored critical studies, expert meetings, and various kinds of practical actions. Its annual meeting provided a forum for indigenous people to make public statements about human rights violations, criticize state and donor actions, and suggest ideas for future deliberations and actions. In 1985, the UN General Assembly approved the UN Working Group's recommendation for the creation of a Voluntary Fund for Indigenous Popula-

Table 1.1.
Reporting Relations of UN Working Group and
UN Permanent Forum within the UN Hierarchy

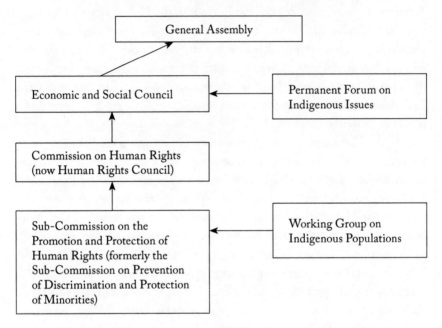

tions to subsidize the participation of indigenous peoples in its meetings. Perhaps most importantly, the UN Working Group discussed, debated, and drafted a Declaration on the Rights of Indigenous Peoples to be approved by the United Nations and then circulated for ratification by member states.

As Andrea Muehlebach (2001) has detailed, during its first two decades (1982–2002), the UN Working Group provided a vibrant forum for indigenous activists from all across the world to meet together, share ideas and approaches, and meet face to face with representatives of UN bodies and international organizations. By the time I attended the UN Working Group in 2004, however, some of this enthusiasm and vitality had waned, as had the participation of African delegates. One reason for the decline was simmering frustrations among activists over the slow pace of revision and approval of the Draft Declaration on the Rights of Indigenous Peoples. A second reason was the structural marginalization of the UN Working Group within the UN system, which limited its effectiveness and influence. The UN Working Group was not itself a "policy-making" body of the UN. Instead, it reported to and made recommendations to the Sub-Commission, which in turn reported to the Commission on Human Rights (now the Human Rights Council), which reported to ECOSOC, which reported to the General Assemble (see table 1.1). Thus, although it was the primary forum for indigenous people to voice their complaints about state violations of human rights, the UN Working Group never had the authority to receive and investigate complaints or to make recommendations to governments. And so the final accomplishment of the UN Working Group was to precipitate its own demise by recommending that the UN create the Permanent Forum for Indigenous Issues as an alternative, more powerfully located structure within the UN system (it would report directly to ECOSOC), which the UN approved in 2000 (UN Resolution 2000/22).[20]

Finally, a number of activists resented what they perceived as the heavy-handed and sometimes hostile actions and words of the long-presiding chair of the UN Working Group, Manuel Alfonso Martínez, a non-indigenous Cuban anthropologist. Many activists I spoke to shared the perspective of "Rita," a representative of a transnational advocacy organization who had attended the UN Working Group annually since 1993: "The peak of the Working Group's dynamism and effectiveness was in the late 1990s and early 2000s. But as the participation of Asians and Africans has increased, the participation of North and South Americans has declined. I think the Working Group is very quiet this year. Very few African delegates are present."[21] She attributed part of the problem to the unrelenting position of the chair of the UN Working Group, Alfonso Martínez, that Asians and Africans were *not* indigenous and should not be involved in the UN Working Group.[22] Alfonso Martínez repeatedly argued that most, if not all, African groups who claimed to be "indigenous" should in fact be considered "minorities," given their complex histories of migration, murky distinctions between who was "indigenous" and "non-indigenous" in Africa, and other differences from more easily recognized indigenous peoples from the Americas, Australia, and New Zealand. He noted two possible exceptions to his position—the San in Botswana and Maasai in Kenya (Alfonso Martínez 1999:para 78, 165).[23] According to a Tuareg activist from Niger, "He [Alfonso Martínez] told me that Tuareg didn't belong at the Working Group; we should go to a conference on minority rights. I told him that we weren't a minority, we were indigenous." Other African activists spoke to me of similar encounters with Alfonso Martínez.

Other long-time activists had grown weary of the format, content, and style of the UN Working Group meetings. As one man told me, "Many of the activists present long statements outlining the history of land alienation and other abuses. But I know all of this, I could write 75 percent of these statements myself. I don't mean to sound like a 'know-it-all,' but it is kind of boring." Others complained that the UN Working Group had become "bogged down by its own success." There were too many statements, too little time, and no clear procedure for prioritizing statements (At the UN Permanent Forum, "collective" statements by caucuses and multiple organizations are given precedence over "individual" statements presented on behalf of just one organization). "It is meaningless to read the first and last paragraph of a statement," remarked a Maasai woman. Finally, many activists were increasingly offended by Alfonso Martínez's combative style. At a meeting of the Indigenous Caucus[24] one morning before the regular session of the UN Working Group, numerous activists criticized Alfonso Martínez for being "loud" and "rude" when he pounded the gavel at the end of the allotted time for a statement. "While the chair of the Permanent Forum [Ole Henrik Magga] is so flexible," said one man, "Alfonso Martínez was so harsh you could feel it in your brain!" As a result, by 2004, a number of advocacy organizations considered the UN Working Group as a "training ground" for neophyte indigenous activists, since its loose organization, inclusive atmosphere, and less formal style encouraged their participation. Once these new activists became more confident and experienced, however, they were advised to participate in the UN Permanent Forum. Even IWGIA shifted its primary advocacy efforts from the UN Working Group to the UN Permanent Forum.[25]

Alternative Paradigms: From "First Peoples" to Self-Identification

As Alfonso Martínez's comments suggest, a key challenge for African groups was to be recognized as indigenous by the United Nations and other international organizations, transnational advocacy groups, fellow indigenous activists, and, ultimately, their nation-states. The late entry of Africans into the indigenous peoples' movement posed a structural disadvantage, as they had to position themselves vis-à-vis the long-standing practices, discourses, and assumptions of the UN Working Group (Saugestad 2001). For

Africans, the first obstacle to political recognition as "indigenous" was the then-dominant definition of "indigenous peoples," which was initially developed as a synonym for "first peoples," that is, autochthonous groups such as Native Americans, Aborigines, and Maori who could clearly demonstrate their territorial precedence prior to conquest and settler colonialism.[26] Clearly the situation in most parts of Africa (and Asia) was very different, with few groups able to claim status as "first peoples" who were permanently dislocated and disenfranchised by settler societies (with the exception of parts of southern Africa).[27]

Parkipuny's eloquent speech to the UN Working Group outlined some of the key reasons why Maasai (and certain other African groups) claimed to be "indigenous." The term was adopted by distinct cultural minorities in Africa (and Asia) who argued that they had been historically repressed by majority populations in control of the state apparatus. Few claimed to be "first peoples" as such. Instead, they argued that vis-à-vis their nation-states they shared a structural position similar to that of indigenous peoples in the Americas, Australia, and other settler colonies. Because of their cultural distinctiveness, they had experienced a long history of political subjugation, economic marginalization, territorial dispossession, and cultural and linguistic discrimination. These arguments are based on what scholars and advocates have termed a "constructivist," "structural," or "relational" definition of indigenous, in contrast to more "essential," "substantial," or "positivist" definitions that depend on evidence of territorial precedence.[28]

As Parkipuny's remarks made clear, the main groups who could be considered indigenous were pastoralists and hunter-gatherers, whose "cultural" distinctiveness was in great part produced by and predicated on their distinct livelihood strategies (especially their reliance on mobility and access to communal lands), which contrasted and often conflicted with the dominant, state-endorsed livelihoods of settled farmers, resulting in their economic, political, and social marginalization as "second-class citizens." Nomadic and semi-nomadic pastoralists such as Maasai had long posed a challenge to colonial and postcolonial state agendas of control, containment, and modernization (e.g., Hodgson 2001a, Kipuri 2001). The sociopolitical organization of most pastoralist groups, with a reliance on a cadre of young men as raiders, protectors, and "warriors," enabled them to resist, to some degree, the intrusions of farmers, game parks, and the state in their lives. But hunter-gatherers, who had no such organization, were even more vulnerable to predation, eviction, enslavement, and extinction (e.g., Barume 2000; Madsen 2000; Saugestad 2001; Sylvain 2002). Tensions between these groups and their respective nation-states escalated in the 1990s with state implementation of the neoliberal political and economic "reforms" mandated by international capital, the United States and its allies, and multinational financial institutions such as the World Bank to reduce funding for social services, privatize formerly state-controlled functions and industries, establish strict private property regimes, and ensure "free" markets and "free" trade for multinational corporations. For most pastoralists and hunter-gatherers in Africa, the implementation of these neoliberal politico-economic regimes has accelerated the alienation of their lands and resources for more "productive" enterprises (such as commercial agriculture, game parks, and mining); carved up their communal territories into bounded, privatized enclaves; intensified socioeconomic inequalities of access to education, healthcare, and other social services; and amplified state campaigns to forcefully restructure their lives and livelihoods through settlement, assimilation, livestock development projects, and more (Lane 1996; Hodgson 2001a; Hodgson and Schroeder 2002; Sikar and Hodgson 2006).

The ability of Africans to make these claims to indigeneity, and the willingness of established indigenous groups to consider them, was facilitated by an emerging principle of the indigenous peoples' movement, the principle of *self-identification*. In a 1986 UN report, José Martinez Cobo proposed a definition of indigenous peoples that relied on evidence of historical continuity and cultural distinction:

> Indigenous communities, peoples and nations are those which have a historical continuity with pre-invasion and pre-colonial societies that developed on their territories, consider themselves distinct from other sectors of societies now prevailing in those territories, or parts of them. They form at present non-dominant sectors of society and are determined to preserve, develop, and transmit to future generations their ancestral territories, and their ethnic identity, as the basis of their continued existence as peoples, in accordance with their own cultural patterns, social institutions and legal systems. (Cobo 1986:5, para. 379)

Cobo's definition outlined the complicated issue of determining "historical continuity" as follows:

> This historical continuity may consist of the continuation, for an extended period reaching into the present, of one or more of the following factors:

(a) Occupation of ancestral lands, or at least part of them;

(b) Common ancestry with the original occupants of these lands;

(c) Culture in general, or in specific manifestations (such as religion, living under a tribal system, membership of an indigenous community, dress, means of livelihood, lifestyle, etc);

(d) Language (whether used as the only language, as mother tongue, as the habitual means of communication at home or in the family, or as the main, preferred, habitual, general or normal language);

(e) Residence in certain parts of the country, or in certain regions of the world;

(f) Other relevant factors. (Cobo 1986:5, para. 380)

Cobo emphasized self-identification as central to the definition of *indigenous* and stressed historical precedence and cultural difference as aspects of indigenous status. In addition, however, Cobo acknowledged the unequal power relations that exist in many states by noting "non-dominance" as another common characteristic of indigenous peoples.

The Indigenous and Tribal Peoples Convention 169 adopted in 1989 by the International Labour Organization (ILO) to replace their earlier 1957 Convention proffered a similar definition (ILO 1989).[29] In contrast to the language of integration and assimilation that pervaded the 1957 Convention, the 1989 Convention recognized the "aspirations of [indigenous] peoples to exercise control over their own institutions, ways of life and economic development and to maintain and develop their identities, languages, and religions, within the frameworks of the States in which they live" (ILO 1989: preamble). Moreover, the ensuing articles outlined a broad set of governmental responsibilities and indigenous rights, including: a preference for customary legal solutions; recognition of the rights of indigenous peoples to ownership of, possession of, and access to their traditional lands and resources on their lands; prevention of discrimination in the terms, practices, and benefits of employment; government provision of adequate, appropriate health services and educational programs in cooperation and consultation with the people concerned; and support for indigenous language instruction for children (ILO 1989). The articles are full of calls for cooperation and consultation between governments and indigenous groups in a manner that recognizes, affirms, and strengthens the rights of indigenous groups to cultural, social, economic, and political self-determination *within* the framework of the nation-states in which they reside.[30] The convention also stated that "*self-identification* as indigenous or tribal shall be regarded as a fundamental criterion for determining the groups to which the provisions of the Convention apply" (ILO 1989: article 1.2; emphasis added).

By the 1990s, during debates over the provisions of the Declaration on the Rights of Indigenous Peoples, indigenous activists refused to include in the Declaration any specific definition of who qualified as "indigenous." Instead, over the vehement objections of many states, they argued that self-identification should be the primary mode for determining who was covered by the Declaration in order to defuse the power of states, the UN, and other bodies to decide who was or was not indigenous.[31] And, indeed, the final version of the Declaration does not define "indigenous peoples" anywhere in the preamble or articles (United Nations 2007).

But the final version of the Declaration, which reflects the input and agendas of indigenous activists and organizations, differs from the 1989 ILO Convention in several significant ways. The Declaration is more radical in its condemnation of the historical and contemporary treatment of indigenous peoples by nation-states and dominant populations. It claims that "indigenous peoples have suffered from historic injustices as a result of, inter alia, their colonization and dispossession of their lands, territories and resources" (UN 2007: preamble). Second, in addition to the rights specified in the 1989 ILO Convention, the Declaration also extends to indigenous peoples the rights to maintain, protect, and develop their material culture (including archaeological and historical sites, artifacts, designs, and technologies), visual and performative culture (ceremonies, arts, and literature), and intellectual and cultural knowledge and property, as well as spiritual and religious sites and traditions (UN 2007: articles 11, 12, and 31). Third, the Declaration repeatedly emphasizes the responsibility of states to "consult and cooperate" with indigenous peoples and "take effective measures" to ensure the protection of their rights. Finally, the Declaration introduces the concept of "free, prior and informed consent" to strengthen the relationship between indigenous peoples and states. In compliance with the Declaration, states and other institutions (such as the World Bank) must obtain the "free, prior and informed consent" of indigenous peoples before relocating them from their lands or territories (article 10); using their cultural, intellectual, religious or spiritual property (article 11); adopting and implementing legislation or administrative measures that may affect them (article 19); or implementing a development project that affects them or their land and resources (article 32).

Triumphs and Tensions: Africans at the UN Permanent Forum on Indigenous Issues

By the time of the first meeting of the UN Permanent Forum in 2001, the UN and most activists from the Americas and elsewhere had accepted the participation of Africans as indigenous peoples. Their acceptance was formally recognized in the structure of the UN Permanent Forum, which had sixteen "expert" members from different regions, but always including Africa.[32] The involvement of Africans in the very formulation of the UN Permanent Forum produced a much more welcoming and inclusive space than the UN Working Group in which to voice their concerns. Not surprisingly then, the presence of Africans and other activists (and representatives of UN agencies, state observers, academics, and others) at the UN Permanent Forum grew steadily. At the six annual meetings of the UN Permanent Forum that I attended (2003–2005, 2007–2009), I saw, met, and heard Africans from all over the continent, including San from southern Africa, Maasai from Kenya and Tanzania, Tuareg from west Africa, Amazigh from north Africa, and Batwa and other "pygmies" (as they called themselves at the UN) from central Africa.[33]

I vividly recall the opening session of the second annual meeting of the UN Permanent Forum in 2003 in New York as a lively, noisy, vibrant occasion. Indigenous representatives, most wearing some rendition of their customary dress, wandered around the huge meeting room greeting one another with hugs, handshakes, bows, and kisses. Many of the delegates seemed to know each other well, presumably from prior meetings of the UN Working Group in Geneva and other international gatherings and networks. I sat in the balcony, trying to make sense of the dizzying kaleidoscope of clothing, jewelry, ornamentation, hairstyles, and other cultural signs—Maori? Yanomami? Saami? I was certainly not alone in my inability to decode the dense cultural iconography displayed in the attire and adornment of indigenous delegates, since many of the outfits drew on common tropes of feathers, cowries, beads, hides, and bright cloth. Soon I realized that my ethnographic zeal to distinguish and identify distinct groups was probably beside the point. Rather, much like the collage of photos of indigenous peoples featured on the UN Web site, posters, and other publicity materials (Hodgson n.d.), the overriding purpose of their dress and appearance was not necessarily to reference specific ethnic groups, but to signify "indigeneity" to each other, government representatives,

UN officers, and others in order to mark their connections to one another and difference from the rest of us, the "non-indigenous." The boundaries of belonging (or not) were visually marked by cultural symbols that at once drew on indigenous sartorial repertoires and were recognized as "indigenous" by indigenous and non-indigenous alike.

Despite my confusion, I quickly identified several Maasai: a young man draped in a short, plain red plaid cloth, wearing tire sandals and a beaded bracelet, carrying a beaded *rungu* (a short stick marking him as a junior elder in the Maasai age grade system), with partially extended earlobes and teased-out hair; two middle-aged men wearing long bright red cotton cloths with circular aluminum dangles sewn along the edges, socks and loafers, and close-cropped hair; a wizened old man wrapped in a well-worn long cloth and red blanket, with extended earlobes, tire sandals, short hair, and an old khaki safari hat, accompanied by a young girl in printed cloth (commonly called a *kitenge*), beaded necklaces, socks and tennis shoes; and a heavy set middle-aged woman with shoulder length, straightened red hair in a dark skirt, a beaded red shirt and red shawl, pantyhose and pumps. While certain key signs such as the beaded jewelry and red cloths signaled that these were Maasai, the differences (tire sandals versus loafers and pumps, plain cloth versus cloth with dangles, natural versus straightened and dyed hair) suggested distinctions of age, gender, class, education, and rural versus urban backgrounds. Other indigenous delegates, donors, and government representatives clearly also recognized them as Maasai and accepted them as "indigenous" in 2003, based, in part, on their distinct attire and prominent presence at the UN Permanent Forum and other sites of transnational indigenous advocacy as leaders, speakers, and performers.

By 2003, several Africans, especially Maasai from Kenya, had become visible leaders of the international indigenous rights movement. Lucy Mulenkei, a Maasai journalist from Kenya, was president of the African Indigenous Women's Organization and co-chair of the Indigenous Caucus in 2004 and 2005. Hassan Id Balkassm, an Amazigh lawyer from Morocco, founded the Indigenous Peoples of Africa Coordinating Committee (IPACC) in 1997 (he eventually served as its second director), based on an informal network of African activists who had been attending the UN Working Group. He regularly presented statements at the UN Permanent Forum and worked to mobilize and coordinate the efforts of other African activists. Mary Simat, a longtime Maasai activist from Kenya, was the deputy chairperson, then chairperson, of IPACC, and also a regular presenter.[34]

These experienced activists networked with their fellow activists from all over the world, sharing handshakes, hugs, greetings, news, advice, and business cards. After I exchanged business cards with one African delegate in 2003, he stuffed it into his wallet, which was already crammed with at least fifty others. "So many cards!" he said, shaking his head. They eagerly courted representatives of donor agencies and transnational advocacy organizations, publicizing their accomplishments, grievances, recommendations, and requests through colorful brochures and posters, media interviews, and, of course, formal statements during the UN sessions. Several activists frequently made presentations as part of the "side events" organized by indigenous organizations to highlight particular issues. Others took advantage of being in New York to set up meetings with sympathetic donors and advocacy organizations. And they all guided first-time participants, introducing them to other delegates, helping them learn how to write and present statements, and teaching them how to navigate the bureaucracy and logistics of the UN meeting.

I also quickly learned how certain informal and formal conventions of the UN Permanent Forum shaped their appearances and participation. For example, most indigenous delegates wore their "indigenous" dress to the ceremonial opening meeting of the forum, which included extended indigenous performances and welcoming remarks by high-level UN officials. On subsequent days, however, they might wear culturally unmarked dress such as blue jeans, pant suits, and dresses, but usually with some cultural accent such as a beaded bangle, embroidered shawl, or head covering. In other words, having established their indigenous credentials the first day, they could choose whether or not they wanted to blend in or draw attention to themselves in subsequent days.[35] Compare, for example, two photos of me with Ndinini Kimesera Sikar, a Maasai activist from Tanzania, at the 2004 and 2007 UN Permanent Forums (p. 146). In the 2004 photo, Ndinini is wearing the elite rendition of Maasai customary dress—a brown cotton cloth (to look like leather) with a beaded border (a similar cloth is wrapped around her waist as a skirt), and a beaded collar, headdress, and bangle. The day after this photo was taken, Ndinini wore a stunning silk dress, a black jacket, and pumps—a "business-like" outfit similar to the one she is wearing in the 2007 photo.

The appearance of Maasai men reflected a similar range of sartorial choices. The few uneducated men who attended wore their everyday Maasai attire of well-worn plaid cloth, beaded accessories, and tire sandals or tennis shoes. In contrast, elite Maasai men, such as the lawyers and NGO leaders from Kenya at the 2004 UN Permanent Forum (p. 147) wore brightly colored red or blue shirts decorated with aluminum dangles and colorful beads. While chatting at the 2005 UN Permanent Forum with one of them, who was wearing a red tunic with beaded designs and aluminum dangles,[36] black pants, and a hat, I asked him about his outfit: "Half Maasai?" I joked. "And half modern [Swahili: *kisasa*]!" he replied, chuckling. His response is telling, and reflects the aesthetic dilemmas of elite Maasai, who seek ways to signal their ethnicity and their class—thus the recent creation of beaded cloth shirts for men and "leather-like" brown cloth drapes for women. For many elites, this was more than a "staged authenticity" (MacCannell 1976:98, cited in Conklin 1997:725) or performed identity, but a nostalgic reassertion and claiming of a still often fiercely held ethnic pride, taking advantage of the elision or slippage between "ethnic" and "indigenous" dress at the UN.

The visibility and acceptance of Africans, especially Maasai, as indigenous peoples at the UN Permanent Forum was marked in other ways as well. When Ole Henrik Magga, a Saami from Norway and member of the UN Permanent Forum, was elected to chair the 2004 Forum, he opened the first session by displaying a beaded Maasai *rungu* (carved short stick) to all the delegates. "Since the last Forum," he announced, "I was able to visit East Africa, especially with Maasai. They gave me this beaded *rungu*. I feel I have the inspiration to guide you through the work we have to do."[37] The next day, as part of the daily opening ceremony in which different indigenous delegates were asked to begin the session with their customary prayers, songs, or rituals (as everyone in the room stood silently), six Maasai delegates performed a praise song to their deity Eng'ai one morning on the main podium. Over the years, the UN Special Rapporteur on the Human Rights and Fundamental Freedoms of Indigenous Peoples visited several African countries, including Kenya, Botswana, and South Africa, to investigate the situation of indigenous peoples. And the UN Permanent Forum in 2006 (which I did not attend) devoted its special thematic session to Africa.

Activists from Africa came from a range of backgrounds and learned about the UN meetings in different ways. Many of those from East Africa, such as Adam, an Ilparakuyo Maasai from Tanzania whom I interviewed, first heard about the UN meetings at the 1999 regional workshop on indigenous rights co-organized by IWGIA:

> I heard on the radio about a conference on indigenous peoples in
> Africa that was taking place in Arusha, organized by PINGOs [a

network of pastoralist and hunter-gather organizations in Tanzania].
I went, met with several representatives of the UN, and realized that
I could attend the UN. I applied twice for money to attend the
Working Group, but I was unsuccessful. But I attended in 2000,
sponsored by the United Nations Fund for Indigenous Peoples. In
2001, I was awarded a five-month fellowship at the UN in Geneva to
learn about the UN, the indigenous rights process, etc., and attend
the 2001 meeting of the Working Group. I also attended the first
Permanent Forum in 2001 in New York.[38]

Similar meetings in other regions created awareness about the UN process
among Africans and sparked their interest in participating. Although a few
activists had college degrees and even doctorates (or other post-baccalaure-
ate degrees), most, like Adam, had completed only secondary school. Some
had extensive prior careers in development, with large international institutions such as World Vision or government agencies. Others had little experience in development or human rights, but had started or worked for small
local NGOs or community-based organizations (CBOs). A few of the "fa-
vored" had developed long-term support networks with IWGIA or other
transnational "partners," which ensured financial support for their regular
participation in the UN meetings. Others scrambled every year to apply for
grants, appeal to friends, and endear themselves to donors.

In our interviews, African activists conveyed a range of reasons for their
participation in the UN Permanent Forum. Some argued that the indigenous rights movement was a political opportunity for voicing their claims
that was not to be missed. As a prominent Kenyan Maasai activist explained
to me in 2007, "If Africans are not present, then we lose out. Indigenous
peoples from Asia and the Americas are much more powerful, present, and
knowledgeable." Several activists described how they had listened to and
learned from other, more experienced activists. Many noted that the UN
Permanent Forum provided an invaluable opportunity to speak face to face
with power, in the form of the World Bank, FAO, and other international
agencies. Some believed that their statements had succeeded in changing the
policies and practices of some of these agencies. "Through our participation
in the UN, we can pressure UN agencies to change. For example, the Food
and Agriculture Organization. Their policies caused a lot of problems, but
now, because of discussions at Permanent Forum, they are recognizing indigenous peoples and working with them."

Fundamentally, however, they hoped to leverage their international visibility and the support of the UN and donors to achieve recognition and protection of their resources and rights by their nation-states. As a representative of Ogiek hunter-gatherers in Kenya told me in 2004:

> We are marginalized and dismissed; no one cares about us. The dominant ethnic groups take over; they won't even register Ogiek as landowners. 'Oh, you just live in the forest and eat honey, why do you need land?' We are trying to fight for our land rights, development, and so forth. Now we want to educate our children, but where are the schools?

Efforts to seek protection from the Kenyan state had failed, so the UN was the only alternative: "This is our space; we have no other space." A Maasai activist from Tanzania explained: "I think the value of 'indigenous' is that everyone can work together to pressure the Tanzanian state without making it an 'ethnic' or 'tribal' issue. But the problem is that everyone has to get along." Of course, as indigenous activists themselves realize, the paradox is that they must demand recognition from the very nation-states that have historically oppressed and disparaged them.

Many activists were frustrated, however, by the failure of most African states to even send observers to the UN Permanent Forum. In 2005, the African Caucus sponsored a side event at the UN Permanent Forum to discuss the prospects and challenges for the region. About forty African activists attended, in addition to donors and academics, but no representatives from African states. "It is too bad that most African governments are not here to meet with us," remarked a Maasai activist. Everyone present agreed that the key problem they faced as Africans was the lack of recognition of indigenous peoples by African states. "Although I am an expert member of the Working Group on Indigenous Populations/Communities of the African Commission on Human and Peoples Rights" (discussed below), explained a Batwa activist from the Central African Republic, "my own government denies the existence of my group and has driven us out of the forest." In 2005, another activist from the Central African Republic described the indigenous peoples' movement on the African continent as at an "embryonic stage," which was "especially noticeable at United Nations meetings." The problem, he explained, was the "lack of recognition" by African states. Among the strategies proposed to address the situation was to convene a session of the UN Permanent Forum in Africa and to organize a regional meeting between indigenous activists and state representatives to discuss the Millennium Development Goals (MDGs) in Africa. Later, over coffee, another activist suggested sending the states direct invitations. When a representative from the Kenyan High Commission attended the 2005 UN Permanent Forum, everyone was intrigued, until, when asked, he identified himself as "just a low-level staff member" to one activist.

Activists were even more hopeful in 2007, when the permanent representative of the Kenyan government to the United Nations, His Excellency Zachary Dominic Muburi-Muita, was scheduled to present a statement for the first time at the UN Permanent Forum and had invited the Kenyan delegates to a dinner party one evening. "A first!" exclaimed one of the Maasai activists. But the difference between the typed, prepared statement (by a junior functionary, presumably) and the hand-edited statement that Muburi-Muita read about recent land policy initiatives in Kenya revealed the ongoing resistance of the Kenyan government to political recognition of indigenous peoples. While the original statement stated that "colonialism created disparities and dispossessed *many indigenous people* of their ancestral land," handwritten edits rendered the statement "colonialism created disparities and dispossessed *all people of Kenya* of their ancestral land" (Muburi-Muita 2007:2; emphasis added). Similarly, the typed phrase "indigenous peoples" in a statement about how such land alienation "relegate[ed] many of the *indigenous peoples* into the so-called 'native reserves'" was struck out and replaced with "Kenyan peoples" (Muburi-Muita 2007:2; emphasis added). In discussing how the new land policy was being formulated in consultation with a broad range of stakeholders, Muburi-Muita noted that "this new land policy is targeting to correct [*sic*] the problems that have affected all Kenyans over the years. No distinction is being made as to who the beneficiary will be: the guiding principle is to deal with the principal [*sic*] rather than deal with personalities or groups of persons" (Muburi-Muita 2007:4). The word "indigenous" appeared only once in the entire edited statement: "The process of formulating this policy has been consultative, participatory, interactive, transparent and inclusive. Groups that identify themselves as 'indigenous' [note: the quotation marks were written by hand on the typed text] were involved in the process every step of the way" (Muburi-Muita 2007:4). A later paragraph addressed the "impact of critical development projects in pastoral community lands," calling for "need to balance public and community interests," in response to criticism about two specific projects (Muburi-Muita 2007:5). Like all political rhetoric, the statement, especially as revised, was carefully crafted to navigate potential political minefields. So while Muburi-Muita acknowledged that some groups identified themselves as "indigenous," he undermined the declarative power of the identity by inserting quotation marks, and never affirmed that he (and therefore the Kenyan government) supported their identity-claims. Moreover, the words "ethnicity" and "ethnic group" were never used, represented instead by the nonspecific "communities," and opposed to the state (or "public").

The disdain, and, more commonly, hostility of many African nation-states toward claims of indigeneity by some groups was exacerbated by the inability of indigenous activists from Africa to form viable, powerful regional or continental networks. As an Ogoni activist from Nigeria complained, "We only meet and network in Geneva or New York. We need to promote more networking among African indigenous peoples' organizations. We are so scattered that we can have no serious impact at the national or regional level." A key obstacle to more effective networking was the complicated cultural politics of inclusion and exclusion within the continent produced, in part, by colonial legacies of boundaries (political, linguistic, and otherwise); postcolonial disparities in wealth, education, and international mobility; and racialized ideas of belonging. Notably, there was a deep mistrust between African activists from North Africa and those from sub-Saharan Africa, all of whom were identified as "Africans" according to UN geographical designations. Ironically, given their support and reliance on the principle of self-identification, some activists from sub-Saharan Africa wondered if their light-skinned, Arabic-speaking northern colleagues were even African, much less indigenous, and accused them of paternalism and even racism. Activists from North Africa, in turn, felt frustrated by the challenges of effectively organizing their often (but not always) less-educated, less-experienced, and less-cosmopolitan colleagues.

Hassan Id Balkassm, the Amazigh lawyer from Morocco who has been involved with the UN Working Group and then UN Permanent Forum since 1994, has been a lightning rod for such debates. While he is well known and well respected by indigenous activists from Latin America, Asia, and other places, many of his own African colleagues suspected his motives, resented his success, and alleged that IPACC, the organization he founded, treated them in a racist manner as "black" Africans. For example, at the 2004 UN Permanent Forum, two African activists complained to me over coffee that the executive committee of IPACC was comprised of Moroccans and South Africans, while other Africans were just members. "But what do they do? Are they really African? Did you see that woman with Hassan? She was really light-skinned . . . who is indigenous there?" Another woman grumbled about a meeting of the African Caucus that she had attended the night before: "It was dominated by people from Francophone Africa; they all spoke French. Nigel [a white socio-linguist who runs the secretariat of IPACC] translated. Many of the people were from Morocco—do you think Moroccans are really Africans?" Hassan's practice of presenting formal statements at the UN in Arabic (even though he is also fluent in French and English) only further upset activists from sub-Saharan Africa, many of whom associated Arabic with historical experiences of Islamic conquest and oppression. Several activists told me that the first time that Hassan ran for a seat as an "expert" member of the UN Permanent Forum, the East African delegates insisted on electing Dr. Ayitegan Kouevi, a Togolese lawyer and member of IPACC who was a full-time resident of France, because they did not want a "Berber from Morocco" as their representative. They quickly regretted their decision, wondering, because of Kouevi's residence in France, "How indigenous is he?" Moreover, remarked a Kenyan activist, "We don't think of him as an African at all."

As some of the above comments suggest, many activists from sub-Saharan Africa were concerned about what they perceived as a racial hierarchy between IPACC's leaders and members. After IPACC was formalized at the 1997 UN Working Group, it established a small secretariat at the San Institute in Cape Town, then became autonomous in 2000. The organization currently describes itself as "a network of 150 indigenous peoples' organizations in 20 African countries."[39] The executive committee is comprised of elected representatives from six African regions (although one person has often represented both East Africa and the Horn of Africa) and a special representative for indigenous women, one of whom serves as chairperson. In addition, the secretariat is run by a director, who for several years has been Dr. Nigel Crawhall, a white Canadian socio-linguist with expertise in African languages who has lived in South Africa for many years. Although several members of the executive committee are from sub-Saharan Africa, the most visible and vocal members at the UN meetings are Hassan, Nigel, and Mary Simat, a Maasai woman from Kenya. As noted above, some African activists voiced suspicions about Hassan and Nigel, and even Mary (who has served as the chair of IPACC) was perceived by some as a puppet figure. A leader of a transnational advocacy organization wondered about Nigel's political sense: "He is a nice guy, but deeply confused. He is a white South African dressing in Berber dress, but he doesn't see a problem in presuming to speak for indigenous peoples."

Whatever their perceptions about IPACC's leadership, most African activists that I interviewed felt that IPACC had done little to help their cause. When I asked an Ogiek activist from Kenya in 2004 if his organization was involved with IPACC, he responded:

> No, I don't have much to do with them. They are not really linked with the grass roots. Instead, they try to direct us, to tell us what to do. They should be helping and nurturing us to grow, but they don't. We sat for two hours in the African Caucus yesterday introducing ourselves, etc., but nothing was achieved. I wish there was another pan-African network. And the white people [Swahili: *wazungu*]—it is fine if they are there and want to help, but they are directing things, so that even the Africans involved with them change and become like them.[40]

In response to their dissatisfaction with IPACC, several sub-Saharan activists formed an alternative pan-African organization, Organization for Indigenous Peoples of Africa (OIPA) in 1999. According to one of OIPA's founders, they had many complaints about IPACC, including: it did not represent indigenous peoples in Africa; it was run by South Africans and led by non-indigenous peoples; there were concerns about how the leadership was elected; since (at the time) IPACC held its General Assemblies to coincide with the UN Working Group in Geneva, only people who went to Geneva could participate; IPACC was more interested in working at the international level, rather than engaging with local peoples; and they disagreed with IPACC's limited mandate, which was just to coordinate indigenous issues within the UN system (see also Kipuri 2001:272). In response, IPACC alleged that despite OIPA's claims to represent all indigenous peoples in Africa, it was merely a regional organization representing East Africans (Cameron 2004). Despite some initial funding, however, OIPA never really established itself financially. OIPA sent representatives to the UN Working Group in Geneva twice. One of the OIPA representatives told me how useful he found the UN meetings: "I enjoyed the opportunity to meet other indigenous people, to think about issues on a higher plane, and to see the connections with other people."[41] But the co-founder considered OIPA's biggest success to be its involvement in the 2003 World Parks Congress: "We held a large preparatory meeting and then sent delegates to the conference in Durban. They really influenced the discussions and decisions that were made" (see also OIPA 2003). By 2005, however, when I was in Tanzania trying to find the OIPA office to read their files and interview the current secretary, the office was closed, funds were gone, and the secretary, a Kenyan, was nowhere to be found (I finally met him at a workshop in April 2006).

Another factor underlying the tensions between North Africans and sub-Saharan activists was a difference in priorities. The primary goal of most sub-Saharan African groups was to protect their remaining lands and resources, as without land, issues of cultural and linguistic rights were moot. "Our main issue is to protect our communal lands and ensure the continuation of migration routes for pastoralists," explained a prominent Kenyan Maasai activist in 2007. "That is the baseline." In contrast, North Africans such as Amazigh already had recognized rights to their territories, so they were able to focus their political efforts on the recognition and protection their linguistic and cultural rights. At the 2004 UN Working Group, for example, Hassan Id Balkassm presented a statement on behalf of IPACC and TAMUT (an Amazigh NGO in Morocco). In Arabic, he stated that he was going to focus on Africa in general and the countries of the Maghreb in particular. He discussed the failure of these states to recognize the cultural rights of indigenous peoples such as Amazigh. Some states were beginning to change, however. He described how the Moroccan state now supported the formal recognition of Alwazi identity and the teaching of the Alwazi language. Similarly, in a subsequent presentation, he claimed that many of the wars and conflicts in Africa were the result of the nonrecognition by states of the cultural and linguistic identities of indigenous people. Only at the end of the statement did he mention the need to protect indigenous peoples' rights to their natural resources.

The legacy of colonial linguistic and spatial politics further complicated efforts to create a viable pan-African network, whether as a formal organization like IPACC or OIPA or just the African Caucus that routinely met during the UN meetings. While the formal UN session provided simultaneous translation in French, English, and Arabic, among other languages, it was far more cumbersome for individuals (such as Nigel) to translate during meetings of the African Caucus. As discussed above, East Africans complained that the African Caucus was dominated by francophone Africans. Many francophone Africans, in frustration over the language difficulties, have aligned with a newly formed francophone indigenous peoples' caucus. Moreover, the postcolonial reality of air travel routes made it far easier (although expensive) for activists throughout Africa to fly directly to a meeting place in Europe than to one in Africa.

For these and other reasons, it was also difficult for African activists to form viable regional and national networks among themselves. In 2007, when I asked a Maasai member of a network of pastoralists and hunter-gatherers in Kenya whether they worked with pastoralists in northern Kenya such as Samburu and Turkana, he replied: "We try, but it is difficult. They face very different issues in northern Kenya, especially the ongoing conflicts among pastoralists. So any time we have a meeting, one group blames the other, who blames the other and so on. But in southern Kenya, the problem is one of land and resources." Similarly, an Ogiek activist told me in 2004 that while there was some networking among Kenyan groups, it was not very far along: "I could be in one corner and someone else in the other, both groups having similar problems. But we don't know about each other."

Even coordination among members of one ethnic group divided by colonial borders into different states was a challenge, as illustrated by the case of Maasai in Kenya and Tanzania. When I asked a Maasai activist from Tanzania in 2003 if the different Maasai delegations worked together at the UN, he replied:

> Yes, slowly, slowly. For example, we tried to put together a joint statement on the alienation of land by national parks and protected areas, but we didn't have time to write it. We realize that we need to work together as Maasai. But we were divided by colonists—not just in terms of the colonial border [between Kenya and Tanzania], but they took advantage of us after our wars. It is hard to work with nomadic communities, but we are trying.

When I asked the same question to a Maasai from Kenya later that day, he said, "Just this morning we were discussing the need to cooperate, to work together to present our issues. But we really haven't done so yet." Maasai from Kenya have been very active in the UN meetings, attending in large groups, presenting statements, obtaining leadership positions, organizing and speaking at side events, and publicizing their grievances and demands. In contrast, since Parkipuny's participation in the 1989 UN Working Group, only a few Maasai from Tanzania have participated over the years. Several Kenyan Maasai whom I interviewed felt that they were far more politically organized than the Tanzanians: "The Kenyans are far ahead of the Tanzanian Maasai, in part because they faced the dilemmas of individual property so much sooner. I am always telling Tanzanians that they can learn from us, that we are a model." The Kenyans generally tried to work with the Tanzanians, although their help was sometimes perceived as paternalistic and even condescending. Although one Maasai from Tanzania acknowledged that the Kenyans were better organized and better funded ("They know how to get grants to support their travel to the Permanent Forum"), she resented it when a prominent Maasai man from Kenya hijacked her time slot in 2004 to speak on behalf of "all Maasai women." The recent decision by several Maasai activists and organizations in Tanzania to disengage from the international indigenous rights movement in order to focus their advocacy activities on more effective engagements with the state has further divided them from their Kenyan counterparts (chapter 4).

Debating Indigeneity at Home: The African Commission on Human and Peoples' Rights

In 1999, several African activists, with the support of IWGIA, decided to pursue an alternative, complementary strategy to promote the recognition and rights of indigenous peoples by African states through mechanisms provided by the newly formed African Commission on Human and Peoples' Rights (African Commission).[42] Delegates to the 1999 Conference on Indigenous Peoples in Eastern, Central, and Southern Africa in Arusha, Tanzania, co-sponsored by IWGIA and PINGOs Forum, adopted the "Arusha Resolutions," a list of declarations, resolutions, and recommendations to recognize and promote the rights of indigenous peoples in Africa. The resolutions included requests to the African Commission to include an agenda item on the rights of indigenous peoples in all of its sessions and to establish a working group "to consider all aspects of the rights of indigenous peoples in Africa and to promote consideration of the matter by African states" (Arusha Resolutions 1999). Barney Pityana, a commissioner from South Africa, participated in the Arusha conference, and raised the issue of indigenous peoples at two subsequent meetings of the African Commission. His overtures were initially rejected by the other commissioners, who felt that the term "indigenous peoples" did not apply to Africa. In 2000, under pressure from NGOs and human rights organizations, the commissioners agreed to include the situation of indigenous peoples as a separate agenda item in their deliberations. Although still suspicious about the relevance of the concept, the African Commission adopted the "Resolution on the Rights of Indigenous Populations/Communities in Africa," which provided for the establishment of a Working Group on Indigenous Populations/Communities (AC Working Group) (African Commission 2000).

The initial mandate of the AC Working Group was to examine the concept of indigenous populations/communities in Africa; to study the implications of the African Charter on Human and Peoples' Rights (African Charter) for the well-being of indigenous populations/communities, especially with regard to several articles of the African Charter; and to consider appropriate recommendations for the monitoring and protection of the rights of indigenous populations/communities (African Commission 2000). The AC Working Group was also tasked with seeking donor support for its work. IWGIA immediately offered financial support, and Marianne Jensen, an IWGIA staff member specializing in Africa, served as an "independent expert" member of the AC Working Group.[43]

After three years of meetings, research, and consultations with human rights experts and representatives of indigenous peoples' organizations, the AC Working Group presented a final report to the African Commission in 2003 that endorsed the applicability of the concept of indigenous peoples to Africa; reviewed the human rights situation of specific indigenous peoples on the continent (primarily hunter-gatherers and pastoralists) in relation to the principles of the African Charter; and recommended specific measures to review and address the needs of indigenous peoples in Africa, including the appointment of a special rapporteur on indigenous issues by the African Commission, the establishment of a forum for regular meetings of "indigenous participants, experts and other human rights activists" during sessions of the African Commission, the permanent inclusion of "the rights of indigenous populations in Africa" as an agenda item in all Ordinary Sessions of the African Commission, and an extension of its own mandate (African Commission 2005). The African Commission adopted the report, endorsed the recommendations, and renewed and expanded the mandate of the AC Working Group to research, study, raise awareness, and make recommendations about the human rights situations of indigenous populations and communities in Africa (African Commission 2003).

African activists were thrilled that the African Commission adopted the report; they hoped it would serve as a potentially powerful tool for them to leverage for political recognition by their reluctant nation-states. But they also recognized the limitations of the report, especially the compromises made to obtain state support. Notably, the report (like the title of the AC Working Group) did not recognize indigenous "peoples," but indigenous "populations and communities." As reflected in debates about the title and wording of the Declaration, the UN Working Group, and the UN Permanent Forum, many states argued that the term "peoples" was a legal concept akin to "states" in international law and treaties, which had been granted the right to self-determination. For African governments (and others) fearful of ethnonationalism, endorsing the existence of indigenous "peoples" in their borders would therefore be tantamount to supporting their right to secede from their existing states and form new states.[44] The repeated response of African activists to the states, to me, and to anyone who asked was that they were seeking more inclusion in their nation-states, not less. Moreover, by "self-determination" they did not mean political secession, but the right to debate, decide, and control their own political representation, economic futures, social organization, and cultural practices and beliefs without outside intervention, in the face of a long history of state efforts to force them to assimilate, change, or refute their heritage. As a Batwa activist told Andrea Muehlebach:

> Self-determination, I think, is about letting the people do what they want by themselves. That is what I understand by self-determination. Sometimes projects are imposed on indigenous peoples, projects which are not good for them, and governors tell them they must agree. So, that is an imposition, and indigenous groups misunderstand this and maybe some projects can't succeed. So I think that self-determination is to let indigenous peoples make their decisions. That is what I learn by self-determination. . . . The second way to explain the concept of self-determination to the Batwa is that they are human beings . . . and that they can do things without other people. It is *us* to say, "We want it this way." It is within our right, our human right to say no. To say yes. And not to be pushed around. We are equal. (Bambanze Vital, quoted in Muehlebach 2003:259; emphasis in original)

As Muehlebach argues, the concept of self-determination described by Vital and other "neophyte" activists is strikingly similar to that advocated by many professional indigenous activists and human rights lawyers, "that the concept must be understood broadly as a fundamental human right that guarantees a peoples' right to make decisions about its present and future freely and without outside interference" (Muehlebach 2003:260).

African States, Indigenous Peoples, and the Politics of Recognition

So what have been the consequences for African groups (and for the transnational indigenous rights movement) of their almost twenty years of involvement in the indigenous peoples' movement? As IPACC noted recently, there have been some concrete achievements in improving the relationship between African indigenous peoples and some African states:

> Cameroon, Gabon and Congo Republic have all entered into dialogue with the World Bank and indigenous peoples about the appropriate protection of rights. Burundi has changed its constitution to guarantee that Batwa have political representation. South Africa has created an interdepartmental working group to negotiate with Khoe and San communities as well as vocally supported the UN Declaration. Congo Republic is adopting legislation to protect the cultural integrity of indigenous people in the rainforest. Morocco unbanned the Amazigh language after 40 years of suppression. Algeria recognises the distinct cultural identity of Amazigh people. Mali and Niger signed peace accords with Tuareg of the Central Sahara without jeopardizing their national territorial integrity. Mauritania has expressed concern over the last hunters of the Sahara, the Nemadi peoples. (IPACC 2006)

But these achievements have been accompanied by continuing struggles between some states and self-identified indigenous peoples within their borders over land alienation and evictions (of, for example, San in Botswana, and Hadza and Maasai in Tanzania); the imposition of state-endorsed "development" projects (such as dams, ranches, oil pipelines, resettlement) financed by multilateral aid organizations (such as the World Bank and FAO) without the "free, prior and informed consent" of affected peoples; and continuing acts of violence, repression, and subjugation (in Congo and Botswana, for example). Moreover, in states such as Tanzania that have embraced neoliberal "reforms," the accelerated, state-supported influx of international investment in such industries as tourism, hunting, and com-

mercial agriculture has eroded the economic resources and ignored the political rights of Maasai, Hadza, and others in more dispersed but cumula-
tively significant ways (chapter 2).

As a result of these ongoing conflicts, some activists and organizations
have voiced frustration with the glacially slow, seemingly ineffective processes and procedures of the United Nations. As a Maasai activist from
Kenya wondered at the 2005 UN Permanent Forum, "There are all these
words and papers, but what really happens on the ground?" Her comments
were echoed by another Maasai activist at the same meeting: "We don't need
a bunch of words and documents; we need resources." "These statements are
so generic, they all begin to sound the same," complained another activist.
Some donors shared their concern, working to help activists connect the
statements and advocacy done at the UN Permanent Forum with their activities and practices in their local communities. As one donor explained, "I
try to tell the indigenous activists that nothing will happen just by making a
nice statement. They need to link it with local pressure and action." Many of
the African activists I spoke with shared the concern of other indigenous
activists that while the UN Permanent Forum was one of the few international sites where they could voice their grievances, it lacked the institutional
structures to implement, evaluate, and monitor its own recommendations.

In response to these frustrations and the enduring hostility of their nation-
states to their claims of indigeneity and collective rights, some individuals and
organizations, such as those representing Maasai in Tanzania, have distanced
themselves from the indigenous movement and withdrawn from active involvement in the UN meetings and other international fora to restructure their
political discourses and practices in order to try to more effectively lobby and
engage state-level institutions and actors (chapter 4).[45] Other activists and organizations have maintained their participation at the UN Permanent Forum,
despite questions about their motivations and accusations that they are just
"jet-setting indigenous" (as one donor complained to me). But as an Ogiek
activist told me, "I don't do this to get rich, but to help my people. Look at
me—I'm not fat. I can't get fat when I am concerned about other people. I don't
care about my body, only my life." Some donors and researchers tried to encourage pastoralists from East Africa to participate in an alternative international network of "mobile peoples," but the Kenyan and Tanzanian Maasai
that I asked about this network just laughed: "We are not interested. What
comes next after 'mobile peoples'?"

The significance of the participation of African groups in the indigenous peoples' movement became starkly clear in late 2006, when several African states launched a last-minute attack to delay (if not prevent) approval of the Declaration. In June 2006, after almost twenty years of negotiation, the Declaration was finally adopted by the UN Human Rights Council (UN HRC) by a vote of thirty votes in favor (including three African states—South Africa, Cameroon, and Zambia), two against (Canada, Russian Federation), and twelve abstentions (including six African states—Algeria, Ghana, Morocco, Nigeria, Senegal, and Tunisia).[46] Given this strong support by the UN HRC, most activists expected an easy approval by the UN General Assembly at its next meeting in November 2006, the final step in the process. Much to everyone's surprise, given the marked lack of involvement of African states in the many years of deliberations over the Declaration, a group of African states, led by Namibia, suddenly voiced opposition to the Declaration, claiming that it conflicted with provisions in the constitutions of many African states. In early November 2006 they circulated a Draft Aide Memoire that detailed their concerns, including the absence of a definition of indigenous peoples; the fear that the recognition of the principle of self-determination for indigenous peoples could lead to secession, and thus was a threat to the "political unity and territorial integrity of any country"; and other specific articles that they claimed conflicted with or undermined the legal, political, and economic rights and sovereignty of states (African Group 2006). Namibia proposed that adoption of the Declaration be deferred for a year to take into account the concerns of these African states, and suggested amendments to the Declaration on behalf of the "Group of African States."[47] (Although some African states, most notably South Africa, supported the Declaration, they agreed on the need to try to seek consensus among all the African states, rather than split their votes.)

The General Assembly approved Namibia's proposal, sparking a year of intense debate and lobbying among indigenous activists, supportive and non-supportive African states, advocacy organizations, and other states over the future of the Declaration. Some indigenous activists from the Americas voiced regret that they had ever recognized Africans as indigenous peoples. African activists, in turn, were angered and deeply embarrassed by the unanticipated actions of their states. After the African Union issued a Decision in January 2007 that supported the Aide Memoire and asked the African states to seek a "united position,"[48] several African human rights experts launched a formidable, coordinated response to the African states with the support of some advo-cacy organizations, especially IWGIA. Among other initiatives, they wrote a detailed response to the Aide Memoire that summarized the findings of the AC Working Group report endorsed by the African Commission; refuted the objections of the states with specific examples of cases where the rights and resources of indigenous peoples were already recognized and affirmed by African states; and argued that the Declaration reaffirmed rather than challenged rights "that are already recognised by virtually all African constitutions and the African Charter" (African Group of Experts 2007).[49] Moreover, they stressed that no indigenous communities in Africa were claiming statehood or threatening secession:

> On the contrary, these peoples or communities are claiming aspects of the right to self-determination that do not threaten national boundaries, including the right to full participation in national life, the right to local self-government, the right to be consulted and to participate in the making of certain laws and programmes, the right of recognition and appreciation of their traditional structures along with the freedom to enjoy and promote their cultures. (African Group of Experts 2007: 6)

Then, with the support of IWGIA, six African experts visited New York in April 2007 to meet with representatives from nineteen African embassies to discuss the Declaration. IWGIA also collaborated with the UN Permanent Forum to organize a roundtable at the 2007 meeting with the participation of seventeen African permanent missions and twenty-five non-African perma-nent missions. Indeed, the 2007 UN Permanent Forum was a frenzy of activity as African activists and others condemned the actions of the African states, lobbied state representatives both formally and informally, and debated how to proceed. After discussion at its May 2007 meeting, the African Commission issued an Advisory Opinion in support of the Declaration that was discussed at the African Union Summit in July 2007 (African Commission 2007). Other organizations, such as IPACC, also launched a series of press releases and public statements, sponsored visits between African indigenous activists and representatives of African states, and lobbied the African Commission and reluctant African states to support the Declaration.[50]

Finally, as a result of all of these efforts, a compromise was negotiated be-tween the African states, indigenous activists, and the states sponsoring the Declaration, and an amended version of the Declaration (reflecting all of

Namibia's suggested revisions) was adopted by the UN General Assembly on September 7, 2007, by a vote of 144 states in favor (including almost every African state except twelve states that were "absent" for the vote),[51] four votes against (Australia, Canada, New Zealand, and the United States), and eleven abstentions (including Burundi, Kenya, and Nigeria) (United Nations 2007). The victory was a stunning one for indigenous activists, and African activists in particular. While African activists successfully mobilized most of their states to approve the Declaration, long-time activists from the powerful settler colonies of Australia, Canada, New Zealand, and the United States witnessed defeat, despite decades of lobbying and negotiations. (Although the Declaration is a nonbinding agreement for states, it does establish a shared international framework of minimum standards for the recognition, rights, and resources of indigenous peoples.)

What the Declaration means for the future political struggles of African peoples is unclear. Will the approval of the Declaration and the African Commission's endorsement of the AC Working Group report encourage further African involvement in the indigenous peoples' movement? Or will the frustrations of activists over the slow pace and byzantine processes of the UN and the acceleration of state-led neoliberal economic and political reforms encourage activists to reposition themselves to make a new political space to seek redress for their grievances? Whatever the future holds, it is clear that the involvement of Africans in the indigenous peoples' movement has reshaped international and national politics in several important ways, as will be discussed in subsequent chapters.

First, by broadening the concept of indigenous to include African (and Asian) claims, the indigenous movement became at once more inclusive and potentially more contentious, as some influential states fought for a narrower, clearer definition of "indigenous" in order to limit the scope of the Declaration. The embrace of the principle of "self-identification" by indigenous activists from across the globe facilitated the recognition of Africans and Asians as indigenous peoples by international institutions such as IWGIA and the UN. Moreover, the creation of the UN Permanent Forum and the eventual demise of the UN Working Group enabled Africans to institutionalize their presence and ignore the hostility of certain powerful non-indigenous participants such as Alfonso Martínez. But their very success in establishing international recognition produced backlash at the national level, as some African states, wary of the validity and potential divisiveness of the claims and desperate to protect their already fragile sovereignty, challenged these new relational and structural definitions of "indigenous" with recourse to older, more essentialist definitions predicated on the historical experiences of "first peoples" in Australia, the Americas, and elsewhere. Yet remarkably, despite initial misgivings, the African Commission eventually endorsed the applicability of the concept of "indigenous peoples" to certain African groups, a testament in itself to the concerted struggles of African activists working with key allies such as IWGIA.

Second, the experiences of African activists and the history of their involvement with the indigenous rights movement suggest that, like other "activists beyond borders" (Keck and Sikkink 1998), they are neither pawns nor dupes, but human beings struggling to create and take advantage of available political spaces to forward their political and economic agendas. Their capacity for political action has been shaped not only by the legacies of colonial policies and practices but also, more recently, by the formidable alliance of capital with African states in the pursuit of privatization, productivity, and profit through the implementation of neoliberal political, economic, and social policies. Despite the tremendous potential for political paralysis in the face of such obstacles, these African activists have creatively positioned themselves to take advantage of the opportunities for political agency and collective action provided by the indigenous rights movement.

Whatever future political course African activists decide to pursue, they have learned tremendously from their participation in the indigenous movement in terms of effective ways to engage their states and donors, strategies to form and maintain viable (if fragile) coalitions and networks that transcend ethnic and national concerns and commitments, and possibilities for being different kinds of citizens within their states. Like Parkipuny, many have been able to see and learn from the larger patterns of structural similarities between their situation and that of Aborigines, Native Americans, and other indigenous peoples, especially about the range of possible relationships between indigenous peoples and nation-states. As discussed in subsequent chapters, the experiences of African activists underlines the need to take seriously the continuing salience of states in shaping how citizens and civil organizations engage with transnational advocacy networks and movements such as the indigenous peoples' movement, suggesting both the effects of neoliberal reforms on state agendas and the possible limits of transnational advocacy.

2

MAASAI NGOS, THE TANZANIAN STATE, AND THE POLITICS OF INDIGENEITY

Shortly after his trip to Geneva in 1989, Parkipuny and seven other Maasai men founded one of the first Maasai nongovernmental organizations (NGOs) in Tanzania, called Korongoro Integrated People Oriented to Conservation, or KIPOC, which also means "we shall recover" in Maa. These men clearly recognized the tensions between international recognition of indigenous peoples and state hostility toward the relevance of the concept in Tanzania: although the word "indigenous" appeared thirty-eight times in the initial twenty-two-page project document written to publicize KIPOC's program and funding needs to international donors (KIPOC 1991), it was mentioned only once in KIPOC's formal constitution (in reference to livestock production: "integrated indigenous livestock and wildlife system") (KIPOC 1990), which was submitted to the Tanzanian Ministry of Home Affairs as a requirement for formal registration as an NGO under the Tanzanian Societies Ordinance. The project document echoed and elaborated many of the themes raised in Parkipuny's 1989 address to the UN Working Group; it was full of the language and logic of the sanctity of the "cultural identity" of "indigenous" peoples and their "basic human rights" to choose the form, content, and pace of changes in their lives. According to KIPOC, the Maasai struggle was "part of the global struggle of indigenous peoples to restore respect to their rights, cultural identity and to the land of their birth" (KIPOC 1991:7).

Since the formation of KIPOC, the number of NGOs started by Maasai and other pastoralists and hunter-gatherers in northern Tanzania has grown exponentially, from ten registered NGOs in 1994 to more than one hundred such organizations in 2000.[1] During the 1990s, most, like KIPOC, were organized around diverse claims of a common "indigenous" identity based on ethnicity (such as "being Maasai"), mode of production (being a pastoralist or hunter-gatherer), and/or a long history of political and economic disenfranchisement by first the colonial and now the postcolonial nation-state. Such rhetorical moves were politically strategic; they enabled these NGOs to link their demands to international networks and institutions preoccupied with ensuring and strengthening the rights of "indigenous peoples." Given their long history of grievances against the Tanzanian state, framing their demands in terms of their rights as indigenous people provided a unique opportunity to challenge disparaging stereotypes, forge a collective identity, and mobilize disparate and often dispirited groups. They gained greater visibility for their groups, increased international legitimacy for their claims, and, inevitably, improved donor support. In fact, after a while, many of these organizations demonstrated an extraordinary ability to attract substantial funds from bilateral and private international donors. Their evident success in mobilizing donor funding—visible in the new offices, vehicles, jobs, and national and international travel—encouraged the formation of even more NGOs.

This chapter explores the emergence and spread of these NGOs and the experience of Maasai activists and organizations in order to analyze the opportunities and obstacles that their involvement in the transnational indigenous peoples' movement has posed for their ongoing struggles for recognition, resources, and rights. As such, the chapter illuminates broader concerns about the structural dilemmas of NGOs, the dynamic relationship between NGOs and state institutions, the tensions between "global" and "local" economic and political agendas, and the cultural politics of indigeneity. As discussed in the introduction, I am *not* concerned with determining the "authenticity" of Maasai cultural identities or the merits of their claims to being "indigenous." Rather, I am interested in exploring *how* and *why* Maasai positioned themselves as "indigenous," how the legacies of colonial and postcolonial policies and practices influenced this positioning and its effects, and probing the opportunities and challenges they encountered, especially in terms of their relationships with the Tanzanian state.

Becoming Maasai

For over a century, Maasai have been perceived by Euro-Americans and increasing numbers of Africans as icons of "primitive" Africa, an image produced and sustained by their prolific representations in colonial travelogues and journals, tourist brochures, "coffee table" picture books, postcards, movies, commercials, newspapers, billboards, fashion magazines, and other venues.[2] As always, these static visual images—of men perched on one leg with cattle grazing in the background and women dressed in elaborate beadwork and colorful cloths milking cows—and stereotyped narratives—of ruthless warriors stealing cattle from defenseless farmers or brutal patriarchs controlling docile women—mask a complicated historical and contemporary reality. As I documented in *Once Intrepid Warriors* (Hodgson 2001a), key points of that history include the following: Maa-speaking peoples migrated into what is now known as Kenya and Tanzania at least several hundred years ago from a homeland they call "Kerio," which some archaeological and linguistic evidence suggests may be in southern Sudan. They were originally agro-pastoralists, but, in time, certain changes in technology (mastery of iron forging), climate (decades of relatively high rainfall), and social organization (the emergence of male age grades) enabled a group of Maa-speakers to specialize almost solely in livestock herding and develop a heightened sense of themselves as pastoralists (Sutton 1993; Galaty 1993). By the late 1870s, the ethnonym "Maasai" was used by early Euro-American travelers and others to refer to those Maa-speakers who specialized in pastoralism (Bernsten 1980). The conflation of ethnonym with livelihood and the reification of Maasai identity as "pure pastoralists" were further reinforced during the colonial period with the division of Maasai social networks by colonial boundaries between present-day Kenya and Tanzania; the creation of Maasai "reserves" in both colonies to contain and control the seemingly chaotic movements of the semi-nomadic herders and take possession of their most fertile rangelands and permanent water supplies; and ambivalent colonial policies that either sought to protect and "preserve" Maasai "culture" by limiting their access to education, healthcare, and other "detribalizing" influences or to demand immediate, radical changes to their lives and livelihoods in the name of "progress," "productivity," and "prosperity" (such as in the Masai Development Project of the 1950s)[3] (Hodgson 2001a; Börjeson et al. 2008). At independence, Maasai were still concentrated in the former Masai Reserve, with few schools, health facilities, roads, or other indicators of "development" in comparison to other groups and areas of the country.

Paternal Politics: Citizens and Subjects under Socialism

For Maasai, a key motivation to participate in the transnational indigenous peoples' movement was their increasingly hostile relationship with the Tanzanian nation-state since independence, a hostility produced, in part, by the colonial legacies described above. The Tanzanian elites who took power in 1961 fiercely embraced the developmentalist agendas of modernity and progress propounded by the British in the 1950s and 1960s. They accused Maasai of being anachronistic relics of "the past" and "the primitive" and ignored how their present predicaments had been shaped by their complicated past. Instead, the new African leaders launched repeated campaigns such as "Operation Dress-up" to force Maasai to modernize, including decrees banning old men from wearing blankets in the daytime, the application of ochre to clothing and skin, leather dresses for women, and pigtails for warriors (Hodgson 2001a:149–50; Schneider 2006). In 1970, Maasai men and women were even temporarily prohibited from riding buses or using public facilities (including shops and government offices) "unless he or she were wearing contemporary attire: shorts, trousers, dresses" (Hatfield 1977:16). Rather than succeeding in enforcing a "modern" dress code, these measures further alienated Maasai from the state and increased their hostility to non-Maasai (whom they called "Swahili").

As part of President Julius Nyerere's African socialist vision of *Ujamaa* ("familyhood"), government officials continued colonial practices of alienating and redistributing the most fertile areas of Masai District (which was eventually broken up into smaller districts—presently Monduli, Longido, Ngorongoro, Kiteto, and Simanjiro Districts; see map, p. 150) to more economically "productive" people and enterprises. For example, the Conservation Act of 1974 removed large areas of grazing land in the Serengeti, Ngorongoro, and Tarangire National Parks from use by Maasai herders in the interests of "preserving" wildlife. In the 1970s, the government took some of the best grazing land in the Ardai plains to build a military training camp. One thousand acres of "unused" land in Emairete (actually Maasai drought reserves and dry-season grazing lands) was allocated to the Tanzania Beer Company (which became Tanzania Breweries) to grow barley and another 1,400 acres to Tanzania Cartons. Arusha, Mbulu, Gogo, and other agricultural and agro-pastoralist groups were encouraged to move into Masai District, while Maasai were discouraged from moving out, further constricting their resource base and straining the already fragile rangelands. In addition, the government forcibly relocated thousands of dispersed Maasai into settled villages as part of the national villagization scheme and launched the Masai Range Management and Livestock Development Project (a ten-year, multimillion-dollar project to rapidly increase the "productivity" of Maasai livestock that was financed, in part, by

USAID) (Hodgson 2001a, 1999b). Finally, as tourism, wildlife viewing, and big-game hunting quickly became the primary sources of foreign exchange, the government promoted Maasai in brochures, postcards, guidebooks, and tours as icons of "traditional" "primitive" Africa in order to expand the increasingly lucrative tourist industry. Ironically, although the Ujamaa policy was designed, in part, to disregard and move beyond ethnicity to build national unity, Maasai were still always identified in discussions, policies, and the (state-controlled) media by their ethnic label, rather than the ubiquitous *ndugu* (comrade) (Hodgson 2001a: chapter 4).

At the time, as Parkipuny explained in chapter 1, there were few avenues available for Maasai to protest state actions and to demand change. The one political party, Chama Cha Mapinduzi (CCM), controlled the political system, stifled political critique, and regulated meetings, organizations, and collective action through a strict system of permits, permissions, and laws. On occasion, elder Maasai men made public speeches to protest specific actions, and Maasai women launched collective strikes against certain Maasai and non-Maasai leaders (Hodgson 2001a). But "civil society" as such was virtually nonexistent in Tanzania at this time, as all mass political movements (women, workers, youth) were under CCM's leadership (cf. Gibbon 2001). As Roderick Neumann (1995:368) concluded: "Essentially, the mass of peasants and workers were denied the right to organize independently, and thus could not counter the formation of a bureaucratic ruling class. The party leadership and state bureaucrats (often interchangeable) facilitated their control of popular politics through coercive practices reinforced by a legitimating populist discourse which represented Tanzania as a classless, egalitarian society." Moreover, with a few notable exceptions, a lack of education and political integration prohibited most Maasai from any meaningful political participation beyond the village level.[4]

My conversations and interviews with Maasai men and women in the mid-1980s and early 1990s revealed that few of them considered themselves as "citizens" of Tanzania; rather, they thought of themselves as "subjects" of unjust rule by postcolonial elites (cf. Mamdani 1996). They spoke bitterly about their disrespectful treatment by "Swahilis"; described the discrimination they experienced from government and CCM leaders in terms of land matters, delivery of social and veterinary services, and political accountability; and wondered how their annual development taxes and other payments were actually used (Hodgson 2001a). A few older men even wistfully wished for the return of British colonial rule: "at least they treated us with respect!" In 1992, almost one third of the seventy-five women I surveyed in three communities claimed to not know what CCM was, responding *"Kainyoo CCM?"* (What is CCM?) to my query about their membership in the political party. Many women indeed did not know what it was, demonstrating the failure of the one state party to reach out to and incorporate them. But some women knew all too well about CCM; their response was intended to mark and mock the discrepancy between the promises and the realities of CCM's initiatives. As one woman replied sarcastically, "What is CCM? The name for people who don't work?" (Hodgson 2001a:190).

Neoliberalism, Civil Society, and Indigenous Rights

By the mid-1990s, after the retirement of Nyerere in 1985, the introduction of multiple political parties in 1992, and the imposition of neoliberal economic policies in the shape of structural adjustment, much had changed in Tanzania (Shivji 2006). The new president, Ali Hassan Mwinyi, signed a structural adjustment policy (SAP) with the World Bank/International Monetary Fund in 1986 that initiated a radical restructuring of the Tanzanian economy from one based on socialist principles of Ujamaa, collective well-being, and communally owned resources to one based on capitalist principles of a free-market economy, privatization of resources, individual success, and profit maximization. Over the next twenty years, through a succession of SAPs, poverty reduction strategy policies (PRSs), and other World Bank–endorsed (and capital-friendly) policy "reforms" and practices, the Tanzanian state dissolved and sold the assets of the parastatals that had controlled tourism, utilities, airlines, banking, and so forth to private (often foreign) investors; instituted a new land policy to replace the communal ownership of lands with the possibility of private land titling (including to non-Tanzanian companies and investors); replaced state-supported social services for education and health with fee-for-services programs; streamlined its own ranks by laying off thousands of bureaucrats and other state workers; and ratified a new investment code and created the Tanzanian Investment Commission to encourage and enable foreign investment in Tanzania, among other measures.[5] Moreover, after mandating the use of acaricides for years to prevent tick-borne diseases (which also reduced the cattle' inherited immunity to such diseases), the state decentralized financial support of veterinary services and infrastructure (dips, crushes, etc.) to localities and quit inoculating cattle for tick-borne diseases—which produced a huge number of cattle deaths.

One result of this dramatic transition was to intensify economic inequalities and political discontent among already marginalized peoples. For pastoralists and hunter-gatherers, one of the most alarming effects of liberalization was the tremendous acceleration of illegal and quasi-legal incursions onto and alienation of their lands (especially their dry-season and drought-reserve grazing lands) for large-scale commercial farms, mining, game parks, wildlife reserves, and other revenue-generating endeavors by the state, elites, and international capital (Hodgson 2001a; Hodgson and Schroeder 2002; Lane 1996; Madsen 2000; Brockington 2002). For example, during the late 1980s and early 1990s, more than five thousand Maasai were evicted from the Mkomazi Game Reserve in order to establish a new national game park (Brockington 2002), large-scale commercial farms spread rapidly in the Simanjiro and Loliondo areas (Börjeson et al. 2008), there was a continued influx of Tanzanian and European settlers into Maasai areas, and the state approved the appropriation of large areas of land for hunting concessions, construction of tourist lodges, and mining. One of the most publicized and scandalous state-endorsed "land grabs" was the infamous "Loliondogate" case in 1993, when the minister for tourism leased the entire Loliondo Game Controlled Area (about 4,000 square kilometers) to a hunting firm owned by an army brigadier from the United Arab Emirates (MERC 2002). Hassan Sachedina (2006:35) has calculated that since 1992 alone (thus long after the creation of Serengeti National Park and the Ngorongoro Conservation Area), eighteen game reserves and national parks have been gazetted in Tanzania, for a total surface area of 27,256 square kilometers. Thus, by 2009, the Arusha Regional Commission (2009) reported that of the 34,526 square kilometers that comprised the total land area of the Arusha Region, 13,664 square kilometers (39.6%) was designated as game reserves (no human settlement), over 1,000 square kilometers (2.9%) as national parks (no human settlement),[6] many (unsurveyed) square kilometers as game controlled areas (human settlement allowed, but restrictions on land use), and 923 square kilometers (2.7%) as forest reserves. The report concluded that the available grazing land was "under pressure as it is almost fully utilized," especially since almost 11 percent of the "available" land was infected by tsetse fly (Arusha Regional Commissioner's Office 2009).

Despite this conclusion, large swaths of land that were used seasonally by pastoralists as dry-season and drought grazing lands have been labeled as "unused" land by state authorities (specifically the Tanzanian Investment Commission) and therefore available for appropriation and purchase by national and, preferably, international investors.

The accelerated land alienation was coupled with reinvigorated state-sponsored attacks on the extensive transhumant livestock management system of Maasai, which was premised on mobility and access to communally managed lands, as "unproductive" and ecologically damaging (discussed in detail in chapter 4). Instead, echoing colonial diatribes, the Ministry of Livestock and other government units tried to coerce Maasai and other pastoralists to improve the "productivity" of their livestock by settling and converting their livestock production system into an intensive, fixed-ranch model (often referred to as "the Botswana model"). Almost every week, articles and editorials appeared in the major Tanzanian newspapers berating pastoralists for their "backward" livestock management practices, with headlines such as "Pastoralists need education on animal husbandry,"[7] "Calls to modernise livestock keeping,"[8] and "Tanzania's herds of cattle are dead capital."[9] Conflicts between pastoralists and farmers escalated, as pastoralists tried to cope with not only the tremendous loss of land, but increasing constraints to their ability to move their cattle across the expanding patchwork of private and commercial farms.

A key hotspot for these conflicts was in Kilosa District, located in Morogoro Region, south of Arusha Region, toward the coast. Conflicts between pastoralists (including Ilparakuyo, Gogo, and Barabaig) and farmers in Kilosa over increasingly scarce land and resources has occurred since at least the 1960s, but has accelerated over the past decades (especially during times of drought), resulting in the destruction of property, attacks on cattle, damage to crops, and more than forty deaths between just 1998 and 2000 (Morindat et al. 2003). The conflicts were exacerbated by contradictory land laws; poor local governance, planning, and oversight; accusations of corruption and negligence; and complicated histories of migration, displacement, settlement and livelihood practices (Morindat et al. 2003; Mung'ong'o and Mwamfupe 2003; Maganga et al. 2008). Many of the pastoralists had lived in Kilosa for decades (a number were in fact agro-pastoralists); some were evictees from Mkomazi who were never allotted any alternative land; and others were seasonal herders searching for grazing land and water. Similarly, some of the farmers had lived in Kilosa for decades, while others were recent migrants encouraged by the government to settle and farm the "unused" grazing land. Despite a series of investigations, consultations, and efforts to reconcile the groups, matters worsened in late 2008, when confrontation between a farmer and a herder escalated into the killing of seven other people.[10] In the spring of 2009, the government called for the immediate removal of many pastoralists from the area and the confiscation of their cattle, but soon suspended the measure to consider "a more comprehensive approach" in response to national and international outcries.[11]

The consequences of these changes were tumultuous for Maasai lives and livelihoods. In the past, Maasai systems of redistribution and assistance such as clientship, stock partners, bride service, and child adoption had supported poorer Maasai and often enabled them to rebuild their herds and reestablish themselves economically. But these institutions have rapidly disappeared in many areas as increasing numbers of Maasai struggle for economic security. As a result, economic stratification, which was always present among Maasai, has intensified and rigidified, compelling displaced and impoverished Maasai to seek new options for survival.[12] Comparative data collected from three communities in Monduli district in 1980 (Ndagala 1982:35) and 1992 (Hodgson 2001a:176) showed a marked decline in total livestock holdings coupled with a significant increase in stratification (measured in terms of livestock holding) in just over ten years. In 1980, only 4 men (7%) out of 60 surveyed had no livestock units;[13] by 1990, 111 households (24%) out of 454 surveyed had no livestock. Conversely, in 1980, 15 men (25%) owned more than 40 livestock units, while only 14 households (3%) held more than 40 animals in 1992. Moreover, in one community, two men owned over 300 head each of the 1,879 cattle, or about one-third of the entire village holdings (Hodgson 2001a:175–176). Comparative data confirms that the marked decline in per capita livestock holdings over the last few decades and stark inequalities in livestock holdings (with most cattle owned by just a few wealthy men) are the norm throughout Maasai areas (e.g., Sachedina 2006, 2008; Sachedina and Trench 2009; Trench et al. 2009; Mung'ong'o and Mwamfupe 2003).

As a result, Maasai communities, as well as individual men and women, intensified their efforts to diversify economically. Building on a long history of small-scale farming by "pastoralist" Maasai in certain areas of Tanzania (Hodgson 2001a), they expanded their cultivation of maize, beans, potatoes, and other food crops exponentially, both as a subsistence strategy and as a means to mark and protect their remaining land from alienation (Hodgson 2001a; McCabe 2003). Over the past few decades, Maasai cultivation has taken many forms, including young men farming individual plots, men marrying non-Maasai women who farm small gardens, hiring of non-Maasai laborers to work their fields, and purchasing or renting of tractors, combines, and other equipment (Hodgson 2001a; Homewood et al. 2009). In the Ngorongoro Conservation Area, for example, where the government has alternatively banned and approved cultivation, Terrence McCabe (2003:105) reports that "by 1994, approximately 85% of resident families . . . were engaged in some form of cultivation." Similarly, Sachedina (2006:19) found that 93 percent of the 228 households he surveyed in Emboreet village in Simanjiro in 2004 reported that they farmed, averaging 12.57 acres per household, which was a significant increase from the average of 8.66 acres they reported just two years earlier in 2002. Moreover, in response to a question about how many acres they aspired to farm, the average "future acres" per household was 128.33 acres. In 2007, the percentage of arable land under crop production in some of the "pastoralist" districts was 35.3 percent in Monduli District, 39.9 percent in Longido District, and 40 percent in Ngorongoro District (this includes subsistence and commercial production) (Arusha Regional Commissioner's Office 2009).

In addition to farming, certain well-placed communities such as Terrat and Emboreet negotiated contracts with photographic safari companies to provide access to land for camping and walking tours in exchange for concession fees (Sachedina 2006; Nelson et al. 2009). In 2005, Emboreet village earned more than fifty thousand dollars from "bed night fees" paid by tourists and other miscellaneous wildlife-related revenue, not including tips from tourists (Sachedina 2006:15). A few communities near the borders of national parks have even taken advantage of the growing interest in "cultural tourism" to build their own lodges and camps, often in collaboration with safari operators, or to enter into "joint ventures" with international tour companies in which the village leases the company land for the construction of a permanent tourist lodge and exclusive access rights for photographic tourism (Nelson et al. 2009:322). Profits from these and other arrangements were usually supposed to be channeled into a village development account, to be applied toward projects of the village's choosing, but evidence suggests that elite leaders have been the primary beneficiaries of these initiatives (Sachedina 2008).

Other efforts at economic diversification have been more gender- and age-specific. Over the past two decades, young men have left their homesteads in droves to seek work as brokers in the expanding Tanzanite mining sector in Mererani or work as night guards or casual labor in Arusha, Dar es Salaam, and even Zanzibar (May 2002; May and McCabe 2004 ; May and Ikayo 2007; Sachedina 2006). Many have used their income to support their homesteads through irregular remittances and to purchase livestock to build their own herds. A few Tanzanite brokers, such as Lengai ole Mako, have become extraordinarily wealthy (Homewood et al. 2009a:257–59). Some older men experimented with contract farming of, first, barley for Tanzania Breweries and, later, flower seed for Multiflower and another international corporation. Women sought any means possible to earn money: producing beadwork to sell to tourists, selling milk and hides at local markets, collecting and selling firewood and medicinal herbs, raising chickens, making and selling illicit alcohol, cultivating not only maize and beans but small garden crops such as tomatoes for sale, and even, occasionally, trading sexual services for cash or food (Hodgson 2001a; Talle 1999; Homewood et al. 2009a). Many homesteads and individuals pursued several strategies simultaneously, taking advantage of environmental differences, social relations, and expanding market opportunities.

As growing numbers of pastoralist men left their homesteads for extended periods to seek work as miners or guards and laborers in towns, pastoralist women often became the de facto heads of household. But their increased workloads and responsibilities were rarely matched by increased rights and decision-making control. Over the past hundred years or so, as resources such as land and livestock became commoditized, men were targeted as political leaders, household "heads," and livestock "owners" by first colonial then postcolonial authorities, and women's moral authority and spiritual significance were dismissed; pastoralist women and their children occupied increasingly vulnerable and dependent positions in their households and homesteads. Most women now held only limited rights to livestock, lacked inheritance rights and significant decision-making power, and had few ways to earn cash. Yet they were increasingly responsible for feeding and caring for their children, including paying any school fees or healthcare costs. Very few were literate or spoke Swahili, the national language.

Initially, in addition to scrambling to ensure their economic security, pastoralists responded to the accelerated alienation of their land and resources through the kinds of "everyday acts of resistance" (Scott 1985) they had perfected in the colonial period, including "trespassing," ignoring permits, and evading authorities (Hodgson 2001a, Neumann 1995). They felt betrayed and angry by the repeated (and often sudden and violent) alienation of their land by the government in the name of "progress" and "productivity," and sometimes in violation of the government's own regulations describing the legal processes for the transfer or sale of village lands. Their sense of bewilderment and injustice was further fueled by the fact that many of these regulations and policies contradicted each other in terms of who (individuals, villages, or local/regional/national government offices) had the right to control access to and profit from different resources (such as the land, minerals under the land, wildlife on the land) and land-based activities (specifically tourism and hunting). From their perspective, "neoliberalism" was less of a contrast with prior postcolonial and colonial policies and practices than a continuation and even intensification of the prejudice and dispossession they had experienced for more than one hundred years.

Economic liberalization, however, was accompanied by political "liberalization" in the form of "democratization," including the transition from single-party rule to multiparty politics, donor-supported efforts to "strengthen" civil society, decentralization of decision-making from central government to local authorities, and the development of an independent media.[14] As such, democratization opened up a new space for more organized political activism and organizing, in contrast to the era when the only political space for activists such as Parkipuny to advocate for Maasai rights was within the CCM party structure in political positions such as member of Parliament (see chapter 1).

As a result of the new political openings produced by democratization and the transition to multi-partyism, increasing numbers of pastoralists took advantage of the opportunity to organize nongovernmental organizations (NGOs) and community-based organizations (CBOs) to advocate for their right to determine their own development, protect their legal rights, and challenge perceived injustices (Neumann 1995; Igoe 2000, 2003, 2004, 2005). Many pastoralist leaders were frustrated by what they perceived as their continued political and economic marginalization at the hands of the state, fearful of the seemingly all-powerful alignment of state and capital, discouraged by the failure of repeated efforts to challenge unjust actions through legal actions, and dismayed by the continued deployment of negative images and stereotypes of pastoralist practices, beliefs, and livelihood strategies by politicians, the media, and everyday people in order to justify these interventions and resource alienation. As discussed in the introduction, the proliferation of NGOs and CBOs in northern Tanzania mirrored a similar explosion of NGOs throughout the

Global South, as multilateral institutions and northern donors shifted their priorities and resources from supporting state-led development projects (now criticized as "top-down," inefficient and ineffective) to those designed and implemented by "grassroots" NGOs and CBOs (which were celebrated as "bottom-up," participatory and empowering).

In sum, these neoliberal "reforms" were deeply contradictory for pastoralists, simultaneously opening the political space for their mobilization through the formation of NGOs and shrinking the economic space on which their livelihoods depended by further alienating their lands and other resources. These contradictions were exacerbated by the related process of decentralization, which involved the "reform" of centralized state planning to shift political control and economic resources from the level of the nation-state to the subsidiary units of the districts, making the latter the key units of development (Pallotti 2008). Decentralization encouraged "local" control but also hampered government and NGO attempts to organize or implement programs that linked these units.

Circumventing the State:
The Emergence of Maasai NGOs

As discussed above, in the context of these changes, Parkipuny and several Maasai leaders (and leaders of other ethnic groups, including Barabaig and Hadza) found the possibilities of starting NGOs to promote their economic and political claims compelling (see p. 148). These organizations took an array of forms: from legitimate groups started by educated men who had worked in development for religious organizations or the government to "briefcase NGOs" run by opportunistic individuals (often laid-off civil servants) seeking a means to make a living. Some were premised on shared ethnic and linguistic identity, others were organized along geographic lines at the village/community level, and a few claimed broad multiethnic representation yet were in reality dominated by one ethnic group or rooted in one community.

During the 1990s, most of these organizations linked their objectives, whether implicitly or explicitly, with discourses of indigeneity. Like many other pastoralist groups, Maasai did not claim to be "first peoples," since their migration from "Kerio" was central to their history, mythology, and identity. Nonetheless, as Parkipuny and others argued, they believed that they shared similar struggles with "first peoples" to protect their distinct cultural identity and their economic and political rights in the face of active discrimination and disenfranchisement by the state and more powerful citizens (Murumbi 1994). By reframing their long-standing demands and grievances against the Tanzanian state in the language of indigenous rights, Maasai NGOs[15] such as KIPOC turned the cultural politics of their treatment by the colonial and postcolonial states on its head. Rather than continue to challenge enduring stereotypes of Maasai as culturally (and even, at times, racially) distinct, inferior, backward, and primitive, these NGOs appropriated and reconfigured these fixed, ahistorical images in order to appeal to global indigenous rights advocates and initiatives. Like the other African activists discussed in chapter 1, these Maasai leaders hoped that they might be able to use their involvement in the indigenous rights movement to leverage changes in their relationship to the state.

The history of the formation of two of the first Maasai NGOs, KIPOC and Inyuat e Maa, and the agendas, styles, and career trajectories of their founders reflects the challenge of political organizing at a time of state distrust, the complicated articulations of "local" and "global" agendas, and the emergent gender, generational, and class politics of these NGOs. As described below, the leaders of KIPOC pursued a confrontational approach to the state, drawing on discourses and lessons from the indigenous rights movement to frame their demands for development and land in terms of "justice" and "rights." In contrast, the leaders of Inyuat e Maa positioned themselves as more conciliatory in relationship to the Tanzanian state, trying to educate and mobilize Maasai themselves to think through and resolve the emerging tensions between their increasing desire for development and simultaneous wish to maintain certain aspects of their cultural and social practices, values, and institutions.

Confronting the State: KIPOC

KIPOC, the NGO cofounded by Parkipuny, pursued a bifurcated strategy —positioning itself vis-à-vis the Tanzanian state as an NGO "devoted to sustainable grassroots community development" and "promot[ing] [the] integrity of the cultural and biological heritage of our land" (KIPOC 1990: cover page) at the same time that it located itself firmly within the indigenous peoples' movement in its communications with international donors and transnational advocacy organizations. For example, in an early document written to describe their vision and seek donor support, KIPOC argued that the dominant "national culture" conceives the "modern Tanzanian" to be a Kiswahili speaker and either an active farmer or of "peasant origin." In contrast, the few "indigenous minority nationalities" in Tanzania were defined by KIPOC as either pastoralists or hunter-gatherers, who had "maintained the fabric of their culture": "They are conspicuously distinct from the rest of the population in dress, language, transhumance systems of resource utilization and relationship to the environment. Pastoral and hunter-gatherer peoples persevered, through passive resistance, to hold on to their indigenous lifestyles, traditions and cultures" (KIPOC 1991). Although stigmatized by the dominant culture as "static, rigid [and] hostile to cultural interaction and exchange," these indigenous cultures had in fact never been "irrationally opposed to economic development nor uncompromising in dealing with external interests and forces." In reality, these people had been "left out of the development process," especially in terms of the allocation of resources to social services and economic infrastructure; "they are looked down at, as backward and evolutionary relics of past primitive ages, condemned . . . as disgraceful to the national image" (KIPOC 1991).[16]

Since KIPOC was one of the first NGOs organized by representatives of the local community themselves (rather than by, for example, religious organizations), Parkipuny and the other cofounders confronted formidable challenges from concerned state authorities. At the time, any organization that was "autonomous from the state" had to be registered under the Societies Ordinance of 1954, a holdover from the late colonial period designed to restrict and monitor potential anticolonial organizing. According to KIPOC:

> Autonomous organizations are not accorded legal recognition as a democratic right of citizens to associate, but at the discretion of the state. The actual process of registration is cumbersome, lengthy and prone to political blockage. Moreover, legally existing autonomous organizations are subject to state surveillance, which may be accompanied by harassment and ultimate banning. In view of these circumstances, in which autonomous existence is at the mercy of the state, it is no wonder that genuine grassroots organizations have been a rarity in Tanzania. (KIPOC 1991:8–9)

It took three years, "a painstaking process," for KIPOC to secure formal registration. Moreover, KIPOC had to revise its original structure and constitution, which was predicated on a representative system based on customary Maasai forms of political organization, to reflect the top-down structure of officers, executive committee, and a general assembly of individual members required by the Societies Ordinance. Even once KIPOC was registered, the organization and its members were subjected to continual harassment, surveillance, and mistrust (KIPOC 1991).

Nonetheless, in great part because of Parkipuny's international reputation and his carefully cultivated connections with Euro-American donor organizations and transnational advocacy groups such as IWGIA, KIPOC was extraordinarily successful in receiving external funding for it projects and initiatives. Two Dutch donors provided immediate support for facilities, salaries, and operating expenses, and more support rapidly followed.[17] As a result, KIPOC grew quickly, from the vision of a few men to a staff of ten (headed by Parkipuny as executive secretary and an expatriate as the program officer), organized into the main office, a "women's wing," and a "youth wing" (mirroring the organizational structure of CCM, the sole political party). Parkipuny decided to base the headquarters of KIPOC in Loliondo, the headquarters of Ngorongoro District, so as to be closer to the people of Ngorongoro whom KIPOC sought to work with. Although the placement of KIPOC's headquarters certainly facilitated engagement with Maasai in the surrounding areas, its location near the Kenyan border, far from the regional headquarters of Arusha (connected by a terrible road), with erratic electricity and no direct telephone service (at the time), produced constant difficulties in communication with donors, transportation of supplies, and other logistics.

The people of Ngorongoro District faced significant pressures to their land and livelihoods, from the onslaught of tourism (the district contained both the famed Serengeti National Park and the Ngorongoro Conservation Area), big-game hunting ("Loliondogate" took place in the district), and commercial farming (one of the first court cases that Parkipuny coordinated was against the Tanzanian Breweries for trying to take over, with government authorization, 100,000 acres of prime dry-season grazing land near Loliondo to grow barley for beer). These contradictory pressures, especially the increasing value of wildlife as a lucrative source of foreign revenue from tourism and hunting, exacerbated tensions between Maasai and certain state institutions, as state officials sought to further strengthen their policies and practices of "fortress conservation" (Brockington 2002), which separated wildlife and humans and prioritized the well-being of wildlife instead of people (Hodgson 2001a; Århem 1985a, 1985b). They also intensified struggles among the two primary sections of Maasai, Purko and Loita, who lived in the district and had a long history of conflict over access to grazing land and other resources, as well as between Maasai and Sonjo, a culturally and linguistically distinct agropastoralist community.

Parkipuny not only challenged these policies nationally through KIPOC's advocacy campaigns, but used the UN to draw international attention to what he described as violations of the rights of Maasai as indigenous peoples. At the 1991 UN Working Group, he presented a statement that challenged the "alien and ill-conceived wildlife conservation policies exercised on our land and their consequent negative impact on the rights of indigenous Maasai people." As he argued, "the very people who have protected their wildlife resources so magnificently that today it constitutes a stock worthy of national and global pride are condemned to blant [*sic:* blatant] deprivation and abject impoverization [*sic*]." In his statement, he reviewed the history of the formation of Serengeti and Ngorongoro, including promises by the government to provide reliable water sources and regular grain supplies to Maasai living in the Ngorongoro Conservation Area. Moreover, he complained about the failure of an endless series of commission investigations and reports over the past ten years to resolve the complaints.[18]

According to Parkipuny and other activists whom I interviewed, KIPOC's initial approach was based on that of ADDO, the Catholic Church's development organization that I had run in the mid-1980s. Like ADDO, KIPOC members drew on Paulo Freire's methodology of conscientization and the DELTA training model[19] to engage community members in a process to reflect on and voice their own concerns and priority issues as a basis for future projects. The difference between KIPOC and ADDO was that ADDO's work was limited to development projects (water, education, veterinary care, etc.), while KIPOC was deeply invested in advocacy work from the beginning. Parkipuny and other KIPOC staff traveled widely in Ngorongoro district to meet with communities, listen to their concerns, raise their awareness about pressing political issues such as illegal land alienation, and mobilize them for action. By 1993, they had organized a study tour for local leaders to Kenya to learn how Kenyan Maasai had designed programs to benefit from wildlife and conservation; mobilized forty women's and youth groups; secured title deeds for seven villages; and funded the secondary school education of twenty students (Kaiza 1992). By the late 1990s, their work had been formalized into four main areas: (1) land rights, including working with ADDO to survey and title village lands; (2) education, including the construction of the Ololosokwan Secondary School, the first secondary school in Ngorongoro District, with the assistance an Italian NGO; (3) leadership training for community members; and (4) the empowerment of women and youth by organizing them into groups for "awareness-creation on development needs, such as the need for formal education, sustainable resource use and the land question" (Kipuri et al. 1998:166).

In addition, KIPOC formed a second "branch" in 1990, KIPOC-Barabaig, in order to help a group of Barabaig pastoralists who were having trouble registering their NGO with the government. As Parkipuny explained, "I offered to let them open up a 'branch' of KIPOC, since we were already registered."[20] One of the leaders of KIPOC-Barabaig was the late Daniel Murumbi, a Barabaig activist and former government official who had also attended the UN Working Group in 1991 with Parkipuny and was his close friend and interlocutor. The purpose of KIPOC-Barabaig was to assist Barabaig pastoralists in their advocacy and activist work challenging the land alienation and human rights abuses that accompanied the implementation of the Canadian Wheat Project, a huge, multimillion-dollar partnership between the Canadian and Tanzanian governments that displaced thousands of Barabaig from their land in order to start a commercial wheat farm.[21]

The district officer, however, quickly closed the KIPOC-Barabaig office, citing a range of accusations that reveal much about the government and party's concerns about the functions and freedoms of NGOs. According to a long article in the *Express,* one of the few independent weekly newspapers in Tanzania at the time, district party and government officials had expressed some of the following complaints about KIPOC:

> They claimed KIPOC was a one-man show and wondered "how an individual could rise up and usurp party functions of bringing development to the people." "Based on this," they resolved, "it was contrary to the *modus operandi* of this country for KIPOC to try and bring changes in the lives of the pastoral people without involving or getting the consent of district leaders." "By concentrating on the pastoralists," they claimed, "KIPOC was discriminating against other inhabitants of the land and was thus unconstitutional." "In any case," they wondered, "where did KIPOC get the guts from to send a delegation of Maasai pastoralists including some CCM leaders to Kenya for four days [on the study tour] without CCM's knowledge?" (Kaiza 1992)

As these comments suggest, the delegates interviewed by Kaiza still viewed development as a prerogative and responsibility of CCM, the sole political party, and worried about the seeming independence and autonomy from party control of these fledgling NGOs (a few even accused KIPOC of being a political party). Some of their concern was probably jealousy; KIPOC-Barabaig had just received 800 million Tanzanian shillings (approximately $2.5 million U.S. dollars at the time) to build a secondary school for Barabaig pastoralists.[22] As Kaiza, who was clearly sympathetic to KIPOC-Barabaig, wondered: "What was so dangerous about the programme to warrant the government's move to frustrate chances of a secondary school built for Barbaig pastoralists?" Or later, after praising Parkipuny's political and academic credentials: "One is bound to ask the political and government leadership in Arusha in whose benefit are they working? Is their mutual misunderstanding with Parkipuny worth the possible loss of a 800 million/- programme to help raise the living standards of the Barbaig people?" (Kaiza 1992).

Despite these challenges, Parkipuny was emboldened by the new possibilities for political organizing provided by KIPOC, as opposed to the inherent limitations of his former position within the government as an MP. He became an even more confident and controversial critic of government practices and policies. Through KIPOC, he mobilized Maasai to challenge the Breweries' "land-grab," fought state efforts to further restrict Maasai rights and livelihoods in the Ngorongoro Conservation Area in the interests of wildlife conservation, and supported the Barabaig in their struggle against the Canadian Wheat Project. In response to their advocacy efforts, Parkipuny and other KIPOC members regularly encountered low-level government harassment in such forms as lost documents, glacial procedures, frequent questioning, and ongoing surveillance. But tensions quickly escalated. According to Parkipuny:

> On May 2, 1993, I was shot by a policeman in Loliondo. The government did not like the civil society organizations; they were engaged in land advocacy, challenging the Arabs [who had been given the huge hunting area as part of Loliondogate]. The policeman was not arrested. When I went to see the head of the police, he said "*Hungera!* [Congratulations!] You survived!" Evidently the OCD [officer commanding district, the senior police commander in Ngorongoro District] had ordered the shooting to get rid of me. (See also Parkipuny's account in Ndaskoi 2009a:60.)[23]

Parkipuny survived and continued his work with KIPOC, but lived in constant fear of further assassination attempts on his life and concerns about the safety of his family and colleagues. In 1996, he left KIPOC under pressure from a donor agency and some fellow Maasai, amid allegations of mismanagement. He started another NGO, Aigwenak Trust, which took over manage-

ment of the Ololosokwan Secondary School started by KIPOC, and continued to work as an activist for Maasai rights. In his absence, KIPOC limped
along for a few years, but was soon mired in the sectional politics of Ngorongoro District (chapter 3).

In 2000, the government tried to silence him once more, fabricating a
corruption case, and threatening him with thirty years or life in prison.
Parkipuny fled and went underground for almost four years, unwilling to
trust the police, courts, or jail with his life. As he told me, "The case was a
complete fabrication, designed to dirty my reputation because I spoke out.
Finally I returned to try to deal with it in court. I turned up every week for
a year, but they never came with their witnesses. Finally the judge gave them
one last time, and then he dismissed the case. The woman couldn't even
recognize me. She said, 'The police just told me to sign the papers.'"[24]

Parkipuny clearly attributed his harassment by the state to his work as an
advocate and activist: "In the language of the state, I am a trouble maker. If
you don't conform, if you speak your mind, if you stand up against the mis-
deeds of corrupt officials, if you defend the rights of the marginalised, then
they label you a troublemaker, I have been working for my people for decades. That is why they want to eliminate me" (Ndaskoi 2009a:60). In retro-
spect, many of Parkipuny's friends and colleagues admired his fierce style
and critical abilities, but thought that his confrontational manner was in fact
undermining rather than enhancing the relationship between Maasai and
the government, especially given the government's still wary and fragile embrace of democracy. As one of his close friends told me, Parkipuny "was
doing the right things at the wrong time."

Probing the Dilemmas of Culture and Development: Inyuat e Maa

A second Maasai NGO that began about the same time as KIPOC was
Inyuat e Maa (also called Maa Pastoralists Development Organization, and
more recently, Maa Advancement Association), which was started by the late
Saruni ole Ngulay, an ambitious, relentless advocate of the cultural survival
(indeed revival) of Maasai peoples. In contrast to Parkipuny and KIPOC's
explicit positioning of their concerns and objectives in the language of indigenous rights, Inyuat e Maa, under Saruni's leadership, positioned itself more
implicitly in alliance with the movement. Especially in international venues,
Saruni made oblique claims about the similarities between the situation of
Maasai and indigenous peoples, emphasizing the issues of cultural survival in

the face of onslaughts by churches and other "modernizing" forces, and social marginalization within the state. But he was always careful to acknowledge the sovereignty and authority of the Tanzanian state. The different position-ings of KIPOC and Inyuat e Maa vis-à-vis the indigenous peoples' movement reflected and shaped their relationships with state actors and institutions, and mirrored the range of positionings of other Maasai NGOs at the time.

I first met Saruni in 1990, during a summer of pre-dissertation field re-search in Tanzania, when he approached me for help publishing a book he was writing in English about Maasai history, sacred sites, and "traditions." Saruni completed secondary school in 1973 and received a certificate in law from the University of Dar es Salaam in 1978. After working as an immigra-tion officer for the Tanzanian government for twelve years, he left (some say was fired from) the civil service in 1986. He was thoughtful, funny, and en-gaging. We met together occasionally when I was in Tanzania and corre-sponded regularly when I was in the United States. In addition to complet-ing his book, Saruni (who at the time described himself as a "free-lance Maasai cultural researcher" [Inyuat e Maa 1991a]) was eagerly trying to or-ganize what he called the First Maasai Conference on Culture and Devel-opment, to bring together Maasai "traditional leaders" (*ilaigwenak*) from all of the Maasai sections and age groups (from Kenya as well), educated Maasai, researchers, development workers, government and party officials, and others to discuss the tensions and dilemmas of simultaneously seeking cultural continuity and economic development "of their own choosing" (Inyuat e Maa 1991a:2). As Saruni described the "great cultural dilemma" in one report: "Torn between the worlds of modernity and tradition, they [Maasai] have long clung to tradition; fostering cultural pride at the sacrifice of development" (Inyuat e Maa 1991b:1). Although he quickly received suf-ficient international funding for the conference, he encountered significant opposition from some factions of the Tanzanian government, especially dis-trict and regional officials, who blocked the conference, sometimes at the last minute. As a result, he had to cancel the conference twice (once when more than 100 delegates were already present in Arusha). Nonetheless, he persevered: writing letters, meeting with government and party officials at all levels of government, and mobilizing support from donors and other sup-porters. The conference was finally held in Arusha for five days in December 1991, with the participation of more than 180 delegates, including me (as a "dialogue participant"). More delegates were expected, but the permission of the Tanzanian government to hold the conference was predicated on the exclusion of Maasai delegates from Kenya (who had been refused permission to cross the border when the conference was scheduled to take place earlier that year). And although Saruni told me that he had considered inviting "representatives of minority groups that have organizations—the Indians in Canada for instance,"[25] no such delegates participated.

As evidenced by the theme of the conference, "Modernity and Tradition: Conflicts or Harmony," the purpose was to bring representatives of Maasai sections together to look "into the Maa-people's cultural dilemma brought about by the forces of modernity versus tradition and to provide pertinent guidance for the future" (Inyuat e Maa 1991b:4). In contrast to Parkipuny's political-economic analysis, which blamed the colonial and postcolonial state for the precarious economic position and marginal political voice of Maasai and other indigenous people, Saruni's analysis focused on attacks by the state, development workers, and mainstream Christian churches on Maasai cultural beliefs and practices (he briefly mentioned land alienation in one small paragraph). His list of examples included efforts by the Tanzanian government in the late 1960s "to abolish the traditional dress of the Maasai Community," attempts by the Kenyan government "to abolish the institution of moranhood (warriorhood)," and attacks by the Christian churches on "matters pertaining to marriage, tribal rituals (customs, traditions, and beliefs), priesthood, traditional Institutions (Oloibani [sic] in particular, which the Church would like to have abandoned)[26] and to trivial matters such as body decoration" (Inyuat e Maa 1991b:3). He asked, "What is the effect of these pressures on enforced dress codes, abolition of tribal rituals and traditional institutions, the taking of land and encroaching Christianity to this community? The Maasai are desperately adopting western dress, abandoning tribal rituals and traditional Institutions and accepting Christianity not because they want it, but because this is what they are told development means" (Inyuat e Maa 1991b:4). Saruni concluded his analysis by describing four lessons that had been learned from these experiences:

> First, people should not be administered like objects in matters that affect their lives, without involving them in the decision-making process. . . . Secondly, a people's culture is the carrier of their values in the course of their economic and political life and needs to be respected. In order to bring about more effective change it is necessary to know their conceptions of what is right and wrong, what is good and bad and what is beautiful and ugly for them. Third, it is also necessary to respect the Maasai religion, even for other church development

workers. Development has to be by and for the people. Their unity, strength and the bonds stored in their tribal rituals and traditional institutions have to be maintained and safeguarded in order to reap the benefits of sustainable development. Fourthly, Maasai lack educational knowledge and technical know-how. By this I mean the necessary means with which to change and mould their tribal rituals and traditional institutions to a contemporary context. . . . Such a debate does not require the government or the church to initiate it. It is the work of the Community, and educated members of the Community in particular. They are best placed to liberate their Community from ignorance. (Inyuat e Maa 1991b:3)

He acknowledged, however, that the educated elite had issues as well: "the worry is that the kind of education the educated members of the Community have, has alienated them from the Community rituals and institutions, clearly creating the extreme of, on the one hand, an illiterate community, going downhill in history, and on the other hand, educated individuals looking and working for their own advancement" (Inyuat e Maa 1991b:4).

The conference took place in the ballroom of the New Arusha Hotel in downtown Arusha, at the same time as a Maasai Women's Cultural Exhibition of beadwork and leather goods was displayed on the outside balcony. The audience was predominately male Maasai, both young and old, a few educated Maasai women, and several other interested parties, including representatives of the sponsoring donor agencies, other donor representatives, members of other Maasai NGOs (including, for one day, Parkipuny), and expatriate researchers (see p. 148, bottom). Organizers tried to create a hybrid conference format that would accommodate the divergent meeting styles of Maasai elders (who usually sat in a semicircle, took turns standing to address the group, spoke as long as desired [often repeating opinions that had already been shared], and decided by consensus) and NGO/academic workshops (where audiences followed agendas and listened to only a few speakers; participation was encouraged through brainstorming sessions, breakout groups, and other strategies; comments were supposed to be short and concise; and decisions could be made by majority rule). Everyone sat in rows of chairs facing a conference table, where Saruni (dressed in a short cloth, carrying a *rungu*) and other members of the conference committee presided. After a Maasai prayer and introduction of the conference committee, a long debate ensued about the issue of language. Conference delegates eventually agreed that Maa and English should be the primary languages of the conference. Most of the discussion took place in Maa, with Saruni and others providing translation into English for the donor representatives who spoke neither Maa nor Swahili (the national language of Tanzania). The hybrid format and ambitious agenda, however, pleased no one: Maasai elders complained that they did not have enough time to speak, while the conference organizers constantly berated audience members for their long, rambling, repetitive interventions. As one organizer complained: "The time is too little, and the people too many. Let's try to have objectives after such talks, not just talking and talking!"

During the first three days, nine case studies were presented to the audience, exploring aspects of Maasai history, experiences of development, AIDS, religion, and current economic impoverishment and political marginalization. The authors/presenters included a remarkable range of people: Saruni himself, Richard ole Koillah (a Maasai MP), John Galaty (an anthropologist from McGill University), Father Eugene Hillman (an American Catholic priest),[27] and Henry Fosbrooke (formerly a British colonial officer and later head of the Ngorongoro Conservation Authority). After each paper, audience members were encouraged to comment, raise questions, and make recommendations. Many Maasai men spoke, from older *ilaigwenak* ("traditional" leaders) wrapped in their wool blankets, to younger educated men in their ironed pants and creased shirts. Their comments described the dilemmas confronting Maasai at the time, especially in terms of the tension between cultural continuity and economic development. But they also revealed the deep gender, generational, and class divides that were increasingly shaping Maasai perspectives and provoking disagreements.

Education was a key topic. One man explained that he was one of the first Maasai to go to school, was blessed with girl children, and decided to send them all to school. "But when they finished school," he said, "no one wanted to marry them. The warriors were scared of girls who had gone to school; they were afraid they would leave them." Another man worried that educated girls would no longer agree to arranged marriages: "she might even run away." He reminded everyone of the recent case of a Maasai girl who had poisoned herself rather than concede to an arranged marriage. Another man noted, "We have realized now that education is useful, but we can't throw away our cultural values. Let's see if we can use them to advance what we want." Others complained about the poor quality of the schools, the dismal number of Maasai who qualified for secondary school placements, and their fears that their educated children would forget their language, culture, and social responsibilities to their family and clan. Several delegates recommended the reinstitution of boarding schools or "mother-cow" schools (where school children lived with their mothers in a homestead near the school).

Land alienation was another recurring topic. According to one older man: "We Maasai are in the dark. We are going up a slippery mountain. We had the best land, but it doesn't belong to us anymore. The British and the Germans took it." A prominent educated Maasai man elaborated: "If we don't develop a new means to protect the land, people will come and slowly take it from us." "People are trying to grab the land from its owners," explained another man. "We should discuss ways to keep the land. Whether it is cultivation or grazing, it is we who should be doing it." An MP provided a detailed overview of the types of land alienation in each of the five Maasai districts, especially from the inmigration of non-Maasai. As for Maasai in other regions, "[they] are just roaming without destinations, wondering where their homesteads are [since all their land has been taken]." Several delegates mentioned the problems of surreptitious land sales by Maasai to outsiders to "get rich quick," "but the people 'drank' their money [i.e., used it to buy alcohol] and have now become watchmen." The MP described the large swaths of former Maasai grazing land "given" by the government to companies such as the Rotian Seed Company and Tanzanian Cattle Products[28] as part of the "joint" commercial ventures between foreign and local companies.

While many audience members commended the organizers for holding the conference as a forum for Maasai to discuss their problems and decide how to act, two constituencies—women and male elders—fiercely disagreed with the structure and format. Several elderly *ilaigwenak* publicly rebuked the younger, educated male organizers for challenging their authority by deigning to organize and facilitate such discussions. As one old man said on the first day, after emphasizing the need for Maasai "to talk and act," "I want two more elders like me here tomorrow. I am shocked. All these [gesturing to the organizers at the front table] are my children. I feel like an elephant among impala." Other elderly men in the audience murmured their assent; the committee nodded, but did not respond. Later that day, several elder men stormed out of the conference, angry over the perceived insolence and insubordination of the elite young men who had positioned themselves in the front of the room as the leaders and decision makers.

In addition, Maasai women were furious that they had been relegated to the balcony to show their beadwork, rather than invited to participate in the conference. When I had questioned Saruni prior to the conference about this gendered divide,

> he replied that including women in the main conference would be "against tradi-
> tion," as "women were never included in the meetings men held to decide com-
> munity affairs." "Since when," I curtly replied, "was a 'First Maasai Conference
> on Culture and Development,' comprising men of all ages, clans and areas, ever
> considered a traditional meeting?" In reply, he just shrugged and reiterated his
> claims of supporting Maasai "tradition." (Hodgson 2001a:234–35)

Women complained to each other, to their male kin, and to the organizers about their banishment to the balcony (except, of course for the two educated Maasai women who were allowed to participate). Finally, on the last day of the conference, a group of uneducated Maasai women, in customary dress, stormed the meeting room to protest their exclusion: "If this is a conference on Maasai development and culture," one woman remarked, "then why were we women not invited to contribute? Are we not Maasai?" Stunned, the organizers tried to placate the women with promises that they were trying to represent the women's best interests, but the women soon walked out.[29]

On the final day, the audience was divided into small groups and as-signed topics to discuss and provide recommendations on to the plenary. Educated Maasai and expatriate researchers were assigned, by name, to the following groups: Education and Christianity, Education and Culture, Tra-ditional Institutions (my group), Economic Diversification, Land, and En-vironmental Protection. Non-elite Maasai were assigned, unnamed, to five other groups based on their area of residence and section membership. They were tasked with making recommendations about all of the areas, as well as proposing a possible name for an organization that would coordinate and implement the final recommendations. Finally, in response to the com-plaints from both educated and uneducated Maasai women about their ex-clusion from the main discussions, a separate women's discussion group was also formed.

The recommendations of the groups reiterated the concerns discussed throughout the previous days in the conference, including the need to protect sacred ritual sites, to obtain title deeds for all Maasai villages, to encourage the education of all Maasai children (preferably at boarding schools), to protect freedom of religion, and to provide additional veterinary and marketing ser-vices for livestock. Several recommendations from the elite groups to change aspects of Maasai rituals were met with laughter and muttering by many non-elite members of the audience, signaling both class and generational disagreement among Maasai about how to bridge cultural continuity and social change. The controversial suggestions included a proposal by the Traditional Institutions group to replace the prevalent form of female genital cutting with a symbolic cutting and by the Education and Culture committee to reduce the period of "warriorhood" to just three years so that boys could go to school. In contrast, there was widespread approval of proposals to strengthen Maasai land rights. For example, many of the Land committee's recommendations were met with loud applause: to seek national and international support against the alienation of Maasai land; to call on international organizations to support Maasai students for further studies in law to advise on law problems; and to demand that revenue from alternative uses of land such as conservation, big-game hunting, and tourist camps be returned to the villages.

The presentation of the women's committee also provoked a powerful response. Initially, the committee had asked a young educated Maasai man to read their statement. But he demurred, saying it would be better if a woman read it. After a long silence, no woman volunteered. Finally, Miriam Alais, a young woman, stood up to read the statement, to much applause. Miriam had just completed her fourth year of studies at the Simanjiro Animal Husbandry Secondary school against her father's wishes, but with the support of her MP. Although visibly nervous, she spoke passionately and clearly about the concerns and demands of Maasai women:

> We women want development, but what is blocking us is you men.
> We women are behind because of development, we have no say. We
> are not viewed as people who have something to say; men don't give
> us this chance. Few women have been able to be educated; we need
> education. Maasai women have no voice in their community. . . . I
> am viewed just like property. Our fathers sell us like cattle. We want
> to speak about our own development, but men don't give us a
> chance. So we propose that first, you start to listen to women and
> give us an equal say; second, girls get a chance to be educated and
> not sold for cows; third, women be allowed to use and apply the
> education they have obtained. If I go home and tell my father he has
> a sick cow, he won't listen to me and tells me that I know nothing.
> And fourth, that women should be invited to these conferences to
> share our ideas. Many women stayed home because they were not
> invited.

As she sat down, the room erupted in rhythmic thumping of chairs and applause.

At the final session, the conference committee presented a summary of the resolutions and proposed the creation of an NGO, Inyuat e Maa, to seek the means and funding to implement the recommendations. They suggested the formation of an interim committee, with Saruni serving as interim secretary, to design the organizational structure of Inyuat e Maa, draft a constitution, seek to register the NGO with the government, and organize a second Maasai Conference on Culture and Development to continue the discussions, elect officers, and formalize the NGO.

The class, gender, and generational politics that had percolated throughout the conference reemerged during the discussions about the membership of the interim committee and its mandate. The conference committee proposed that the twenty-eight members of the interim committee include three *ilaigwenak* elected from each of five relevant political districts (not Maasai localities or sections), five educated Maasai, six members of parliament as ex officio members, and two well-known and influential *ilaigwenak*. The conference committee proposed the inclusion of the five educated Maasai, since they were "so few," and would never be chosen as the district representatives. Christopher, a young educated Maasai man (with highly educated sisters), immediately asked whether any women would be members of the committee. After some debate, the delegates decided that the women could sit together and elect one or two representatives to the committee: "This is democracy," said one man. Another man was concerned about the number of younger men sitting on the committee, and the implications for the authority of elders. "In all societies," he said, "elders advise the youth and guide the youth, especially in matter of culture." Several people wondered about Maasai living in the districts of Moshi, Same, and elsewhere; how would they be represented?

In the end, however, the debate over the composition of the proposed interim committee became so complicated and contentious that participants decided to just keep the conference committee as the interim committee. "But," one older man warned, "the interim committee needs to look at the resolutions again, because the majority of participants didn't agree with them. It would have been better if the resolutions had been discussed before they were presented."

And so began Inyuat e Maa. Eventually, despite difficulties with government officers and departments similar to those experienced by Parkipuny and

KIPOC, Inyuat e Maa was registered as an NGO in 1993. The Second Maasai Conference on Culture and Development: Environment and Sustainable Pastoral Development took place in 1994, with the sponsorship of the International Institute for Environment and Development (IIED), based in the United Kingdom. More than two hundred Maasai-speaking pastoralists participated, including two (male) representatives from each of the forty-five customary localities, twenty (educated, male) Maasai "facilitators," twenty-five women displaying their wares in the cultural exhibition, and "observers" from the Kenyan Maasai community, as well as expatriate researchers (not including me this time), donor representatives, and other interested parties (Inyuat e Maa 1994a:3). In addition to receiving updates on Inyuat e Maa's activities, participants debated and approved proposed amendments to Inyuat e Maa's constitution (Inyuat e Maa 1991c), elected officers, and listened to and discussed papers on such topics as land use planning, resource alienation, wildlife-livestock interactions, land rights, pastoralist poverty, and the relationship between Maasai and Barabaig. As before, people were divided into small groups and presented draft recommendations for everyone to discuss and approve in order to direct the future work of Inyuat e Maa.

By 1994, Inyuat e Maa had organized itself (at least on paper) into three departments ("1. Developmental; 2. Cultural and Religious Affairs; 3. Research and Economic Diversification"), hired five full-time employees (these included a driver, an office attendant, and a guard), established an office, obtained a vehicle, planned and facilitated the second conference, become involved in addressing the problems of Maasai evicted from the Mkomazi Game Reserve, and worked toward formalizing community ownership of a key Maasai sacred site. Since 1991, the organization had received almost 50 million Tanzanian shillings (approximately U.S. $125,000) in grants, primarily from Nordic donors.[30]

In March 1996, excited by his fundraising success and the seeming interest of donors, Saruni circulated a ludicrously ambitious "Medium Term" four-year plan to seek over $7.5 million U.S. of donor support for a radical "scaling-up" of Inyuat e Maa's staff, institutional resources, and programs (Inyuat e Maa 1996a). The seven proposed programs included organizing forty-five Maasai communities into "grassroots organizations" (GROs), implementing a community conservation program, expanding the provision of veterinary services to pastoralists, engaging in "community outreach" and "development education," planning and hosting two more Maa conferences, and establishing a Vocational Training Centre for Maasai to train as drivers, tour guides, and other tourism-related positions. Saruni also proposed starting a radio station, establishing a resource and advocacy center, publishing a quarterly newsletter, and setting up an award for customary leaders who have "shown excellency in mobilizing the communities in their areas of jurisdiction" (Inyuat e Maa 1996a:14). To buttress his requests, Saruni claimed that Inyuat e Maa represented all Maa-speakers ("a community of 400,000") and had recruited "over 100,000 active members who paid . . . membership fees" (Inyuat e Maa 1996a:8).

By this time, Saruni had leveraged his position as the head of Inyuat e Maa and his claims that the organization represented all Maasai to become an active representative of "the Maasai" at international conferences and workshops, many of which addressed the topic of indigenous peoples. His first trip overseas was in 1991, when a friend paid for him to travel to the United Kingdom. In addition to visiting various tourist sites, he met with Charles Lane, a social scientist who had worked with and advocated for the Barabaig in Tanzania, and was now working for IIED. He also met with Jens Dahl, the head of IWGIA, as well as officials from DANIDA and NORAD "who have shown an interest to help the Maasai community."[31] By 1996, however, he was a seasoned international traveler. He presented a paper at the landmark 1993 IWGIA conference on indigenous peoples in Africa discussed in chapter 1 (Ngulay 1993a), which was later published in the edited volume produced from the conference (Ngulay 1993b). Although he never used the word "indigenous" in the 1993 papers, or explicitly claimed that Maasai were indigenous peoples, his discussion of efforts to disparage and even abolish Maasai cultural practices and beliefs, the problems of land alienation, and the encroachment of Christianity supported IWGIA's arguments for the applicability of the concept of indigenous peoples to certain African groups such as Maasai. Later that year he was one of two Africans (the other was a member of the Nyae Nyae Farmers Cooperative in Namibia) to present a paper at a workshop in Amsterdam called "Voices of the Earth: Indigenous Peoples, New Partners and the Right to Self Determination," sponsored by the Netherlands Centre for Indigenous Peoples, where he did explicitly use the term "indigenous" to explain the situation of Maasai (Ngulay 1994) and joined other workshop participants ("we, the indigenous peoples") in signing a series of recommendations about the rights of indigenous peoples.[32] In addition, over the next few years he visited England, Canada, Italy, and the United States, among other places.[33]

During his 1995 visit to the United States, he drew on the extensive net-work of American acquaintances that he had cultivated over the years (in-cluding me) to actively seek speaking engagements at universities, commu-nity organizations, and other venues. In response to a fax that I forwarded from Saruni, one of his acquaintances in Colorado replied:

> Thanks for sending Saruni's letter to us. Our hearts and support are
> strong for Saruni, his efforts, the Masai and their efforts to survive
> as a race and culture and live in the modern world. If we, the world,
> looses [sic] these Indigenous cultures and the entire world follows
> the collapse of the family, community, human values that the
> western World is plunging into, we will be loosing [sic] one of the
> true treasures of the world and life. Saruni is one of the true heroes
> and great people, leaders of the world who has placed personal gains
> and financial success aside and replaced it with a dedication and
> sacrifice to help others, his people.

This response suggests much about how Saruni presented himself to pro-spective supporters and donors, and his success in positioning himself as *the* representative, if not the savior, of Maasai. From his perspective, Saruni told the Second Maasai Conference that his participation in these seminars "en-riched us with information, knowledge and experience. Likewise, we see these forums as place [sic] we can sell our ideas, and experiences. It is a way of making contact and get [sic] rid of isolation" (Inyuat e Maa 1994a:7).

In October 1996, however, Saruni suddenly collapsed and died while facili-tating a workshop for customary leaders in Simanjiro. His temporary replace-ment was Francis ole Ikayo, a young Maasai man whom I had known for over ten years, since he was a student at the secondary school where I lived and taught from 1985 to 1987. Francis had worked for World Vision for three years in Longido, then started his own NGO in 1994, the Ngorongoro Highlands Pastoralist Organisation (NHPO, which was later renamed the Ngorongoro Indigenous Association) in the Ngorongoro Conservation Area Authority, which incorporated his home village. When I spoke to Francis about NHPO in May 1995, during a research visit to Tanzania, he told me that the primary objective of the organization was to conscientize people about their land rights and political rights. Political rights were key, he said, since people needed to understand the new political landscape of multi-partyism, the difference be-tween CCM (the former sole political party) and the government, new voting procedures, and more. According to Francis, "NGOs have only become possible with multi-partyism, which has created new spaces for these kind of organizations. Before, if groups of Maasai tried to meet together regularly, they would be banned." Nonetheless, he lamented the reluctance of the government to accept the presence of NGOs. For example, when the government called a meeting of various officials to discuss land rights in Ngorongoro in 1994, they initially refused to let the leaders of NHPO participate. According to Francis, some NHPO members attended the meeting anyway, and insisted on being heard. "After the meeting," he continued, "we formed a Pastoral Caucus to coordinate activities and campaigns on land rights [as an advisory body to the Ngorongoro Conservation Area Authority]. We also created a list of recommendations for the government about the land policy."[34]

During that time, Francis was also one of the first Maasai activists to take full advantage of two new technologies—videos and the Internet—to publicize his message. In 1995, with the assistance of the Forest, Trees and People Programme (FTPP, an international community forestry program supported primarily by the UN Food and Agricultural Organization), he videotaped interviews with residents in Ngorongoro that explored their perspectives on a proposed new management plan for the Ngorongoro Conservation Area Authority (NCAA) that had been developed by the NCAA and the International Union for the Conservation of Nature (IUCN, a huge international environmental network). The government claimed that the proposed plan had been discussed and approved by "broad range of stakeholders" through "an intensive participative process" that included representatives from each of the Maasai villages in the NCAA (Taylor and Johansson 1996). But Francis's videotaped interviews with men and women, young and old, suggested otherwise—people were overwhelmingly negative in their views of the plan. Francis translated selected excerpts to compile a fifty-minute video, *Enkigwana e Ramat* (Maa for "Meeting of the Caretakers" [of the Ngorongoro/Serengeti Highlands]), which he showed, with the approval of six of the leaders interviewed, to the head of the NCAA and the Pastoral Council (presumably the NCAA board members viewed it as well). In addition, he worked with two FTPP staff members to post a long article on the Internet, explaining the background to the NCAA, presenting excerpts from the video interviews, and challenging the legitimacy of the management plan.[35] The videos, with English translations, were a moving, powerful explanation, critique, and lament over the long struggles of Maasai to secure their lands and livelihoods. The NCAA (and the IUCN) were not pleased by the publicity. They tried to discredit the videos and Francis, and ultimately banned further video recordings by NCAA residents. And, ultimately, the original management plan was approved.

When I returned to Tanzania for a short research trip in December 1996, Francis was still adjusting to his new job as acting executive director of Inyuat e Maa. The office of Inyuat e Maa was now housed in a renovated shipping container in the backyard of the stately home that served as the offices for the African Wildlife Foundation's (AWF) Community Conservation Service Center. Two desks faced each other, file boxes with titles such as "Indigenous People—General" lined the floor, and a pile of books about development, environmental issues, and indigenous affairs was stacked to the side. In addition to Francis, other staff positions included a community coordinator (held by Peter Toima, a young Maasai man who was completing his MA in sociology at the University of Dar es Salaam at the time), a secretary (staffed by a man who had formerly been a ward secretary), and a driver. Francis told me that he found the job hard: "There are so many conflicting interests, so much work to do. I am not sure that I am qualified enough."[36] At the time, Inyuat e Maa was actively working with AWF to form local grassroots NGOs to implement community conservation programs in the wildlife corridor buffer zone to the east of Tarangire National Park. They had started a spin-off NGO, Inyuat e Simanjiro, to coordinate these efforts.

According to Francis and Peter, Inyuat e Maa was also actively trying to lobby the government to consider the interests of pastoralists as it drafted the new Land Act, which they (like many pastoralist leaders) thought was designed with only agriculturalists in mind. In one action, Francis and Peter had developed a list of recommendations, made 270 photocopies of them, then stood outside the Tanzanian Parliament building and handed them to MPs as they entered for a meeting. They both described their initiative as a "courageous" move: "No one had done that kind of lobbying before."[37] Another time, they heard at the last minute about a workshop scheduled in Arusha by the land minister to discuss the new land law. With three other Maasai, Peter and Francis "stormed" the meeting, demanding to be heard. As a result of those discussions, they were planning to submit some revised recommendations to the MPs and ministries when they traveled to Dar the following week to go, as they called it, "donor-shopping," to seek donors such as USAID and SIDA to fund components of the Medium Term plan.

Peter replaced Francis as head of Inyuat e Maa shortly after I returned to the United States in January 1997. With the assistance of an "expatriate consultant" (Jim Igoe, an American doctoral student in anthropology at the time who was studying and working with Maasai NGOs for his thesis), Peter wrote and circulated a revised proposal in July 1997 that concisely addressed the problems in Saruni's approach, Inyuat e Maa's structure, and the Medium Term proposals (Inyuat e Maa 1997). They claimed that their revised proposal followed Saruni's philosophy, but acknowledged the "major flaws" in his earlier four-year plan, including that it was "top-down and drafted without consultation with its intended beneficiaries"; proposed programs that were "overly ambitious" and exceeded "the current institutional capacity of Inyuat-e-Maa"; sought "unrealistic amounts of funding" and made "no provisions for community contributions to the funding process"; was "geared more closely to donor agendas than to community needs"; and, despite Saruni's claims to have developed an integrated program, "the various elements of the Medium Term Plan [were] actually poorly integrated" (Inyuat e Maa 1997:1). They characterized Inyuat e Maa as a one-man show and blamed Saruni personally for many of its problems: "In spite of his rhetoric of participation, Mr. Ngulay (as the sole drafter of the Inyuat-e-Maa Constitution) in fact designed a very hierarchical organizational structure. He placed himself at the top of this structure, with virtually unlimited power and very little accountability" (Inyuat e Maa 1997:5). They alleged that Saruni's "dictatorial approach to administration alienated almost all of the original leaders of Inyuat-Maa" and that "during the last two years of his life, he was running the organization by himself. None of the other executive organs ever functioned or met." Most drastically, they claimed that Saruni had stolen huge sums of money from Inyuat e Maa: "By the time of his death, in October of 1996, Mr. Ngulay had systematically disappointed all of his donors. Most donor organizations refuse to even consider funding Inyuat e Maa. Mr. Ngulay's financial indiscretions have left his organizations with a legacy of debt, which present a major challenge to his successors" (Inyuat e Maa 1997:6). They thanked AWF for financial and logistical help as the organization confronted the challenge of a major restructuring to regain its credibility and effectiveness in order to "truly serve the Maa speaking community of Tanzania, while remaining true to Mr. Ngulay's dream of Development through Culture" (Inyuat e Maa 1997:7).

Their plan, they claimed, was "more realistic" and "more modest," both "in terms of what it seeks to achieve and in terms of funding requested." They proposed four programs: "1) Institution Building and Community Mobilization;

2) Support for Community Based Organizations; 3) Community Conservation; 4) Education." They argued that Inyuat e Maa should narrow the scope of
its work to just a few areas; cooperate rather than compete with other Maasai
NGOs; not affiliate with any political party; and include participants from all
ethnic groups (especially when working in "ethnically mixed areas"). The core
of their vision was that "Inyuat e-Maa should never concern itself with service
delivery or economic activities. Its main function should be as a coordinating/
support body for Maa GRO's, which also engage in advocacy work" (Inyuat e
Maa 1997:18). Despite their claims to ground Inyuat e Maa's objectives in the
will of the people, they argued forcefully that the primary work of Inyuat e
Maa (and the GROs it was supposed to cultivate) was to "work with AWF, the
private sector, and the community to create a programme of Community Conservation" (Inyuat e Maa 1997:10). Community conservation was, of course, the
dominant policy agenda of their main supporter at the time, AWF, as well as a
number of other international environmental NGOs. AWF wanted to create a
patchwork of wildlife management areas (WMAs) throughout Maasai areas in
order to "strengthen the symbiotic relationship that exists between livestock
and wildlife" (Inyuat e Maa 1997:10) and encourage pastoralists to conserve and
protect the interests of wildlife in the hopes of deriving direct financial benefits
from tourism and big-game hunting.

Since the current draft was designed to elicit input from "experts" and "the
communities themselves," in order to draft a final plan, no budget was attached
for all of the programs. They did, however, include a brief proposal to USAID
(through AWF) for $8,340 to fund modest salaries, office expenses, and vehicle
costs in order to develop "some basic institutional capacity" over the next year.
They also requested $10,000 to fund a series of three community workshops in
Simanjiro with the goal of establishing "viable" WMAs. They specifically
asked USAID to direct the money to AWF to administer, rather than to
Inyuat e Maa. They received some funds and support to stay afloat, primarily
from AWF, while they considered how to move forward.

In 1998, a team of Tanzanian and expatriate consultants conducted a thorough assessment of Inyuat e Maa's institutional structure, management style,
finances, relationship to constituencies, and more. As part of their evaluation,
the team visited and met with six Maasai communities around Tarangire and
Lake Manyara, all of whom, according to the report, "accepted, trusted and
were prepared to work with IEM in planning and implementing Wildlife
Management Areas" (Inyuat e Maa 1998:3). Moreover, "they denied sugges-

tions that IEM was politicized or that any of its management was involved in political undertakings. The Communities knew of only one other Maasai CBO—Ilaramatak, but did not trust or believe it to represent their interests. They were not prepared to work with Ilaramatak" (Inyuat e Maa 1998:5).

As a result of the recommendations, Inyuat e Maa was restructured, re-registered, and a new constitution was drafted under the new English name of Maasai Advancement Association (or MAA). Saruni's vision of a hybrid authority structure that incorporated customary leaders was replaced by a more corporate structure of a board of trustees and board of directors (all elite Maasai) elected by the General Assembly (at least three representatives from each village served by Inyuat e Maa) (Inyuat e Maa 1999a). AWF funded a three-day workshop in July 1999 for fifteen staff members, board members, and AWF personnel to develop a new strategic plan for Inyuat e Maa (Inyuat e Maa 1999b, 1999c). Funding was secured from AWF and a Dutch donor to support the institutional "capacity-building" of Inyuat e Maa, community outreach and "awareness-raising" activities, and the enhancement of service delivery (such as improved healthcare, land-use planning, and income-generating projects).

The primary goal of Inyuat e Maa, however, under the influence of AWF,[38] continued to be to set up WMAs as part of an AWF project funded by USAID.[39] A Memorandum of Understanding was drafted in 2000 between AWF and Inyuat e Maa, which specified that AWF would provide logistical, administrative, and technical support to Inyuat e Maa, in return for the agreement of Inyuat e Maa to, among other things, "work with local communities, district councils, ward and village councils, Wildlife Division and other specified partners in establishing wildlife management areas, Eco-tourism activities and other efforts for community based conservation" (Inyuat e Maa 2000:4). Although it is unclear if the memorandum was ever signed, the draft provisions reflect the structure of the relationship between AWF and Inyuat e Maa at the time, whereby Inyuat e Maa seemed little more than a proxy for AWF's agenda, mediating between AWF's staff and the Maasai communities it needed to convince to fulfill its mandate of creating WMAs.[40]

The Right Things at the Wrong Time?

Since 2000, Inyuat e Maa, like KIPOC, has continued to change its approach, institutional structure, and mission in response to both internal and external pressures, transformations that are explored in chapter 3. By comparing their institutional histories until 2000, however, we can identify certain patterns in the relationships among NGOs (as a newly emergent institutional form), the Tanzanian state, and donors, and their complex and at times ambivalent relationship to the transnational indigenous peoples' movement and other international agendas.

Jim Igoe and Tim Kelsall have aptly characterized the situation of African NGOs as caught "between a rock and a hard place":

> On one side they must deal with western donors, on whom they depend for support, and whose agendas frequently do not match their own. On the other they must deal with government officials who feel threatened by their activities and who may be competing with them for legitimacy and/or funding. It also includes other NGO leaders, some legitimate and some not, who are competing with them for the same limited pot of money. Finally it includes NGO opportunists who cast suspicion on everyone in the NGO sector. (Igoe and Kelsall 2005:9–10)

Of course, as Michael Bratton has argued, there is always a tension between "the government's urge for order and control and the NGO quest for organizational autonomy" (1989:570). According to Bratton (ibid.), governments seek to control NGOs through a range of strategies, including monitoring, coordination, cooptation, and dissolution; and NGOs in turn have a range of counterstrategies, such as maintaining a low profile, selectively choosing when and how to collaborate with the government, or using explicit policy advocacy. David Hulme and Michael Edwards (1997:13) categorize government interventions as either "carrots" (tax-exempt status, access to policy-makers, and public funding) or "sticks" (closure, deregistration, investigation, and coordination).[41]

Both Parkipuny and Saruni struggled for several years to even get their NGOs registered with the government, confronting an array of bureaucratic and logistical barriers. Different departments and levels (region, district, ward, village) of the government and, initially, CCM, the sole political party (whose organizational structure mirrored the state's) variously treated them with suspicion, regarded them as threats to state and party power, and envied their success with donors.

Once registered, however, the organizations and their leaders positioned themselves in markedly different ways in their relationship to the Tanzanian state. Despite (or because of) his prior tenure as a member of Parliament,

Parkipuny (and therefore KIPOC) was known for his deeply confrontational style as he advocated fiercely for the political and economic rights of Maasai. As "Christopher," an older Maasai leader told me:

> When Lazaro [Parkipuny] started KIPOC, he had a good vision. He knew what we needed. He had lots of energy. But he lacked one very important thing, public relations with the government. He was totally, totally, totally unable to realize good relations with government. If you are a radical person, then you can't do public development. Always, regardless of what you think, you have to be careful how you play your cards.
>
> DOROTHY: In other words, be diplomatic?
>
> CHRISTOPHER: Yes. As soon as you as an individual lose credibility with the government, then you are ineffective. Parkipuny kept putting things "hard," he created absolute enmity with the government.[42]

Christopher acknowledged that part of the problem was the timing: "Maybe today, if Lazaro was doing what he was doing then, it would be OK, but not in Nyerere's time." He elaborated, "[First], the government was not ready for criticism. Second, the government administration didn't want to do anything. If you went to them for help, they would just sit back [mimics this, sitting back from his desk with hands crossed]. This frustrated Parkipuny." The combination of KIPOC's efforts to mobilize Maasai in Ngorongoro District to demand protection of their rights, Parkipuny's incisive political economic analysis of the causes of Maasai marginalization (which laid the blame on the colonial and postcolonial state), and his adversarial style antagonized state officials at all levels of government. His strong international connections, especially with proponents and supporters of the indigenous rights movement, protected him to some degree, but not enough to evade an eventual assassination attempt.

In contrast, Saruni's approach to the government was more conciliatory, almost ingratiating. He strategically framed his interest in the revival and protection of Maasai culture as an apolitical concern that depended on Maasai from different areas and sections meeting to collectively debate and determine their future vision and then work with the state to implement it. Moreover, from the beginning, prominent government officials, including district commissioners, regional commissioners, and MPs, served on the coordinating committee, and eventually the board of trustees and board of directors, of Inyuat e Maa, blurring the boundaries between a "governmental" and "nongovernmental" organization. As Christopher explained, "[Saruni] Ngulay had a traditional movement, he knew how to get things done *pole pole* [Swahili: slowly]. I don't remember [Inyuat e Maa] rooting development strategies in advocacy. He was working on building a mass movement through meetings and slaughtering many cattle." Saruni invited government officers to participate in and address the Maa conferences, and often spoke publicly about the need to respect and work with the government. For example, in 1994, the Arusha regional commissioner opened the Second Maa Conference with some remarks. According to the conference report, he praised the work of Inyuat e Maa, but warned all NGOs "that they should be for and by the people; and not for individual benefits. He cautioned them not to undermine the government, and instead they should cooperate with the government in order to improve the living standard of their beneficiaries" (Inyuat e Maa 1994a:4–5). In response, Saruni stated clearly that everyone needed to recognize the role and rule of the Tanzanian government, "irrespective of which political party is in power. Inyuat e Maa and the government are not competitors, but rather working partners for the development of our community and the whole country at large" (Inyuat e Maa 1994a:8). In the formal, written report he described an incident where he was accused by leaders of another Maasai NGO of "going against the aspirations of the Maasais [*sic*]," in part by "prevent[ing] a demonstration against the authorities over land issues" and "cooperat[ing] with land grabbers and government leaders who are suppressing our voices" (Inyuat e Maa 1994b:11). Although he vehemently denied the allegations, his explicit willingness to work with rather than challenge the government produced constant accusations of cooptation from other Maasai leaders.

Moreover, the career trajectories of Parkipuny, Saruni, and other Maasai NGO leaders troubled any clean distinction between governmental and nongovernmental organizations. As did Parkipuny and Saruni, it was common for other Maasai leaders to begin NGOs after a period of government work, whether as politicians or civil servants. A number of Maasai leaders, such as Peter Toima, however, used their experience and success as the leaders of NGOs to launch their government careers as district commissioners, MPs, and other high-ranking officials. Once Peter left Inyuat e Maa, he had a successful career in a string of district commissioner appointments. A few men seemed to ricochet back and forth over the years between working for an NGO and serving the Tanzanian government. And some did both at the same time, such as the district commissioners and MPs who served on the Inyuat e Maa (and other Maasai NGO) boards. NGO staff members were often former civil servants or low-level elected officials such as ward secretaries and district councilors.

More disturbingly, in at least one case, a Maasai NGO that I will call "Maasai Development Organization (MDO)" seemed to have replaced the local government. In 1997, I visited the town where MDO's headquarters were located with three companions, two members of another Maasai NGO and the ward secretary (a low-level government official) of the area. Having traveled freely and without incident for years throughout Maasai villages and homesteads, I was struck by their increasing apprehension as we neared the town in order to fix a slow leak in one of the car's tires. When I asked what they were worried about, they explained that they were wary of being seen with me in the town. According to them, MDO's leaders tried to control all development and research that happened in the area. As such, "whenever they saw an *mzungu* [Swahili: a white person, a Euro-American], they immediately went to the ward secretary, demanding to know who the person was and what they were doing." Despite their concerns, I asked them to walk with me to see MDO's headquarters while the tire was being repaired. They agreed reluctantly: "People will be suspicious and ask questions. Let's pretend you are taking a tour of the entire village." The "tour" was insightful (in terms of seeing the impressive headquarters of MDO) and uneventful, but their paranoia was palpable.

The ward secretary's fear of reprisal from MDO signaled a troubling power relationship between the NGO and local government, especially given differences of accountability and representation in the two institutions. The ward secretary was an elected official, who served for a specific term as an intermediary between the village governments in his ward (a section of district, the larger political unit) and the district council. In contrast, although NGOs claimed to represent their constituencies, their leaders were usually appointed (even self-appointed) rather than elected, often for no specified term and with no provisions for a planned transition in leadership. In this case, MDO was started in the early 1990s by one leader, who is still, almost twenty-five years later, the head of the organization. Over the years, many NGOs have instituted a board of directors, responsible, among other duties, for the appointment, evaluation, reappointment, or termination of the executive director of the NGO. While this structure introduces a measure of accountability and oversight, at least on paper, the reality is that some boards are very weak and reluctant to disrupt the status quo, and many executive directors have personal, even kinship, relationships with key board members.

The introduction of multi-partyism in 1992 further complicated the relationship between Maasai leaders, Maasai NGOs, and the government. Since independence, representatives of the Tanzanian state and CCM, especially elected officials such as members of Parliament and district council members, had premised their legitimacy on their ability to bring economic development to their constituencies. As the new opposition parties were started, some of them copied this arrangement by starting or aligning themselves with NGOs as the "development" arm of their party. Even if an NGO tried to avoid identifying itself with any particular political party, the political allegiances of its leaders (and board members) were carefully scrutinized and discussed. Moreover, as will be discussed more in the following chapter, the efforts by some Maasai NGOs and Maasai activists such as Parkipuny and Saruni to align themselves with the international indigenous rights movement further antagonized the government. In September 2006, overwhelmed by the proliferation of NGOs, suspicious of their intentions, and challenged to distinguish legitimate from illegitimate NGOs, the Tanzanian government temporarily suspended the registration of new NGOs in order to study the problem and review and revise their NGO registration policy. Registration was soon reopened, but the government continued its efforts to strengthen its ability to monitor the activities and agendas of NGOs through revision of the NGO act and heightened registration and reporting procedures.

Despite these controversies and tensions, by the late 1990s NGOs were no longer novel institutions in Tanzania, but pervasive, if not always respected and trusted. This chapter has explored their emergence in the context of Tanzania's abrupt and fierce embrace of neoliberalism with the concomitant, if reluctant, recognition of an increasingly autonomous civil society and the range of their early positionings vis-à-vis the Tanzanian state, the transnational indigenous rights movement, and each other. The stark contrasts between the approaches of Parkipuny/KIPOC and Saruni/ Inyuat e Maa to the Tanzanian government and the indigenous rights movement underlines the importance of recognizing that not all NGOs were alike and suggests some reasons why it was difficult for them to work together as a network or coalition. Moreover, the history of KIPOC and Inyuat e Maa also demonstrate the tremendous importance and influence of NGO leaders in determining the positioning of their organizations, and the shifts in these positioning over time with new leaders, new donors, and new development agendas. Chapter 3 builds on this history and discussion to analyze the tensions that beset NGOs in the late 1990s as they struggled to reconcile the sometimes deep divergences of expectations between and among themselves, community members, and donors.

3

PRECARIOUS ALLIANCES

Maasai, like other groups in Africa marked by distinctions of culture, language, and livelihood, had a long history of challenging the injustices and disparaging stereotypes perpetrated on them by first the colonial and later the postcolonial nation-state. The political dynamics of these struggles were generally confined within national boundaries, as a matter between Maasai and the colonial administrators and later national elites who ran the government. By representing themselves as indigenous people, and thereby linking their situation and struggles to those of indigenous people elsewhere, Maasai activists and NGOs expanded the dynamics of their efforts to include the transnational advocacy organizations, multinational institutions such as the UN, and international donors involved in the indigenous rights movement, thereby establishing international recognition and support for their demands.

In addition to regularly attending the annual meetings of the UN Working Group and UN Permanent Forum, Maasai activists from Tanzania (and Kenya) participated in the international indigenous rights movement in several ways. Perhaps most importantly, they built strong ties with several international organizations that advocated on behalf of indigenous peoples, including IWGIA, Survival International, and Cultural Survival. These organizations and others sponsored local, national, and international workshops and meetings to educate Maasai and other African groups about indigenous rights and to provide opportunities for activists to meet one another to share their experiences, learn new strategies, and build an international coalition.

In addition, with the encouragement and sponsorship of certain advocacy organizations and eager individuals, several Maasai NGOs and leaders developed relationships with specific indigenous groups. One of the most publicized associations took place between Tanzanian and Kenyan Maasai and Australian Aborigines from 1998 to 2000. Pilotlight UK, a charity founded by

Jane Tewson, the wife of Charles Lane, an Australian social scientist who had long studied and advocated for the rights of Barabaig pastoralists in Tanzania (Lane 1996), organized an exchange program (funded by the UK Lotteries Commission) between "indigenous East African Livestock Herders" and Aborigines "so that they can learn from each other and inform their own efforts to secure rights to their lands."[1] In 1998, nine East Africans visited Australia for six weeks, hosted by Aboriginal communities. The delegates included seven prominent Maasai activists, one well-known Barabaig leader, and a Tanzanian lawyer who was actively involved in defending Barabaig land rights.[2] According to an Australian friend of mine who happened to meet with them, "Matei [a Maasai member of Parliament at the time] kept pretty much to himself, made some great speeches but didn't mingle much even with his colleagues, and Martin [head of a Maasai NGO] seemed rather shy (although gorgeous— he, Naomi, and Joseph wore Maasai clothes and looked resplendent)." As she concluded, "It's mostly a profile-raising and public education exercise and also inspirational for the actual delegation members."[3] In return, Maasai in Kenya and Tanzania hosted a delegation of four Aboriginal activists from Australia in 2000, who were accompanied by a BBC team filming for a planned television documentary, *Common Ground* (later retitled *Meeting the Masai Mob*). According to one reporter's account, "Many points of connection emerged between the Aboriginals and the Maasai. . . . As our host in Lorkisale, Tanzania put it; 'It's the first time in this zone that we've had guests like this . . . sitting together, exchanging ideas together. . . . We're both traditional people and it's similar. . . . There are Maasai in Australia!'" (Rose 2000). (Similarly, IWGIA encouraged the development of ties between Maasai in Tanzania and Saami reindeer herders from Scandinavia.)

All of the activists that I spoke to acknowledged that one benefit of their success at gaining significant international visibility and recognition as an "indigenous people" was a tremendous flow of resources from international donors. In effect, international recognition enabled them to circumvent the Tanzanian state to access signnificant resources for social and economic development initiatives such as water, education, health services, and livestock restocking, at a time when the state had withdrawn its support for these services. For example, in addition to the projects described in chapter 2, Danida spent almost $5 million on a livestock development project in Ngorongoro, working through the auspices of a Maasai NGO; HIVOS and NOVIB (two Norwegian donors) worked with another Maasai NGO to support water projects, women's income-generating projects, and several land-rights claims; and other donors funded NGOs to build health clinics, pay for secondary school education, and more. And, of course, these donors and others spent large sums of money funding endless workshops, training sessions, meetings, and "capacity-building" seminars for NGO leaders and their staff. A few donors assisted Maasai in their scramble to defend and protect their remaining lands, through either advocacy or, more pragmatically, help for villages to survey their lands to obtain titles.

Despite these successes, and the initial enthusiasm and high expectations of donors, by the late 1990s the NGOs were in disarray, beset by a host of divisions and tensions among themselves, and in relationship to donors, the state, and their constituencies. Each of the over one hundred NGOs had its own (sometimes overlapping) agenda, leaders, constituencies, and, often, donors. Many had made positive contributions to improving people's welfare, including delivering services such as healthcare and water to remote areas avoided by government workers; raising critical awareness among their constituencies about the reasons for some of their problems and possible solutions; and facilitating collective consideration of, and approaches to, community problems (Morindat 2000; Sangale 2000a, 2000b). Perhaps most importantly, several NGOs, such as KIPOC, were relentless advocates for pastoralist and indigenous rights, especially land rights. Despite these accomplishments, however, numerous instances of corruption, misuse of donor funds, and failure to implement promised projects (such as those documented for Inyuat e Maa in chapter 2) had discouraged many donors, who responded by withdrawing funds and sponsorship. Local people themselves were increasingly troubled by the arrogance, lack of responsiveness and accountability, and corruption they perceived in some NGO leaders (Igoe 2000). Moreover, several attempts to coordinate the assorted groups within the movement and instill a more transparent, systematic relationship with donors had failed dismally.

This chapter reviews the sources and expressions of these tensions in order to examine the structural predicaments confronted by NGOs as an institutional form during the intensification of neoliberal policies in the late 1990s. After a brief overview of the key axes of friction and factions (which are explored further in chapter 5), the chapter explores the efforts of Maasai leaders themselves to understand and resolve these differences through the formation of an umbrella group and, later, a workshop to evaluate the failure of the umbrella group and other efforts to form a viable alliance.

Representing "the Maasai"?

The brief histories of KIPOC and Inyuat e Maa, especially the extended discussion of the First Conference on Maasai Culture and Development, convey the complicated social dynamics that beset all of the Maasai NGOs that claimed to represent the interests of "the Maasai." From the beginning, uneducated Maasai were deeply suspicious of this new institutional form and its advocates. As Marjorie Mbilinyi and Timothy Nyoni reported in 1999, after conducting extensive meetings with Maasai individuals and communities in Ngorongoro District:

> Many villagers were cynical about the NGOs. They were perceived locally as personalised development projects which benefited leaders, not the communities in which they worked. Informal information suggests that most local NGOs/CBOs faced problems of transparency and accountability that were partly rooted in the top-down bureaucratic structures and leadership styles they had adopted. Structures to involve members and leaders of local communities in basic decision-making were absent, according to FGDs [focus group discussions]. According to local perception, they appeared to be operating in some cases as intermediary agencies on behalf of external donors, not on behalf of the community. (Mbilinyi and Nyoni 1999:50)

Similar sentiments were echoed by many community members whom I spoke to and interviewed over the years (see also Hodgson 2001a; see discussion in chapter 5). From their perspective, they regularly voiced their needs and priorities in endless meetings, workshops, and seminars (including political campaigns during election cycles, village council meetings, and other non-NGO-organized fora), were promised assistance, yet rarely saw any results. Their frustrations were intensified by years of meeting with state officials, listening to demands to change certain aspects of their lives, and hearing empty promises of material gains.

One source of the distrust voiced by communities about NGOs was the difference between the advocacy agendas of many of the NGOs and the development expectations of their constituencies. Rural Maasai who depended on herding, farming and, increasingly, other production strategies for their subsistence wanted immediate, tangible services (especially health care and veterinary care) and products (like a water pump, grinding machine, school, or clinic) that they believed would help them improve their lives. As such, they did not always understand or appreciate the repeated efforts of many of the

Maasai NGOs to "mobilize" them, increase their awareness of their rights, and build their capacity for advocacy. While they were willing to protest and respond when their own community was suddenly immersed in a land conflict or subject to a perceived injustice, issues of policy, advocacy, and rights (especially "indigenous rights") seemed remote from their everyday concerns.

Of course, as many NGO leaders told me (and their constituents), "without any land, there would be no pastoralists and no development." For them, advocacy and awareness-raising were primary, not secondary, especially during what they perceived as a time of accelerating land alienation and rapid abrogation of pastoralists' rights. In recognition of the priorities of community members, however, few NGO leaders tried to share or translate the current discourses of their advocacy efforts (like "indigenous rights") with community members. Instead, they focused on raising community awareness about their legal rights and tried to design and implement some development projects as well.

Community mistrust of NGO leaders was amplified by the often vivid, visible material improvements in the lives of (successful) NGO leaders. At the same time that many community members were struggling with increasing impoverishment, NGO leaders used their often generous salaries to purchase personal vehicles, build large houses, and educate their children in private schools. Even if they did not own their own car, many leaders took advantage of having a work vehicle to transport foodstuffs, people, building materials, and other goods.[4] A few NGO drivers even charged fees to passengers to subsidize their incomes. These disparities in income and lifestyle, coupled with the focus of most NGOs on advocacy rather than service delivery, provoked some community members to accuse the NGO leaders of corruption and greed. A Maasai friend told me a story about visiting the offices of a Maasai NGO in Simanjiro District one day in 1996 in order to learn more about their work. None of the program officers were around, so he spoke to some staff members, who gave him a brochure. When he asked his friends in the surrounding village about the NGO, they laughed. They all told him that the NGO was a way for the leader to get vehicles, buy a farm, and have "the good life." But there was no evidence that he or his NGO had helped the community. A year later, after I had visited the same offices, which included a huge main office building, staff housing, and other buildings on a large compound, I asked one of the Maasai men accompanying me about what the NGO had accomplished. "Not much, besides the buildings!" he replied.

As a result of these and similar experiences, illiterate community members, in particular, perceived some leaders as elitist and worried about the "power of the pen" to transform their lives (Hodgson 1999c, 2001a). As Peter ole Toima and Jim Igoe commented in their assessment of Inyuat e Maa:

> The few local leaders who have studied (both in government and NGOs) often use their knowledge to deceive their constituents and misappropriate land and money. These educated elites also use their knowledge to protect and maintain their positions of power. They create images of themselves as the only people capable of bringing development and money. Even those individuals who are aware that these elite are corrupt, are hesitant to appose [sic] them as they believe that they will lose the few development projects that they have. (Inyuat e Maa 1997:24)

While Toima and Igoe arguably overstated the prevalence of deception and corruption among NGO leaders, their accusations had some merit. Part of the problem was, as one thoughtful NGO leader told me,

> the capacity of the people who initiated NGOs. Some, of course, are just "briefcase NGOs"—they hire a lawyer to draw up a fancy constitution, but there is nothing there. Others have the problem of "know-how"—they just lack ability, but have the good will. And others just lack the "will to assist." The desire to help the community is just not there, even among some of those with master's degrees. There is a problem about not having a sense that one is a change agent.

The extended absences of the NGO leaders from the communities—whether to work in the office headquarters in Arusha or travel nationally and internationally to participate in workshops, attend UN meetings, and meet with donors—only further intensified community suspicions that NGOs were organizations merely for personal improvement rather than for community empowerment and development.

Generation

In addition to these emergent class differences, a related set of problems concerned the significant social differences of age and gender between NGO leaders and their constituencies. NGO leaders were almost all younger, educated men. Yet, historically, Maasai society conferred specific rights, responsibilities, and powers to men according to their age set. With the subsequent formation of new age sets, older men assumed new responsibilities, respect, and power, moving from the categories of uncircumcised boy (Maa: *olayioni*, pl. *ilayiok*) to "warrior" (Maa: *olmurrani*, pl. *ilmurran*), junior elder, elder, senior elder, and venerable elder (Hodgson 2001a). Junior men were supposed to listen to, learn from, and follow the advice of older men, although the age system produced and incorporated some structural tension, such as between the demands of "unruly" warriors and their more staid elders, and friction between adjacent age sets (Spencer 1988; Hodgson 2001a). Of course, this ideal system had already been changing as increasing numbers of Maasai men (and some women) pursued education, converted to Christianity, and became bureaucrats, lawyers, politicians and, now, NGO workers.[5]

Thus, as evidenced at the First Conference on Maasai Culture and Development, by assuming the leadership of NGOs, junior men provoked generational tensions by challenging the customary authority of elder men. Although some NGOs, such as Inyuat e Maa, tried to include elder men (often referred to as "traditional leaders") in their decision-making structure, advocacy initiatives, and development programs, other NGOs forged ahead without them, unable (or unwilling) to work through the generational differences of perspective, process, and power (which also, of course, often reflected differences of education and class).

Age differences also shaped relationships among male NGO leaders, despite shared educational and class backgrounds. Younger male leaders were expected, according to Maasai age-gender protocols, to show deference and respect to the few older leaders such as Parkipuny. And, mostly, they were properly respectful, at least in public. Junior men sat patiently if their elders spoke at length in workshops and conferences. They recognized and praised the accomplishments of their elders. They were careful to phrase any critique or challenge to the ideas or practices of their elders in the most diplomatic way possible. In private, however, they characterized some of these older leaders as "has-beens" who were obstacles to progress and should just realize their obsolescence, step down from power, and advise the younger men only when asked. Conversely, the older leaders often characterized their juniors as "young bulls," eager to act before thinking and lacking the experience and wisdom necessary to lead well.

These generational differences sometimes produced radically different perspectives, politics, and positionings. For example, by the time I returned to Tanzania in 2005, Parkipuny (as one of the oldest leaders) was pursuing what I would call a "neo-traditionalist" strategy. Echoing his 1989 speech to the UN Working Group and common debates among indigenous peoples, he argued repeatedly and forcefully, at workshop after workshop, that Maasai leaders and people needed to "go back to our roots." He spoke eloquently about the cultural and social alienation produced by education and the lack of accountability of NGO leaders who were often self-appointed representatives of their communities. He affirmed his arguments with his sartorial strategy, which was to wear the clothes of a Maasai elder (red blankets, tire sandals, and the appropriate adornment) during his visits to Arusha for meetings, workshops, and events. His dress contrasted markedly with that of the other NGO leaders, most of whom wore pants, shirts, and jackets, with perhaps a beaded bracelet, necklace, or anklet to reflect their ethnic heritage (see p. 149). A few of these leaders chose to wear Maasai dress at certain public occasions, but most were clearly more comfortable in slacks and shirts. Although many disagreed with his arguments and approach, most of the junior leaders respected Parkipuny deeply as, in many ways, the founder of their movement. At every workshop that he attended, they approached him during the breaks individually or in groups to greet him, ask for his advice, and share ideas and concerns. Many shared the belief of one prominent leader: "[Parkipuny] is our hero."

In February 2006, PINGOs (one of the Maasai "umbrella groups"; see below) organized a workshop for its members, MPs, and invited guests to discuss how to more effectively work together to influence national policies for the benefit of pastoralists. On the second day, after a long presentation about the history of pastoralist advocacy on natural resource issues, a Maasai MP commented that "to fight for our rights, we need unity" (the lack of unity had been a recurring theme in the discussion). In response, Parkipuny proclaimed:

> The lack of unity is about us. It is the problem of those of us who are leading our society. Those of us who are educated have lost our roots. We need to regain our roots by returning to our traditional systems of leadership. In our traditional system, leaders have binding taboos to follow. If you accept certain responsibilities, then there are sanctions and consequences for failure. We have to go back to our roots.

"But the question is *how*?" asked another senior leader. Parkipuny replied, "We need to accept that we have been alienated by our education, that globalization is changing us. We talk about indigenous pastoralist hunter-gatherer societies, but who are we?"[6] Most younger leaders, who were very familiar with Parkipuny's arguments, but disagreed with his position, responded politely. "We can't change our history, but we can change our future," said one. "We need to learn from our past to change our future." A few were annoyed, and found Parkipuny's interjections a diversion and waste of time from the "real" issues at hand. Moreover, they rejected his notoriously confrontational style as a failure and no longer suitable for the current political situation. Several younger leaders tried to reconcile the group. "The issue is not to condemn what happened before," said one. "The approach then was appropriate to the circumstances, especially the lack of democracy. We learned from it as well. The cases of Mkomazi [the eviction of Maasai for a game reserve] and NAFCO [the eviction of Barabaig for the Canadian wheat project]; we were young then. But those who were fighting are here with us today [he named three older men, including Parkipuny], and we should learn from them."

Gender

Similarly, during the 1990s, women, young or old, were rarely included in NGO leadership or consulted in their programming, thereby reinforcing women's ongoing economic and political disenfranchisement (Hodgson 1997, 1999a, 1999b, 1999d, 1999e, 2000, 2001a). Although some NGOs had "women's wings," these were often more to satisfy donors interested in ensuring that gender was considered than effective structures to empower women. As a woman who worked for the "women's wing" of KIPOC from 1990 to 1994 told me:

> When it started, KIPOC was a good organization, addressing
> development issues in a holistic manner. But I was not satisfied
> working with KIPOC. It was run by a committee of twelve people,
> only three of whom were women. I was forming women's groups,
> working on women's issues, but when I would bring my ideas or
> issues to the board, they would always laugh. When I talked about
> the need to send more girls to school, they didn't take it seriously. It
> was very frustrating.

Her experiences and frustrations were shared by other women I spoke to who were involved in the "women's wings" of other NGOs.

Those women who were involved with the Maasai NGOs, even symbolically, were often the educated wives or relatives of the male Maasai leaders. In

February 1996, Inyuat e Maa, with funding from HIVOS, finally sponsored a "First Maa Women's Conference on Culture and Development," as a vehicle to develop its women's wing, Olamal lo-Indomonok (Maa for Commission of Women). Although I was unable to attend, I did read the conference report and see pictures of the event. The photos showed about five men and forty-five women in a room, some in Maasai dress, but most in Western dress and wearing token beadwork. At the front table, facing the audience, were three people: Saruni, dressed in a suit, crisp starched white shirt, and tie; a heavy woman with straightened hair, wearing an elite version of Maasai dress (I was told she was a businesswoman from Dar es Salaam); and a skinny man in a Kaunda suit (a board member). Of the forty-seven Maa women listed among the eighty-four participants in the conference report, I recognized many names: the wife of a MP, three sisters of a wealthy, elite Maasai family, and the wives of several Maasai NGO leaders.

According to the conference report, one of the first items of business was to change the name of the proposed organization from Olamal lo-Ing'oroyok (which also means "commission of women") to Olamal lo-Indomonok because "participants agreed that 'ing'oroyok' is a man-centred name for women and customarily does demean women" (Inyuat e Maa 1996b:6). Participants debated such "cultural practices" as bridewealth (supported because it strengthens marriage bonds and binds the families of the bride and groom), polygyny (no longer economically sustainable), arranged marriages ("the cause of old men marrying young girls"), wife-beating (which came under "scathing attack"), female circumcision ("not a pressing issue"), and intermarriage (which was so far minimal) (Inyuat e Maa 1996b:9–10). They also described the "macro-environment" of Maa women, including high illiteracy, poverty, lack of income-generating activities, lack of health and education facilities, land alienation, and lack of access to and control over natural resources (Inyuat e Maa 1996b:10). "The core of the problem," they concluded, "lies on [sic] the distribution of wealth produced. Men control livestock that constitutes over 60% of family total income. They control farm produce, for those practicing agro-pastoralism. . . . Left without any source of income, women in Maasai society are burden [sic] with other chores in the family, which men do not value" (Inyuat e Maa 1996b:11). To rectify this situation, participants called for the "mobilization" and "empowerment" of women through the creation of a network of women's grassroots organizations (GROs) designed "to get them organized within their customary socio-organizations and show them the way of doing things for self-advancement." Participants clearly contrasted empowerment with service-delivery projects: "Empowerment is not taking a milling machine here and there, because women need it. It is not starting credit schemes (for instance, there is one in Monduli, which has not benefited many pastoral women), nor is the empowerment of women engaging in handcrafts [sic]. Maasai women, for example, are good in beadwork; but markets for these products are also limited" (Iyuat e Maa 1996b:12). Nonetheless, they strongly recommended that Inyuat e Maa sponsor income-generating projects such as transport, grinding machines, and handicraft production.

Both before and after the conference, Saruni sent project proposals to an array of donors, seeking funds for village grinding machines and handicraft production, with no success. The list of donors that he contacted is telling, for both their geographical breadth and their orientation. It included the embassies of Denmark, Norway, Sweden, and the United States; Friedrich Ebert Stifung (Germany); SELF-HELP Crafts of the World (USA); and the Danish Volunteer Service. But the network of GROs never materialized, as few of the elite women officers of Olamal lo-Indomonok had either the time or the interest to travel through remote Maasai areas, facilitate meetings, and engage in the often slow and frustrating process of organizing.

More recently, some Maasai NGOs have been more successful in obtaining funds to support women's development programs, although most of these projects are fairly typical income-generating and labor-saving projects. For example, in 2005, one NGO, CORDS (described below), ran a large women's development program that included the provision of grinding machines, construction of a dairy processing plant, and the support of small income-generating projects. According to the coordinator, "We do a lot of traditional things like grinding machines, not so much empowerment. But our hope is that by reducing women's labor and time, perhaps give her more time for other perhaps more empowering activities . . . we see it as a 'point of entry.'"

CORDS, like other NGOs involved, at least symbolically, in women's development included women on its board and staff. Sometimes these women seemed to be mere figureheads. Two of the three women on Inyuat e Maa's board of directors in 2000 were the wives of fellow board members. Other female directors and staff, however, were committed to women's development and empowerment, but confronted constant disparagement, even outright hostility, from some of their male counterparts about their concern for gender issues. For example, at a 2005 workshop in Monduli for NGO leaders about land policy, I witnessed the following exchange between male and female program officers from different Maasai NGOs. After learning that village land committees were required, by law, to include at least four women as members, "Peter" scoffed, "Many women don't want to run, they can't read, can't write, can't speak language." "Elizabeth" and a few other women present laughed at the outrageousness of his comment. "Can't speak the language?" they muttered. "Swahili? Or is the problem that men don't permit them to run?" "Yes, say the truth!" exclaimed some of the other women and a few men. Then "Stephen," a well-educated Maasai activist, intervened in a mocking, deeply patronizing manner. "What [Peter] is saying is that he thinks that bringing women in, who may just sit there with their eyes closed [in exaggerated pantomime, he mimics a woman sitting at a table, head slumped against hand, eyes closed] is a waste of time. But that is not true; it is important to include women, to educate and teach them, then they learn." Now the women were clearly upset. Everyone muttered and raised their hands to speak as Stephen walked out of the room. Finally, Elizabeth, who was visibly angry, said "[Peter] just supports discrimination." "No I don't!" interjected Peter. "He doesn't want women to participate," she continued. "If men were not educated, then they wouldn't participate either."

This public exchange mirrored more private exchanges within NGO offices, as the women in charge of "gender affairs" or "women's development" struggled to gain attention, resources, and understanding for their causes. When, toward the end of my year in Tanzania (June 2006), I asked the gender officer of a large Maasai NGO if she thought that attention to gender issues by the leaders of her NGO was improving (a topic we had discussed throughout the year), she laughed. "[The coordinator] says that gender doesn't matter. We have four women on the board, but they don't have same capacity as men. They don't speak up at all. They are very weak in comparison."

In part because of the challenges of including gender projects as part of the broader mandates of pastoralist NGOs, some Maasai women decided to start NGOs dedicated to women's and gender issues. In the early 2000s, two NGOs were started by Maasai women for Maasai women—Maasai Women Development Organization (MWEDO) and Pastoralist Women's Council (PWC). Although there are important differences between MWEDO and PWC in terms of their leadership and approaches to gender issues, they are two of the most successful NGOs that I studied in terms of the effectiveness of their programs, their presence in local communities, and the commitment of their leaders to improving the lives of their constituents.

MWEDO was registered as an NGO in 2000 "to work towards the empowerment of disadvantaged Maasai women economically, politically, culturally and socially through implementing activities in capacity building, advocacy, and promotion of human rights within the Maasai community" (MWEDO 2005:6). In 2005–2006, work was conducted by a staff of five from the regional headquarters of Arusha through more than thirty-five village-based membership groups spread throughout four of the so-called pastoralist districts (Monduli, Simanjiro, Kiteto, and Longido). Their main programs included maintaining a fellowship fund to support the secondary and tertiary education of pastoralist girls; providing advice, start-up grants, and marketing assistance to women's groups for income-generating projects; and bringing rural women together for workshops on aspects of women's rights, including their political rights as citizens, legal rights (marriage, divorce, and inheritance), land rights, and rights regarding HIV/AIDs, which MWEDO framed as a women's rights issue, as in their right to know how to protect their bodies and decide who would be their sexual partner (see p. 151).

MWEDO was founded by three Maasai women, including Ndinini Kimesera Sikar, who became its first executive director. Ndinini is an educated Maasai woman who was taken from her rural Maasai homestead as a small child to live with her uncle in Dar es Salaam for health reasons. As a result, she was educated and easily assimilated into the guiding norms of urban, elite, "Swahili" society, yet maintained strong ties with her rural base. After secondary school, she studied finance and then worked as a banker for several years before marrying an older Maasai man, moving to Arusha, and helping to start MWEDO.

I first met Ndinini at the United Nations in New York in 2004, at the annual meeting of the UN Permanent Forum. She was browsing through a table of pamphlets and posters outside the main assembly room, dressed in a stunning rendition of customary Maasai dress, with a long beaded skirt and cloak, headdress, and jewelry (see p. 146). I approached her and greeted her in Maa, which at once surprised and pleased her. We spoke for a while, and then continued to meet and talk throughout the week long session. We discussed many things, including news about mutual friends in Tanzania, her unusual life as one of the few well-educated Maasai women, MWEDO's work, and current policy debates in Tanzania. At the time, Ndinini felt very drawn to "indigenous rights" as a useful frame for pursuing Maasai political struggles: "It allows everyone to work together to pressure the Tanzanian state without making it an 'ethnic' or 'tribal' issue. But the problem is that everyone has to get along." She had only just learned about the UN Permanent Forum at a meeting for East African Pastoralists in Nairobi, and IWGIA had sponsored her trip to New York. But she was very disappointed that she was the only representative from Tanzania at the UN Permanent Forum that year, in contrast to the many Kenyan Maasai who were present.

Although Ndinini has continued to maintain contacts with IWGIA and attended some subsequent UN Permanent Forums, her primary concern has been to maintain and expand MWEDO's programs by courting donors, meeting with community members, and networking with other NGOs, government bureaucrats, and NGO coalitions. She is adept at making contacts, and has developed strong relationships with major bilateral donors such as USAID and the African Development Bank, as well as smaller independent donors such as the Flora Foundation. She is also skilled at obtaining media coverage about MWEDO.[7]

The Pastoralist Women's Council (PWC) was founded in 1997 "to promote sound cultural, political, environment and education development of pastoralist women and children to facilitate their access to essential social services and economic empowerment." It works in the Loliondo area of northern Tanzania, providing awareness-raising workshops on critical political, policy, and rights issues and small loans for income-generating projects through a network of more than thirty-five community-based "women's action groups." In addition, it also supports the education of pastoralist girls through granting fellowships and running a local secondary school for Maasai girls and boys. Finally, PWC established the "Women's Solidarity Boma" to house and support abandoned, widowed, abused, and destitute women through a revolving livestock project (discussed in chapter 5).

The founder of PWC is Maanda Ngoitiko, a formidable woman who, with the assistance of Parkipuny, fled an arranged marriage to pursue further education in Dar es Salaam. After a few years working with a well-known feminist NGO in Tanzania, Tanzania Media Women's Association (TAMWA), she returned to Loliondo to lead the "women's wing" of KIPOC under Parkipuny's leadership. I first met her in 1990, when I discussed my proposed dissertation project with KIPOC leaders in Loliondo. I remember her as young, quiet, and intense. By the time we were reacquainted in 2005, she was a fierce, fearless, and tireless advocate for the rights of Maasai, especially Maasai women. In addition to running PWC, she worked for another NGO, Ujamaa Community Resource Trust (CRT), which mobilized people to understand, defend, and secure their land rights and create plans to manage their resources in sustainable ways (CRT won the prestigious Equator Prize in 2008 for its work), and served as an elected district councilor in Ngorongoro District.

Although Maanda is less educated than Ndinini, she is not less worldly. She has also traveled outside of Africa to attend development workshops (including completing a one-year diploma in development studies at Kimmage in Ireland), court donors, and educate Americans and others about the needs, perspectives, and priorities of pastoralist women. I hosted her for a few days in April 2009 during a whirlwind tour of the United States organized for her by an American woman she had met in Tanzania. During her visit, she gave numerous talks about the work of PWC (using a PowerPoint presentation), met with potential donors and partners, and patiently answered endless questions about the lives of Maasai women and men. Maanda was thrilled by the opportunity to forge some international connections, since PWC's location in northern Tanzania (a ten-hour drive from Arusha, when the roads are passable) means that it (and she) is very isolated from the networks of donors and NGOs in Tanzania that Ndinini and MWEDO are involved with.

Although both MWEDO and PWC seek to "empower" Maasai women, they are perceived by other NGO leaders and donors as taking somewhat different approaches. MWEDO, with its focus on education and income-generating projects, is characterized as more mainstream, pursuing a fairly conventional, conciliatory, gradual approach to improving gender relations. In contrast, although PWC runs similar programs, its reputation as a haven for girls fleeing arranged marriages and its sustained efforts to organize women to demand their rights from male family members and village leaders has earned it a reputation as a more radical and confrontational organization. When a twelve-year-old Maasai girl from the Loliondo area was beaten to death in 2006 by her older husband for refusing to stay with him, Maanda and other PWC members helped to publicize the incident with the police, government, and media and to mobilize public outrage, including a rally by secondary students from Dar es Salaam.[8] Despite these differences, Maanda and Ndinini have started to consult with one another, share advice, and work together to help Maasai women improve their lives. My interviews throughout Maasai areas (chapter 5) suggested very strong knowledge of and support for MWE-DO's and PWC's programs by the women involved.

Frictions and Factions

In addition to the challenge of bridging differences of class, generation, and gender between themselves and their constituents, Maasai NGOs confronted an array of centrifugal pressures that made it difficult to advocate together on policy issues. Some of these stresses were predictable, such as competition with one another for the attention and resources of donors (discussed more below). Others were, like the generational tensions described above, historically produced and structurally inherent in Maasai society. Notably, this included conflict between Maasai sections (Maasai belonged to different named sections that each had slightly different ritual and social practices, occupied different territories, and had a long history of fighting over livestock, land, and leadership). For example, the Maasai NGOs in Ngorongoro District were renowned for not getting along, because their leadership and membership often aligned along section lines. Parkipuny was successful and effective as MP, founder of KIPOC, and activist because, in part, he was not a member of the two dominant sections in Ngorongoro, the Purko and Loita, but from the Kisongo section. Although Kisongo Maasai were the majority in other Maasai districts, such as Monduli, they were scarcely represented in Ngorongoro, and not part of the long history of conflicts between Purko and Loita over land, water, and other resources. As such, Parkipuny was relatively neutral, and often served as an intermediary in section-based conflicts in Ngorongoro.

Another source of discord between Maasai NGOs were their different approaches to the government, which, like KIPOC and Inyuat e Maa, ranged from confrontational to deferential. In addition to KIPOC, another Maasai NGO with a reputation for directly challenging the government, especially on land rights, was Ilaramatak Lorkonerei (Orkonerei Integrated Pastoralist Survival Programme). Ilaramatak was founded in 1991 by a group of Maasai men concerned about "land-grabbing" in sixteen villages in Simanjiro District. The organization grew quickly from a small CBO staffed by twenty-one volunteers to, by 1996, a medium-sized NGO operating in three locations, with thirty full-time staff members, several buildings, two vehicles, and a financial "turnover" in 1995 of more than 43 million Tanzanian shillings (Mwau and Reynders 1996:1). The executive secretary of Ilaramatak, Martin Saning'o (who had formerly led another Maasai NGO, Inyuat e Moipo), was an educated Maasai who had worked for several years with a Lutheran church-sponsored mobile eye clinic throughout Maasai areas, and traveled overseas on several occasions for short-term training programs. From the beginning, Martin adopted an oppositional stance toward the government, using the language of human rights (Swahili: *haki za binadamu*) to frame Maasai struggles and the phrase "indigenous pastoralists" (Swahili: *wachungaji waasili*) in its publicity and reports.[9] In a conversation that I had with an officer of Inyuat e Maa in 1997, he criticized Ilaramatak for spending all of its time fighting with the government, blaming the government for everything. Moreover, he claimed, "Ilaramatak is responsible for breaking up families. They claim that when a husband beats his wife, it is a 'human rights violation,' so they get involved, and tell the wife to go to court and send her husband to prison." He scoffed: "There are traditional ways to deal with these kinds of problems. There is no need for outside interference, which only results in permanent breakups."

This harsh assessment was prompted not just by a difference in approaches to the government, but by a long, bitter rivalry between Ilaramatak and Inyuat e Maa (or, more accurately, between their leaders), which constantly undermined efforts to form a viable coalition. Leaders of Inyuat e Maa frequently complained to me that Ilaramatak had "hijacked" their ideas (such as a Maa-language community radio), by claiming them as their own and successfully seeking donor funding. More disturbingly, they alleged that Ilaramatak had undermined several of their projects by trying to convince community members and local government leaders to "kick us out." In contrast, some members of Ilaramatak characterized Inyuat e Maa as a government stooge, afraid to stand up to state-led affronts to Maasai rights. Parkipuny described the rivalry between Martin and Saruni as a war (Swahili: *vita*): "They hated each other. I tried to mediate, but I was unsuccessful." Unfortunately, the rivalry between the organizations continued even after Saruni died. And, as was often the case among Maasai, the disputes dissolved into rumors and accusations about who was "really" Maasai. (Ironically, given his lifelong interest in Maasai traditional practices and beliefs, Saruni was constantly rumored to not be Maasai.)

Another tension faced by these NGOs, common to NGOs everywhere, was between following a mission of advocacy or one of service delivery. Most

NGOs, at least initially, were, like KIPOC, organized to advocate for broad political agendas of land rights and social justice in the face of heightened large-scale land alienation produced by economic liberalization policies that encouraged large commercial farms, the often illegal "sale" of village lands to government officials and nonresident entrepreneurs, and the increased, government-sanctioned immigration of agriculturalists into lands formerly used for livestock herding, small-scale cultivation, hunting, and gathering (cf. Hodgson 2001a; Hodgson and Schroeder 2002; Neumann 1995). Many were very active in the late 1990s, when the Tanzanian government sponsored a review and then "reform" of its land policies, shifting from a communal system of land use and leases to demarcation of land for individual, collective, and commercial sale. In 1996, for example, Ilaramatak helped Orkesumet village in Simanjiro District successfully charge government officials with illegal alienation of their village lands without village consent (Saning'o and Heidenreich 1996). Ilaramatak, Inyuat e Maa, and other NGOs were also actively involved, with the assistance of such international donors as NOVIB, CUSO, IWGIA, Trocaire, and Survival International in assisting pastoralists displaced from the Mkomazi Game Reserve to challenge their removal and demand restitution (Saning'o and Heidenreich 1996; Ilaramatak 1997; Brockington 2002).

In addition to filing court cases against the government, several NGOs also tried to work with national coalitions to argue their case. In 1997, for example, Francis (representing Inyuat e Maa), Parkipuny (Aigwenak Trust), a representative of Ilaramatak, and three other pastoralist NGO leaders were among thirty-one participants in a 1997 national workshop on land rights funded by OXFAM GB. They called themselves a "National Land Forum" and signed a "Declaration of NGOs and Interested Persons on Land" that criticized both the process of formulating the law and its content, and urged the government to allow full debate on the new Land Bill before it was presented to Parliament.[10]

But other NGOs, especially those formed later, were more oriented to economic programs such as "development" or "service delivery" in the form of water projects, veterinary medicines, schools, and health facilities (cf. Cameron 2001). One of the most successful service-delivery-oriented Maasai NGOs was CORDS (Community Research and Development Services), founded in 1998 by Benedict ole Nangoro, a Maasai former diocesan priest who had coordinated ADDO (the Catholic Church's development organization) for six years after my departure. Benedict, whom I have known for almost twenty-five years, is a quiet, intense, and extraordinarily smart and perceptive man. After he left ADDO, he completed a masters of philosophy in development studies at the University of Sussex in 1995. As he told me, "After all of that practice, I wanted to think about theories."[11] His MPhil thesis explored the history of land alienation and the problem of land rights among Maasai pastoralists in Tanzania (Nangoro 1995). Although he contemplated pursuing a PhD, he returned to Tanzania to work as a development consultant, at which time he left the priesthood and married.

In 1997, Benedict and four other researchers and development practitioners[12] conducted a thorough survey of the social, economic, and political situation of pastoralists in the four primarily pastoralist districts of Kiteto, Monduli, Ngorongoro, and Simanjiro (Longido district was created from Monduli district after this time), including a review of development interventions and development actors, both governmental and nongovernmental (Kipuri et al. 1997). The findings and recommendations of the 214-page report provided the foundation for CORDS's mission, which, as of 2008, was "to work with NGO's, CBO's and local communities to enhance the security of resource tenure among the pastoral communities in Kiteto, Monduli, Ngorongoro, and Simanjiro and to promote sustainable livelihoods."[13] To this end, CORDS "promotes community based development initiatives (land rights, water, human and animal health and education)."[14]

CORDS's current mission statement reflects a gradual evolution of its programs, from a primary involvement in assisting villages to demarcate, register, and seek collective titles for their land to supporting a broader array of development activities. At ADDO, Benedict had expanded programs that I had begun to assist Maasai villages to obtain collective titles to their land. He continued those programs at CORDS, with support from some of ADDO's key funders, especially CORDAID. As he explained: "CORDS' main work was in land security and land titling, modeled after what ADDO had been doing. We started first in Monduli District, but it was very political, a lot of powerful politicians tried to get involved. So we moved to Kiteto District, where we did land use planning for nine villages." "But," he continued, "people were pressuring us to do something about their livestock as well. 'Land for what?' they asked us. So we began a program in animal health and one on indigenous breeds [of livestock], helping them to select and adapt them."[15] Other development programs followed, so that now CORDS positions its land-titling work as an economic initiative that is a prerequisite for any other development efforts, rather than a political challenge to government injustice.

Thus, while KIPOC and other Maasai NGOs supported court cases against the government, advocated for changes to the land law, and educated pastoralists about their rights, CORDS followed a more pragmatic and less politically charged approach. In fact, CORDS was the only NGO actually working with pastoralists to demarcate and title their lands in accordance with current Tanzanian land legislation, rather than just "educating" them about their rights and complaining about historic and contemporary injustices. Of course, having researched and written a thesis about land conflict among Maasai, Benedict was well aware of these injustices. But he carefully followed a two-pronged strategy of positioning CORDS as a service-delivery NGO in the eyes of the Tanzanian government, while positioning himself as an advocate of Maasai rights as indigenous peoples among transnational donors and advocacy groups. For the land-titling work, Benedict and CORDS worked closely with government officials, even shifting their focus from Monduli to Kiteto when the situation became too "political." Although "human rights" are occasionally mentioned in CORDS's publicity materials, the phrases "indigenous rights" and "indigenous people" are absent. Nonetheless, Benedict was actively involved in the work of IWGIA (which was one of CORDS's donors). He served on IWGIA's advisory board, published articles about Maasai land rights in IWGIA's quarterly newsletter, *Indigenous Affairs* (Nangoro 1999, 2003) and yearbook, *The Indigenous World*, and worked with IWGIA to promote the idea that Maasai and certain other African peoples were indigenous peoples. He also participated in numerous international meetings and workshops, including at least one UN meeting, as an indigenous representative.[16] In addition, he was one of the signatories to the "Response Note to the Draft Aide Memoire of the African Group" (African Group of Experts 2007) when several African states tried to derail final ratification of the UN Declaration in 2007 (see chapter 1).

When I asked Benedict in 2005 whether he found the concept of "indigenous" useful, he responded that "it is a powerful label that promotes specific interests. It is now accepted by the UN and the African Commission, so I think that we should pick it up and use it strategically. But it needs to be communicated and articulated carefully. The African governments deny that there are any indigenous peoples . . . we have to teach them."[17] "But," he cautioned, "we also have to be careful that it is not equated with ethnicity, then it is too dangerous. It is up to the people in power to provide a rationale and a justification, or else the government will just close the doors." "Does the concept have any pitfalls?" I asked. "Yes," he replied. "The concept can be divisive. But we can choose to either give in [by giving up the use of the concept of indigenous] or look for new strategies." Some of the strategies he listed included involving scholars to help articulate the issues, popularizing the concept among groups, building "strategic alliances," and learning from other movements. "But we need to make the concept specific to our own situation." As he concluded, "Being indigenous doesn't exclude being a Tanzanian, a pastoralist, a Maasai and so forth."[18]

Bridging Differences

During this period, several attempts were made to establish forums for pastoralist leaders to try to work through their differences and disagreements. Maasai and other pastoralist leaders already met together frequently on an informal basis in their offices, over meals, and at social events to exchange information, brainstorm, and plan together. Eventually, a number of them began to call themselves the "Pastoral Caucus." The purpose of the Pastoral Caucus, which met occasionally in the mid-1980s and early 1990s, was to bring together Maasai politicians, NGO leaders, and others to share information, consider future directions, and serve as what one participant called a "pressure group" to forward pastoralist political and economic agendas vis-à-vis the state. In 1995, the Pastoral Caucus sponsored a workshop for pastoralist organizations, researchers, wildlife experts, and government representatives to meet and make recommendations about the proposed national land policy (Pastoral Caucus 1995).[19] Eventually, however, the Pastoral Caucus was taken over by a more structured, formal institution, PINGOs Forum (discussed below).

One idea that emerged from these discussions was the need to create a regular opportunity for pastoralist leaders, donors, and government officials to come together to discuss their common interest in pastoralism. To this end, in 1992, Martin Saning'o, Parkipuny, and others established the Pastoralist Network of Tanzania (PANET), an informal network of researchers, donors, and pastoralists interested in pastoralism:

> The PANET is a loose and informal organization that aims to provide pastoralists in Tanzania with opportunities to interact at a personal, individual and

informal level with researchers, policy makers and executive officers of the Government. It is a non-profit and non-political alliance of people interested in the development of pastoral peoples. It is an alliance that will publicise pastoralist viewpoints, and discuss issues and problems raised by the alliance, in an effort to improve mutual understanding between pastoralists and the government. (IWGIA 1993:139)

The first meeting was strategically held in Dar es Salaam to attract government and donor representatives—twenty-three people attended. Most of the subsequent meetings were held in Arusha, with donor sponsorship.[20] Almost seventy people participated in the third (December 4–5, 1992) and fourth (May 5–6, 1993) meetings, which I attended, including MPs, high-level government representatives, donors, researchers, and pastoralist leaders such as Parkipuny, Daniel Murumbi (a Barabaig leader), Martin Saning'o, and Saruni ole Ngulay. A different topic was discussed at each meeting, such as "pastoralism, tourism, and wildlife" or "pastoral livestock production." After a formal presentation on the topic by a researcher, development expert, or pastoralist leader, an open and often heated discussion among all participants ensued. I witnessed several angry outbursts between government representatives and Maasai leaders over such issues as the proposed land policies and the government's enduring negative stereotypes of pastoralism. A chair facilitated the discussion at each meeting, encouraging participants to reach consensus and make formal recommendations. On occasion, NGO leaders such as Martin described the work of their organization, and site visits to select projects and women's groups were organized after one meeting. After each workshop, an anonymous "editor" at the FAO wrote, copied, and distributed *PANET News*, an eight- to ten-page newsletter in English that summarized the papers, discussions, and recommendations. After the first few years, however, interest in PANET among pastoralists waned, as they became frustrated with the endless discussion of recommendations followed by the seeming failure by the government to translate words into action. As a 1996 report remarked, "since PANET has no mandate and cannot make recommendations to policy makers, few pastoralists see any future in the network" (Mwau and Reynders 1996:46). Instead, Parkipuny and other pastoralist leaders increasingly saw the need to revive the Pastoral Caucus in a more institutionalized form, to enable pastoralists themselves to organize as an advocacy group, not just to share information and exchange ideas with the government, but to pressure and lobby for change.

According to Parkipuny, the idea for an umbrella group had been discussed since 1990 (in such forums as the Pastoral Caucus), but it took time to design an appropriate structure. Participants (including Parkipuny, Martin, and a representative from Inyuat e Maa) in a small 1993 workshop for NGOs and donors on pastoralism and development agreed on the need for a "resource and advocacy center" to collect and disseminate information about "the pastoralist economy and human rights violations afflicted on pastoralist communities by the government, institutions, and or [*sic*] individuals," for a regular "NGO-Donor Forum," and for the creation of an "umbrella organization" to promote collaboration among NGOs and provide a link between the NGOs and the government and other institutions (Bulengo and Scheffer 1993). As a result, Parkipuny and Martin helped to formally establish the Pastoralists Indigenous Non-Governmental Organisation (PINGOs, sometimes PINGOs Forum) in 1994. The purpose was to create an umbrella organization to try to resolve the tensions among pastoralist organizations, coordinate the work of the NGOs, and represent their interests in regional, national, and international fora. As another Maasai leader told me, "PINGOs emerged at a difficult time, out of a real need for coordination."[21]

Initially, PINGOs comprised six Maasai NGOs (including KIPOC, Ilaramatak Lorkonerei, and BULGADA, a Barabaig NGO). Two prominent pastoralist organizations were notably absent, however: Inyuat e Maa and KINNAPA, a successful pastoralist organization working in Kiteto District since 1992. Other NGOs could apply to join PINGOs, with the possibility of being rejected (Igoe 2000:284).[22] PINGOs' mission, according to its leader, was "to build solidarity among pastoral organisations, and to strengthen their capacity in community development through training and the dissemination of information. PINGOs takes a holistic approach to development arguing that economic development goes hand in hand with democracy, constitutional law and human rights" (Bradbury et al. 1995:4; see also IWGIA 1996:227). PINGOs received financing from donors in the United Kingdom, Canada, and the Netherlands, among others.[23] It quickly opened an office in Arusha, started a small resource center, and hired some staff.

Unfortunately, from the start, the legitimacy and success of PINGOs as an umbrella group was weakened by the rivalries between the leaders of certain NGOs as to who was the legitimate representative of all Maasai, and the appropriate structure for such an umbrella group. Saruni had envisioned Inyuat e Maa as an umbrella group of sorts, organizing and representing all Maa-speaking peoples. But when he held the First Conference in 1991, Parkipuny, Martin, and other pastoralist leaders scheduled a capacity-building workshop for the exact same time, thereby making it difficult for representatives of its member organizations to participate in Inyuat e Maa's conference. Although a representative from Inyuat e Maa attended the 1993 workshop, Saruni refused to let Inyuat e Maa join PINGOs when it was officially registered, despite the pleas of Parkipuny and other NGO leaders. Saruni was not only frustrated by the establishment of a rival umbrella group, but upset that Martin was selected to head PINGOs. According to Francis, Saruni disagreed with the structure of PINGOs; he thought that there was no need for PINGOs to become a formal institution, as it created an unnecessary hierarchy among organizations by producing a distinction between members and nonmembers, interfered with the legal status of other pastoralist organizations, and would eventually disempower other local pastoralist NGOs. Instead, Saruni supported the continuation of something like the Pastoral Caucus, a "loose forum" in which all local organizations had direct membership, elected a chair, and met whenever needed, without donor assistance (Francis claimed that one such organization, Maasai Indigenous Non-Governmental Organization, or MINGO, existed for a while in the early 1990s).[24] In 1994, the institutional antagonism between Ilaramatak and Inyuat e Maa and personal hostility between Saruni and Martin was one of the topics discussed at a workshop on conflict resolution sponsored by PINGOs (Bradbury et al. 1995). But this and other efforts at reconciliation failed, and their personal antagonism forced other NGOs to take sides, however reluctantly.

Additional recognized challenges to the effectiveness of the Pastoralist Caucus, PANET, PINGOs, and other efforts to transcend just Maasai concerns and build a coalition among all pastoralists groups (and some hunter-gatherer groups) in Tanzania were significant differences among these pastoralist groups and the domination of Maasai in all of these initiatives. Other pastoralist-identified groups in Tanzania, such as Parakuyo and Barabaig, and hunter-gatherer groups such as Ndorobo and Hadzabe, had, like Maasai, suffered from the alienation of their land and other resources, exclusion from state-led development efforts, and disparaging treatment by government officers and elites. Despite these similarities, however, these ethnic groups had some significant differences in their historical and contemporary relationships to the state, donors, and each other. For example, Maasai, Parakuyo, and Ndorobo (as well as the agropastoralist Arusha) all spoke variations of a common language, Maa, while Barabaig and Hadzabe spoke distinctly different languages. Similarly, although they both strongly identified as "pastoralists," Maasai and Barabaig shared a long history of hostility, fueled in part by competition over the same range resources (cf. Igoe 2000). Finally, for a variety of reasons, including a long history of intense scrutiny and celebration in travelers' tales, coffee-table books, and now tourist propaganda, as well as more (albeit limited) political presence in Tanzania, Maasai were by far the most visible and well-known of these groups to the government and donors. As a result, not only did Maasai leaders dominate efforts to bring together pastoralist organizations, but Maa-speaking groups such as Parakuyo and Arusha who had, in the past, sought to distinguish themselves from Maasai, now, at least in the company of donors, asserted that they were "Maasai."

Finally, in addition to trying to build a pastoralist coalition within Tanzania, some Maasai leaders tried to encourage and facilitate pan-Maasai discussions and advocacy among Maasai in Tanzania and Kenya. For example, Saruni tried to bring Kenyan Maasai leaders to the First Maasai Conference. Although they were prevented by the Tanzanian government from participating, several of them traveled frequently to Arusha to meet with Saruni, Parkipuny, and other Maasai leaders. In May 1995, when I was attending a celebration at the Maasai Girls Secondary School in Monduli with my American friend Trish, a young Maasai man approached me to ask if Trish (who was videotaping the event) was with the media. He introduced himself and explained that he was from Kenya. He was visiting Tanzania to meet with representatives of various Maasai and pastoralist organizations to discuss common issues, especially ongoing struggles to protect the remaining pastures from alienation by corrupt government officials. "Maasai in Kenya have organized," he claimed. "We have frightened the government, and now we are trying to mobilize, to lobby, and to file court cases." He said that he had linked with Survival International, but was trying to find an American sponsor, since Kenya was so dependent on U.S. aid. I recommended that he contact Cultural Survival, which he had not heard of. These informal cross-border visits have continued to the present.

The Future of Pastoralist NGOs?

In sum, despite attempts to foster unity, promote common political agendas (such as the protection of land rights), and coordinate their activities through innumerable meetings and workshops and the creation of at an "umbrella" coordinating group, by 2000 NGOs in Maasai areas had splintered into even more groups and became fractured by sometimes quite hostile disagreements over priorities, competition over resources, and tensions over membership and representation. The following section explores the complicated causes and consequences of these fractures and tensions by focusing on the discussions, disagreements, and silences that occurred as part of a focused effort to reconcile these groups, a workshop in 2000 on the "The Future of Pastoralist NGOs in Tanzania" that took place in Arusha, Tanzania.[25] Representatives from ninety-six NGOs attended the three-day workshop, meeting with each other, donor representatives, and assorted researchers ("experts" and observers such as myself). As participants assessed the problems that had plagued them in the past in order to try to promote future collaborations and alliances, the topics of representation and accountability—between the NGOs and their constituencies, among coalitions of NGOs, and between NGOs and donors—were central to the discussion and debate and invoked issues of cultural identity, power, and history.

I include an extended analysis of the workshop here because it echoes and amplifies earlier insights in this chapter about the sources of friction and factions and the challenges to bridging these divides. The critical self-reflection and debates that occurred during the workshop reveal the cultural, political, and historical dynamics shaping the formation of civil society at this time, the principles and practices of inclusion and exclusion that defined and shaped the contours of political action, and the internal and external stresses that made alliances among the NGOs, the donors, and the government precarious, at best. It exposed the fraught political landscape of the movement and the willingness of most participants to engage in an honest appraisal of the key problems; it also exposed the enduring difficulties of forging and maintaining political alliances under the broad rubric of "indigenous" or even the narrower platform of "pastoralist."

The primary language of the workshop was Swahili, followed by English and occasionally Maa. Its structure was straightforward: prior to the meeting, the workshop organizers circulated a position paper authored in English by a Maasai NGO leader (Benedict Nangoro, the director of CORDS) and a donor representative (Nangoro and Daborn 2000) to leaders of the invited NGOs for comment. They received and circulated written comments in English and Swahili (Anonymous 2000; Daborn 2000; Meitanga 2000; Mwarabu 2000;

Richard 2000). The workshop organizers also commissioned two other key-note papers by Maasai leaders (Morindat 2000; Sangale 2000b), which were distributed to workshop participants, presented orally, and followed by a presentation of a "donor's perspective." Facilitators then worked with the participants to discuss the issues raised and identify the most pressing problems and issues "facing pastoralists." The twenty-three issues noted during the period of discussion and brainstorming were then grouped into one of three topics: political representation, coordination among NGOs, and specific matters such as land alienation and education. Members then split into groups to address each topic. They discussed the causes of and contributing factors to the problem; explored what accomplishments, difficulties, and failures had taken place; and made recommendations for how to overcome these problems and difficulties. Each group then reported back to all of the participants and then engaged in a discussion of "the way forward."

Despite discussion of a broad array of issues, the central concern of the participants was to debate and decide the complicated issue of political representation: Who was choosing to and being selected to speak on behalf of others? Who, exactly, was being represented? What was the mechanism for selecting representative people or organizations? What was the mandate for these representatives? How should these representatives be held accountable to their constituents? Of course, issues of discursive representation were implicit in much of the discussion as well; "the cultural struggles of social movements over meanings and representations are deeply entangled with their struggles for rights and economic and political institutional power" (Alvarez et al. 1998:xi; cf. Brosius et al. 1998).

Debating Representation

The first position paper clearly set forth the workshop's main agenda, which was to deliberate how best to form an organization to coordinate and represent the interests of relevant NGOs. Claiming that "there is a lack of effective co-ordination and co-operation within and between these various organisations, technical services and donors," the authors proposed a series of initiatives "to effect full and sustainable coordination and cooperation between all the concerned parties" (Nangoro and Daborn 2000:2). Their main proposal was to create a national umbrella pastoralist organization to which all pastoralist representative organizations would belong (ibid.). They referred specifically to the failure of PINGOs to adequately include and therefore represent "all pastoralist representative organisations." The choice, to them, was clear: "*Either* strengthen PINGOs to achieve its stated mission and objectives to properly and effectively represent the pastoralist community *or* create a new organisation to take over this vital function" (ibid.). This decision became the key issue that framed the workshop, as participants analyzed the reasons for PINGOs' failure, debated whether these problems could best be addressed through rehabilitating PINGOs or forming a new organization that would not be burdened by PINGOs' history, and discussed the content and structure of the umbrella group they wanted to institute (whether it turned out to be PINGOs or a new organization).

Discussion was long and heated, both in the formal workshop sessions and in the innumerable informal conversations and debates that took place over meals, in hushed (and not-so-hushed) whispers outside the workshop room, and late into the night at the restaurant and bar. The PINGOs leadership felt (rightly so) under attack and held hurried meetings amongst themselves to discuss the accusations and to consider their response. During the workshop, their position changed from one of accepting the legitimacy of the workshop participants to determine the fate of PINGOs (since a quorum of PINGOs' membership was present) to challenging the right of participants to intervene in PINGOs matters (since the workshop was not formally called as a general assembly meeting of the PINGOs membership, and many non–PINGOs members were in attendance). The ensuing debates focused on three levels of representation: the representation of local people by NGOs, the representation of NGOs by PINGOs or a new "umbrella group," and the representation of the NGOs and umbrella group to the state and donors.

First, many workshop participants discussed the personal and structural problems of some NGOs that prevented them from being reliable representatives, reiterating comments made in the position papers (Morindat 2000; Sangale 2000b): a lack of a clearly defined vision, including short- and long-term objectives; poor leadership qualities, especially a lack of commitment or spirit of voluntarism; the selection of weak or ineffective governing boards comprised of "handpicked stooges" or members elected for popularity rather than ability; poor administrative, management, and financial reporting systems that resulted in the misuse of funds and resources; and a lack of transparency and communication in relations with community members (cf. Sangale 2000a). A key problem was the failure to ensure proper (or any) transition of leadership, so that community members saw some NGOs as the "property" (Swahili: *mali*) of one person or a small group in the name of the community. Often these NGOs were perceived as just platforms to advance the political motives and ambitions of their leaders or for leaders to use donor funds for personal ends. Several participants even accused NGO leaders of neglecting to visit the communities they were suppose to represent: "Some just want to stay in their nice office in town and never go to the bush." Here it is important to remember that these accusations were not made about all NGOs or even most, but the problems of certain organizations contributed to a composite picture.

At a broader level, some participants speculated about the cultural politics and identity claims of certain NGOs and their leaders. Who, exactly, was "indigenous"? Who, for that matter, was a "pastoralist"? Few families, even Maasai families, subsisted on pastoralism alone anymore; most had diversified into small-scale cultivation, foraging, wage labor, and other economic activities. Nonetheless, some participants challenged the "authenticity" of some NGOs and their leaders as merely "pretending" to be pastoralists or Maasai in order to attract donor attention. As one participant commented, "Some people just put on red cloths and call themselves pastoralists!" He reiterated the same point later: "Who is a pastoralist? Who is it we are trying to help, those families who have one or two cows, or those whose life depends *entirely* on cattle?" The unstated subject here was Arusha people, Maa-speakers who were primarily agropastoralists and had only recently come to reclaim their Maasai heritage in light of donor preferences to help "the Maasai," not "the Arusha."

Several participants mentioned, directly and indirectly, how differences of gender, age, and class shaped the relationships between NGOs and their constituencies and among NGOs themselves. Others discussed the problem of "conflicting representation" noted by Nangoro and Daborn (2000:6): NGOs competed with other institutions—customary leadership structures, village government, district government, and even other NGOs—to represent community interests (cf. Cameron 2001:59). "There are often," they explained, "no clearly defined lines of demarcation between the roles and responsibilities of these different structures" (Nangoro and Daborn 2000:6). Indeed, NGOs often complicated the picture by aligning with one or more of the structures or by sparking power struggles among these representative structures, producing confusion, if not alienation, of their supposed constituencies. But as another commentator cautioned, "Different pastoralist peoples may feel more comfortable with different systems of representation. Is standardisation the way to go?" (Anonymous 2000:7).

Finally, there was the related question of how each NGO was formed, which had significant consequences for the accountability of NGOs to their supposed constituencies: Was the NGO created through a "bottom-up" process of community discussion and selection? Or through a "top-down" process whereby one or more people decided to form an NGO and then sought community support and approval (or just claimed it all along)? Several NGOs had reputations of being purely opportunistic, created by educated men with few job prospects as more of a "private business" with no popular base as an NGO (cf. Bebbington and Riddell 1997:111).

The second set of concerns focused on the challenges of creating a viable "umbrella" group to represent pastoralist NGOs. Participants voiced many grievances about PINGOs' ineffectiveness as a coordinating group, including its poor communication with members; its lack of transparency in decision making and financial matters; its exclusion of certain NGOs (including Maasai NGOs) from membership; the dominance of Maasai NGOs and, therefore, Maasai interests; and its failure to ensure an inclusive agenda and strategy. Several participants implied that PINGOs was an oligarchy, representing the interests of a few in the name of many (cf. Fisher 1997:456). As one Maasai activist complained, "I've been a member of PINGOs since 1996, and I have never been invited to a meeting." A Barabaig participant scoffed at PINGOs' claims to have worked with non-Maasai pastoralist groups for over ten years: "If so, the Barabaig knew nothing about this!" Another man claimed that his NGO had applied to PINGOs for membership over four years before and had still never received a reply. Several participants accused PINGOs of being a "donor-driven" organization in terms of its finances and agendas (see also Sansom 2000). Some acknowledged, however, that a significant cause of PINGOs' demise as an umbrella organization had to do with the problems of mistrust, competition over resources, and minimal communication and information sharing among the NGOs themselves.

As before, the cultural politics of ethnicity, collective identity, and livelihood were central to debates about whether *common interests* or a *shared identity* (and, if so, *which* identity) should determine membership in the umbrella group. Should, as a Hadzabe man repeatedly asked, PINGOs or the umbrella group represent just pastoralist NGOs or include hunter-gatherers as fellow "indigenous" people? In the ensuing debate, some participants argued that hunter-gatherers should be included: they shared common resources with pastoralists (especially land)—"we are all marginalized people"—and they had already decided at previous meetings to work together since they shared common interests. "But they need to tell us what their needs are," explained one man; "then we can begin to address them." One participant believed that livelihood rather than ethnicity should be foregrounded in deciding about inclusion. Thus, he contended, although Ndorobo spoke Maa (and could therefore be considered Maasai), they were more like the Hadzabe because they were hunter-gatherers. Other participants were less sympathetic:

> We pastoralists decided to meet together, then the hunter gatherers
> decided to attend. Fine, but they shouldn't complain that the
> meeting does not address their concerns. This is a meeting of
> pastoralists. Or perhaps we should retitle the name of the workshop
> as a pastoralists and hunter-gatherers conference?

One claimed that most hunter-gatherers were merely "poachers," hunting for theft rather than subsistence. Another framed the problem in elitist terms, invoking ideologies of modernization and progress: "Hunter-gatherers are very different from Maasai, and very far behind. A Hadzabe man attends school until Form Two then returns to hunt; what good is that?" Some just expressed frustration: "We are being diverted from our purpose by these surprises. We are searching for our self-identity *as pastoralists:* Where are we? Which way forward? From where?" In the end, the group decided to invite the few representatives of hunter-gatherers present to form a breakout group to discuss concerns and then report them to the plenary. Despite this debate, however, the workshop continued to focus on pastoralist issues, as reflected in the discussions and final workshop report (Sangale 2000a).

A related debate occurred about power hierarchies among pastoralist groups themselves in the formation of alliances. PINGOs was accused of being dominated by Maasai NGOs and therefore marginalizing the concerns of non-Maasai pastoralist groups such as Parakuyo and Barabaig. For example, PINGOs named its newsletter *Ngatitin ol Maasai* (The Voice of the Maasai), claiming, when some Barabaig complained, that it was an oversight (Igoe 2000:290). These discussions echoed long-standing historical tensions between Parakuyo and Maasai over cultural identity, and Barabaig and Maasai over rangeland and range resources, as well as jealousy over donor obsession with "the Maasai." Moreover, even some Maasai NGOs were excluded from PINGOs because of personal jealousies and rivalries. One commentator, who claimed to be playing "devil's advocate," questioned the entire premise of a coalition based on a shared mode of production: "Why do you need a pastoralist forum? Is there a mountain community forum? Is there a coastal people (fishermen) forum? Can a pastoralist forum really be truly representative of the disparate aims and views of the many different pastoral peoples in Tanzania?" (Anonymous 2000:2)

The third set of concerns voiced by workshop participants, which echoed many of the problems identified above, was about the representation of the NGOs and umbrella group to the state and donors. Donors complained that many NGOs, especially PINGOs, suffered from a lack of communication, inadequate and infrequent financial reporting, and ineffectual leadership and project management skills. One donor representative explained that although his organization had been involved with PINGOs for years, there had been very little communication. "In my two and a half years," he remarked, "I don't recall receiving any reports or requests for information from them. I have no sense of their agenda or issues." A few participants, however, wondered whether donors would actually liaise with such an umbrella group of pastoralist or indigenous NGOs to coordinate their activities. "Donors," noted one commentator, "especially small donors, often work directly through [NGOs] precisely because they have direct contact of the recipient communities and are more likely to be representatives of and sensitive to specific community needs" (Anonymous 2000:2).

For many participants, PINGOs' inability to effectively coordinate, mobilize, and represent its member groups in relationships with the government was one of its greatest weaknesses. Several activists bemoaned the most recent consequence of their ineffective, fractured coalition—the failure to successfully advocate pastoralist interests (such as collective land titles) in national land reform decisions, arguably the most important political opportunity and challenge in decades. One activist compared their failure with the striking success of women's organizations in Tanzania, which were able to form a viable political alliance to lobby for certain progressive reforms (such as codifying women's rights to own and inherit land). Some claimed that the lack of an effective working relationship between PINGOs (and many other NGOs) and the nation-state had contributed to government mistrust of NGOs (Morindat 2000:5).

The Way Forward?

Some participants argued forcefully that efforts should be made to re-form and restructure PINGOs to be a more effective and representative umbrella organization. As one activist commented, "If we abandon PINGOs to create another umbrella group, we will be like an *enaruk mingani* [Maa, lit. "a woman who goes from husband to husband"]." Most eventually decided to form a new organization that could learn from the problems that plagued PINGOs but avoid the taint of its damaged reputation. "Resurrecting PINGOs," one man remarked, "will only resurrect its problems."

After deliberating in groups about the structure, purpose, and name of the new umbrella organization, the workshop formed a taskforce to review and synthesize the group reports and to prepare a draft proposal and registration documents for the new organization. Not surprisingly, the cultural politics of representation were central to debates about the appropriate composition of the taskforce membership. There was a general consensus that women needed to be represented (they needed two women, argued one facilitator, "because women often have trouble getting to meetings"), as well as hunter-gatherers. Which pastoralist groups and the proportionality of their representation was a more contentious issue: Everyone agreed that Barabaig needed a representa-tive. But Parakuyo? Some participants argued that Parakuyo did not need a separate representative because they were Maasai, but a few Parakuyo dis-agreed: "We need our own representative, or else we will be silenced." Similar debates ensued about Arusha—would Maasai adequately represent their inter-ests? At this point, one man became quite annoyed. "If we start dividing up by groups," he asked, "why not clans or sections? We are all the same, but we could have endless divisions such as Laiser, Mollel [clan names], and so forth." There was also a discussion about ensuring the geographical representation of Maasai from all five government regions. Finally the ten-member taskforce was appointed as follows: three Maasai, two Barabaig, one Hadzabe, two women (one Arusha and one Barabaig), and two (Maasai) experts.[26]

Structural Predicaments

Participants were remarkably open and perceptive in their analysis of the problems that had plagued the NGOs, but most of their critiques implicitly and often explicitly blamed NGOs and NGO leaders for their problems, disregarding (often intentionally) some of the external causes contributing to their dilemmas. Except for a few references to the government's involvement in land alienation, no participant publicly questioned the role of the government or donors in provoking some of their problems, especially their efforts to form and sustain an umbrella group. As one facilitator argued when colonialism was invoked, "The main problem is pastoralists, ourselves; we blame colonialism, yet it has been over for almost forty years now." Obviously this was in part a strategic silence, given the number of donors and scattering of government representatives at the workshop.

But this strategic silence ignored the complex historical context in which these NGOs were formed and operated. By 2000, these Maasai and pastoralist NGOs had changed in at least two significant ways: they had shifted from a few NGOs struggling for donor attention and support into a collection of dozens of groups with substantial national and international visibility vying for significant donor resources; and their objectives (with a few notable exceptions) had changed from advocating broader political mandates such as land reform to supporting much less overtly political agendas of community development and service delivery. These two changes were not unrelated and were in fact central, I believe, to explaining some of the tensions, or "structural predicaments," troubling the movement at the time of the workshop (cf. Mercer 1999).

It is important to remember some of the external pressures that contributed to, produced, or exacerbated the problems identified by the workshop participants (and, of course, community members and NGO leaders). As previously discussed, by the early 1990s, the economic and political landscape of Tanzania, like many other so-called Third World countries, had changed dramatically under the impact of three related processes—"democratization," "economic liberalization," and "decentralization"—that provided both new constraints and new opportunities for NGOs. These three processes were deeply contradictory for pastoralist and indigenous people. By alienating land and exacerbating conflicts over natural resources, neoliberal economic policies and practices produced increased impoverishment and economic stratification among pastoralists. At the same time, however, the advent of multi-partyism and encouragement of "civil society" created opportunities for political mobilization, collective action, and public challenge to government actions. Yet efforts to mobilize and coordinate translocal development and advocacy initiatives were frustrated by the devolution of state control, decision making, and oversight to "local" government authorities.

These processes aggravated tensions between NGOs and the national government in at least three ways. First, as discussed in Chapter 2, shifting international development assistance away from state-based development programs toward "local" NGO initiatives promoted the proliferation of NGOs. Moreover, the ability of NGOs to capture significant amounts of donor funds also, on occasion, sparked the jealousy, resentment, and suspicions of the Tanzanian government. In turn, the tremendous increase in the availability of donor funding, the decentralization of political power and economic resources, and the sheer number of NGOs hindered government efforts to monitor and control NGO activities. Although the government oversaw NGOs through its centralized registration and reporting process, efforts to coordinate NGO and government development initiatives occurred primarily at the district or village level, hampering efforts for more systematic oversight, planning, and coordination. These endeavors were further complicated by the vast differences that existed among regional and local government agencies, as well as individual officials, as to their attitudes, effectiveness, and practices with regard to NGOs and local communities.

The failure of NGOs to build a viable coalition significantly hindered their effectiveness as advocates at the national level. As a result, they engaged in piecemeal rather than systematic lobbying and sporadic rather than sustained political pressure. According to Greg Cameron, even when PINGOs was a viable organization, it "neglected to engage the Tanzanian government via lobbying and campaigning and instead did international advocacy with Western donors" (2001:57).[27] Of course, this presumed that the Tanzanian government was even interested or willing to recognize PINGOs (or another umbrella group) as a duly representative organization and negotiate with it accordingly. As Li (2000, 2001a), Saugestad (2001), and Werbner (2002), among others, have discussed in the case of other indigenous rights movements, the "politics of recognition" (from Taylor 1994)—that is, demanding and attaining national and international recognition of first the identity (and later the rights and claims) of an "indigenous" group—takes place in complex fields of power:

> The "others" with whom those who seek recognition must engage include government departments with diverse agendas; colonial and contemporary legal codes, subject to interpretation; individual politicians and bureaucrats with more or less populist inclinations; international donors; national and international "non-governmental organizations"; and the media which both forms

and responds to the common-sense understandings and sentiments of the "national-popular." (Li 2001a:653–54)

For all of the reasons detailed above—fear of ethnic revitalization, resistance to the acknowledgement of collective rights, jealousies over donor attention and resources—and, more, working for and achieving recognition by the Tanzanian nation-state was a grueling, time-consuming, and ongoing challenge.

In addition to their sometimes troubled relationship with the government, the demands and pressure of donors themselves exerted tremendous, at times fracturing, stresses on NGOs (cf. Bratton 1989; Fisher 1997; Hulme and Edwards 1997). Like NGOs, the "donor community" was no monolithic entity with a common form, function, or agenda—they included multilateral and bilateral funding agencies, international NGOs, religious institutions, the environmental lobby, and more. Their reasons for supporting certain NGOs varied tremendously and even, at times, conflicted. For example, at the same time that AWF funded Inyuat e Maa to create community wildlife management areas (described in chapter 2), another donor financed a Maasai NGO to lobby against the further encroachment of game reserves onto pastoralist and hunter-gatherer lands. The political orientation of donors differed as well, especially in terms of their willingness to support groups that challenged or criticized government policies in some way. Such differences among donors promoted differences, even conflicts, among NGOs and contributed to the proliferation of NGOs as each donor sought its own partner NGO. As a result of their structural position as "gatekeepers," NGOs had to navigate and negotiate the often contradictory demands of their constituencies and donors. As one NGO leader explained, "Some NGOs only have 'upward accountability' to their donors; they pay no attention to their legitimacy among communities. Some are just 'floating up there' with no links to the ground, to any group, they are not really working with any community." Or as a facilitator at the 2000 Arusha workshop asked: "Who owns the NGOs? Their leaders? Members? Communities? Donors?"

Furthermore, as the case study of Inyuat e Maa (chapter 2) suggests, the dependence on donor aid, and the unwillingness of most donors to directly challenge state policies, depoliticized the agendas of some NGOs, producing a shift from primarily "political" concerns (that make some claims on the state) to more "economic" concerns that, at least to the state and donors, seemed more politically benign (cf. Cameron 2001; Igoe 2005). The demand that NGOs emphasize service delivery (education, health delivery, water projects) was, of course, increasingly necessary as the Tanzanian state, as part of structural adjustment and subsequent neoliberal policies, withdrew its already limited support for these social services. But the dependence of NGOs on donor funds, as several workshop participants mentioned, created vulnerability to, and pressure to comply with, donor political and economic agendas. (Ironically, the very unwillingness of NGO leaders to publicly critique donors at the workshop was in itself strong testimony to such pressures.) Moreover, the small scale and large numbers of NGOs made them even more susceptible to such pressures (further highlighting the need for some kind of coalition to negotiate with donors). Fisher (1997:454) has described this process as the "cooptation" of NGOs by donors from "empowerment/social mobilization" to "service delivery/development" as NGOs reconfigured themselves to attract and retain donor funds. Rather than set their own agendas and selectively recruit progressive donors, PINGOs and a number of NGOs were seduced by the availability of donor funds to adopt development programs and projects shaped by donor interests, at the expense of the land reform efforts they believed were crucial to the long-term survival of their constituents.

The tendency of NGO programs, under donor pressure, to shift focus from political to economic issues further fractured the original unifying agenda of NGOs. All NGOs shared a mutual interest in lobbying the nation-state to protest land alienation and to demand legal rights to their customary land; land reforms at the national level would have been advantageous for all of them.[28] In contrast, their shift to primarily economic agendas that sought funds for community development projects of various types produced disagreement and disunity, as NGOs competed with one another (as well as with PINGOs, their supposed umbrella group) for donor attention and funds. Attempts to coordinate donor funding foregrounded this conflict of interest: newer, less-funded groups wanted to "share the wealth" and demanded equitable distribution of donor aid while older, established NGOs wanted to protect and maintain their special, lucrative relationship with certain donors. Moreover, as the workshop made clear, NGOs did not share a common vision for their economic future beyond the protection of land rights. Should communities be encouraged to rely primarily on pastoralism for their livelihoods, or should they be encouraged to diversify economically? What role should education play in their future? What would be their ideal relation to the Tanzanian state? What was their position on certain cultural practices, language issues, and identity claims? What did it mean, inquired one commentator, to organize around a shared identity as pastoralists "when the future development of existing pastoralist communities is that they decide to forego pastoralism as a way of life? . . . Is there a vision for the future of pastoralist culture and way of life?" (Anonymous 2000:1).

Furthermore, the zeal of donors in courting and supporting the NGOs and especially PINGOs sometimes blinded them to the personal, political, and structural problems of NGOs. Even when they became aware of such problems, a common response was simply to infuse more cash rather than demand institutional reforms, thereby exacerbating the problems of financial management and accountability. Greg Cameron, for example, who briefly worked for PINGOs as a Canadian volunteer in the 1990s, wrote about

> donors who felt the aims of the organization [PINGOs] were so significant and the struggle so intrinsically valuable that basic development sustainability of NGO financing, due process in decision making, etc. could be overlooked in the name of Maasai cultural survival. Others dreamed that PINGOs would spearhead a social movement of all pastoralists, but could not concretise this aspiration except by throwing as much money as possible at it. (Cameron 2001:65)

In addition, as discussed above, the blizzard of donor attention and demands on the time and resources of PINGOs and NGO leaders—in the form of seemingly endless workshops, meetings, short courses, study tours, and overseas travel—further alienated leaders from their local constituents and commitments.

In addition to the challenges of working with the government and the complicity of donors, a third external influence on the indigenous movement was the cultural politics inherent in the strategic decisions by activists to link their efforts to transnational discourses and networks of indigenous peoples. Such a link, as comparative evidence suggests, created both opportunities and risks (see, e.g., Conklin and Graham 1995; Jackson 1995; Saugestad 2001; Warren 1998). The positive effects, as mentioned before, included increased visibility, resources, and leverage against the state. But mobilizing around the label "indigenous" implied that members shared common interests because of their common identity, an assumption that may have reflected more rhetoric than reality. The potentially volatile and splintering effects of debates over the criteria for inclusion and exclusion in the indigenous movement were clearly evidenced in the workshop discussions.

Less evident were the consequences of organizing around the label of "indigenous" for non-indigenous groups. Most communities in northern

Tanzania were ethnically mixed, which meant that only certain members of a community—whether because of their ethnicity or their primary liveli-hood—were singled out for representation and resources, while the needs of other community members were ignored. In some areas, the formation of NGOs catalyzed ethnic tensions over local resources and political control. Jim Igoe (2000), for example, documented the increased hostility between Maasai and non-Maasai in the community of Moipo after the formation of Inyuat e Moipo, an NGO run and staffed by Maasai. Non-Maasai villagers complained about their lack of inclusion in NGO projects, their lack of ac-cess to the NGO tractor, and other disparities. Moreover, those villages or communities that did not have an NGO to represent their interests were unable to contribute to, or benefit from, the indigenous movement. The pro-liferation of NGOs was, in part, one response to this issue, as every village or community formed an NGO or CBO to seek development funds.

Finally, the structural problems of some NGOs were intensified because of the timing of their formation. As Saugestad has argued,

> "established" indigenous organizations that were formed in earlier periods in Canada, the United States, Scandinavia, Australia, and New Zealand under-went a long period of internal mobilization to develop and consolidate local or-ganizations before they engaged in dialogue or litigation with their respective governments over land rights issues. In contrast, INGOs that were started in the 1990s were: (a) immediately supported by an existing international indigenous network offering both solidarity and information, which meant that (b) they im-mediately set out to address the most complex of all possible issues: rights to land and water. Inevitably, this means that extremely controversial issues are being addressed before what we might call the "normal" process of local mobilisation and awareness-raising has run its course towards the consolidation of regional and national organisational structures. (Saugestad 2001:233)

As Saugestad cautioned, "the kind of 'flying start' the new organisations receive on the international circuit helps in many respects, but cannot sub-stitute for painstaking grassroots mobilization" (2001:234). In other words, immediate access to substantial donor funds may short-circuit or substan-tially condense some of the slow, painful, but necessary stages of organiza-tional maturation and coalition building.

My purpose in analyzing these "structural predicaments" is to place the issues raised in the workshop in their broader context to explore how many of the problems identified by the workshop participants were produced or aggravated by outside political and economic processes and institutions over which they had little control. It is not meant, however, to absolve NGOs of all responsibility for their actions. In fact, as the workshop discussions made clear, NGO leaders and members realized that they would not achieve an effective political lobby and working relationship with their donors and the Tanzanian government until they sorted out the basis for their claims to be recognized as "indigenous," established a common political agenda, and formed, by participatory and accepted procedures, a truly representative umbrella organization with the legitimate authority to represent constituent members in national-level political efforts.

Ndinini Kimesera Sikar and author in the United Nations cafeteria, New York, during the 2004 UN Permanent Forum meetings.

Ndinini Kimesera Sikar and author on the United Nations patio, New York, during the 2007 UN Permanent Forum meetings.

Representatives of Mainyoito Pastoralist Integrated Development Organization (MPIDO), a Kenyan Maasai NGO, present their case against the Magadi Soda Company Limited during a side event at the 2004 UN Permanent Forum.

Three activists who first promoted involvement with the international indigenous rights movement and were also founders of some of the first NGOs in northern Tanzania—Moringe Parkipuny (Maasai), Daniel Murumbi (Barabaig), and Richard Baalow (Hadza)—sitting together at the Advocacy Training Workshop sponsored by PINGOs, Arusha, 2005.

Delegates to the First Maasai Conference on Culture and Development, New Arusha Hotel, Arusha, 1991.

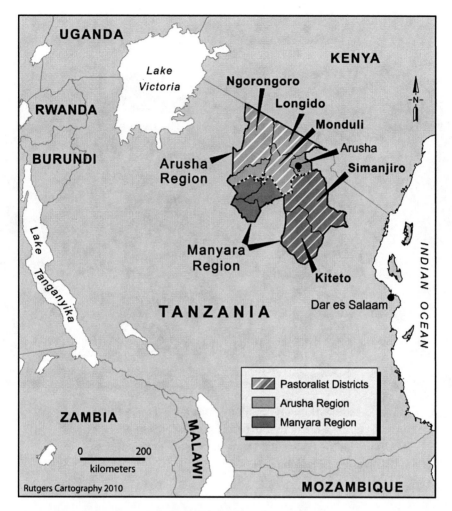

Map of Tanzania showing the "pastoralist districts" located in
Arusha Region (Ngorongoro, Longido, Monduli) and Manyara
Region (Kiteto and Simanjiro) as of 2010. All of these districts
were formerly one district, Masai District, until the 1970s.

Author debating Moringe Parkipuny outside the Equator Hotel,
Arusha, during a break in the Joint Pastoralist Stakeholders'
Workshop on the Policy and Legal Framework Environment
for Pastoralism in Tanzania, 2006.

An older woman speaks while younger women care for their children
at a MWEDO workshop on democracy and human rights, 2005.

A MWEDO women's group
from Longido displaying the
beadwork they have produced
for sale to tourists, 2006.

Members of the
Pastoralist Women's
Council, Soit Sambu,
2006.

A Maasai man using pliers to
cut tiny ruby shards from the
slag, Mundarara, 2006.

4

REPOSITIONINGS

*From Indigenous Rights
to Pastoralist Livelihoods*

While the involvement of Maasai activists with the international indigenous rights movement in the 1990s was tremendously successful in terms of increasing their international visibility and attracting donor funding, it backfired with regard to their relationship with the Tanzanian state. Like leaders in most African states, Tanzanian officials regarded all Tanzanian citizens (except, for some, those of Asian heritage) as "indigenous" and refused to recognize Maasai (and donor) claims that Maasai, like indigenous peoples in the Americas and elsewhere, were discriminated against because of their cultural distinctiveness, mode of production, and political-economic marginalization within the state. In the face of tremendous government hostility, Maasai activists resorted to increasingly confrontational strategies, especially court cases to demand rights and recognition. But, as described in previous chapters, they faced failure after failure—from a lackluster effort to inform the revised land laws, to the state-sanctioned transfer of prime grazing land to wealthy Arab hunters (dubbed "Loliondogate" in the Tanzanian press), to the mass eviction of Maasai from Mkomazi to make way for yet another game reserve.

For these and other reasons, Maasai activists eventually decided to refocus their advocacy efforts from the international arena to the national arena. They sought ways to engage rather than fight the government, to be more pragmatic and less political, to practice what one activist called "advocacy by engagement." As part of the conscious effort to find less confrontational and more effective ways to engage state policy (and policymakers) in Tanzania, Maasai activists and NGO leaders reframed their political struggles from the language of "indigenous rights" to that of "pastoralist livelihoods" and started calling themselves civil society organizations (CSOs) instead of

NGOs. After briefly exploring the reasons for these changes, this chapter assesses the effectiveness of these new positionings for Maasai political struggles through a close examination of their efforts since 2005 to inform and improve a new livestock policy proposed by the Tanzanian state.

The Limits and Lessons of Indigenous Politics

According to Maasai activists themselves, perhaps the most important reason for replacing the language of "indigenous rights" with that of "pastoralist livelihoods" was in response to the vehement hostility of the Tanzanian government over the widespread international recognition and acceptance of Maasai claims of "being indigenous." As a Maasai activist told participants in a 2005 workshop:

> As many of you remember, about four or five years ago we had a big debate about the concept of "indigenous people." We had several organizations that identified themselves as "indigenous organizations" and many discussions. But at the level of the nation, there was lots of discussion about who are "indigenous people," since everyone was claiming to be one. Most politicians ruled out the phrase "indigenous peoples."

As a result of this resistance and hostility, he continued, most leaders had agreed to "leave the phrase 'indigenous peoples' out of their policy recommendations." "If we start debating these words now," he added, "we will not finish today—especially the phrase 'indigenous peoples.'"[1]

The Tanzanian government was suspicious of the very terms of their mobilization, especially the unsettling fusion of assertions of cultural difference with demands for collective rights. By organizing around the identity claims of "being indigenous," premised in part on ethnicity, Maasai NGOs revitalized ethnic identifications and challenged democratic liberalism's championing of the individual rights and responsibilities of "citizens" with their claims of collective grievances and rights (cf. Muehlebach 2001). The Tanzanian government was wary of appearing to endorse "ethnic favoritism" (Anonymous 2000:8), equated political organizing along ethnic lines with "tribalism," and feared that such ethnic mobilization could strengthen political opposition, produce economic and political instability, or even foster violence (see, e.g., Neumann 1995).

Thus a key reason for shifting to discourses about pastoralist livelihoods was to seek less confrontational approaches to influence government policies and practices. According to a Maasai activist I will call Samuel, "Before, we had lots of court cases against the government . . . but they were not very fruitful."[2] Samuel is trained as a lawyer and was the head of one of the pastoralist umbrella groups when I interviewed him. Initially, he was a strong proponent of indigenous rights, including being an active member of the Organization of Indigenous Peoples of Africa (OIPA; see chapter 1). But in recent years, Samuel has all but abandoned the rhetoric of indigenous rights for the language of pastoralist livelihoods. As he explained, "the language of indigenous has strong political connotations, while the language of pastoralism is about development." "Initially," he continued, "we thought we could change our present situation by engaging in the international struggle, but we have learned that we can't neglect the national struggle. For a number of years we tried to use reporting to the UN system, working with international advocacy groups, and so forth, but those efforts did not have a big impact. So in the past three to four years we have reflected on our struggle and made some changes."

Samuel has been a key player in the new emphasis on engaging the Tanzanian government, using his training and skills as a lawyer to read, decipher, communicate, and critique the voluminous policy documents and draft policy proposals produced by the government as it tries to quickly "reform" key policies and laws to accommodate and facilitate neoliberal mandates. Just in the past few years, Tanzania has tried to "reform" its livestock policy (to increase productivity and offtake through the settlement of pastoralists and creation of ranches), land policy (allowing full ownership and sale, including by foreign investors), and local government (to decentralize funding and authority) and has created a new policy to formalize the informal sector (MKURABITA), which was designed and implemented by Hernando De Soto's Institute for Liberty and Democracy based in Peru. The Tanzanian government has, however, tried to temper the social and economic pain of these reforms by simultaneously sponsoring national policies such as Vision 2025 and MKUKUTA (the latest poverty reduction strategy proposal; see below) to reduce poverty and promote development (albeit within a neoliberal paradigm of individual initiative, private capital, and personal investment). As such, the government has had to pay attention to demands for development by pastoralist activists, however much its vision of "livestock development" differed from pastoralist visions of "livelihood security and development."

Second, as Samuel's comments also suggest, not all the activists found the UN meetings and other international workshops and conferences productive. As one Maasai woman commented to me over coffee at the 2004 Permanent Forum, "I find that nothing real takes place here. It is a waste of time. These people come as representatives, but I wonder who they really represent. Probably just a few people. They come here, say a few words, but what really happens?" Both experienced and first-time delegates expressed deep frustration over the formalistic procedures at the UN; the limited spaces for dialogue, debate, and discussion with other activists; and the glacial pace and byzantine processes for instituting changes in international and national policies. As another Maasai activist complained to me in response to a question about her experience at a workshop the night before sponsored by several UN agencies: "It was OK. There was lots of writing. I wonder what all that writing accomplishes? There are lots of policies, but what really happens on the ground?"

Other reasons for the repositioning, however, had less to do with the perceived limitations of linking their struggles to transnational indigenous rights advocacy, and more to do with the lessons learned from their involvement. As described in chapter 3, pastoralist organizations were maturing, in part because of their international experiences, opportunities, and affiliations, but also because of increasing self-awareness and acknowledgment of their own failures and weaknesses. In addition to being frustrated by the limited impact of their international advocacy on their national struggles, many were concerned about competition and jealousies among themselves, a lack of accountability to their constituencies, their ongoing inability to inform and influence government policies and programs, and their unhealthy dependence on donor funds and agendas. Drawing on lessons learned about advocacy, alliance-building, and strategies for political engagement from the international indigenous rights movement, they debated how to reform themselves and build a "more positive relationship" with the Tanzanian government.

The maturation of pastoralist organizations also reflected the growing strength of what calls itself "civil society" in Tanzania, by which activists themselves mean organized, non-state actors who have the political freedom to comment on, criticize, and challenge government policies and practices. Long-time activist organizations such as the Tanzania Gender Networking Program and coalitions of CSOs such as the Policy Forum drew on the expanded range of media options (television, radio, billboards) to pressure the government and expand critical awareness among their constituencies of their rights and responsibilities as citizens. Pastoralist organizations reframed themselves as CSOs in part to align themselves with these prominent civil society coalitions, as well as to distance themselves from increasing questions and suspicions about the accountability, financial transparency, and representativeness of NGOs.

Finally, the Tanzanian government has also changed in recent years. Now it slowly and somewhat grudgingly encouraged the "participation" of its citizens in policy making, under pressure from a strengthening coalition of progressive civil society organizations and the watchful gaze of international proponents of "democracy." But some members of the government, especially the "old guard" who were in power during the days of CCM, were still sensitive to criticism, reluctant to engage representatives of civil society, and dismissive of Maasai. When a highly respected Maasai activist presented a list of suggested revisions to the proposed livestock policy prepared by a task force of pastoralist activists and others to a senior government official, the official was furious. "Who are you," he demanded, "to criticize government policy!?!" With his usual calm, the activist responded: "Well, first of all, I am a citizen of Tanzania. And second of all, I am a representative of over 100 pastoralist CSOs . . ."

For these and other reasons, according to Samuel, "now we focus on building alliances with the nation, not with international actors." As he explained, "one problem with 'indigenous' is that everyone who hears it thinks 'Maasai,' so it worked at the national level to limit rather than expand our possible alliances and collaborations." Emphasizing "pastoralist" livelihoods has enabled organizations to strengthen their links with non-Maasai pastoralist communities such as Barabaig, and increasingly with agropastoralist communities as well. Although Maasai leaders still dominate the movement, most are careful to reach out to and include non-Maasai pastoralists in their organizations, deliberations, and advocacy. Hunter-gatherers, however, now occupy an even more liminal position—while their histories of marginalization were acknowledged in the discourse of indigeneity, their issues are generally sidelined in debates over pastoralist livelihoods. Nonetheless, almost all agree that the government has been much more willing to listen to claims made in the interests of "pastoralist livelihoods" than "indigenous rights."

But, as discussed below, the capacity of pastoralists to engage with the Tanzanian state have been complicated by the emergence, in the wake of the conclusions of the 2000 workshop described in chapter 3, of two "umbrella groups" seeking to coordinate advocacy by pastoralist and hunter gatherer NGOs. Given the detailed allegations made about PINGOs, participants in the workshop agreed to create a new umbrella group called Tanzania Pastoralists and Hunter Gatherers Organization (TAPHGO). But the supporters of TAPHGO took a long time to get it registered, encountering logistical, political, and funding delays. During this time, PINGOs was reformed and restructured, with a new set of bylaws, new leadership, and a renewed sense of accountability and transparency. And so by the time of my field research in Tanzania in 2005, there were two umbrella organizations existing in uneasy relationship with one another and with the NGOs, CBOs, and CSOs they were both supposed to represent. Although a few organizations were members of both groups, most organizations belonged to one or the other, limiting the potential for effective coalition building and unified advocacy. According to one NGO leader, whose organization was a member of TAPHGO, but not PINGOs, "at a 2001 workshop, PINGOs said that we have to choose—either we could be members of TAPHGO, or we could be members of PINGOS—but not both." By 2005, neither organization made such explicit demands for loyalty, and the leaders of both organizations tried hard to work together, but there were inevitably jealousies, competition, and rivalries between them and their member organizations.

In Defense of Pastoralist Livelihoods

The term "livelihoods," especially as used in the phrase "sustainable livelihoods," emerged as an important alternative development paradigm in the mid-1980s, most notably in the work of Robert Chambers (1987, 1999; Chambers et al. 1989), who taught and worked with the Institute for Development Studies at the University of Sussex. According to Chambers (and his associate, Gordon Conway), "a livelihood comprises the capabilities, assets and activities required for a means of living. A livelihood is sustainable when it can cope with and recover from stresses and shocks and maintain or enhance its capabilities and assets both now and in the future, while not undermining the natural resource base" (Chambers and Conway 1992:9). The idea of "livelihoods" as a development agenda appealed to many progressive development scholars, policy makers and practitioners because it was people-centered, holistic, and dynamic and paid attention to people's access to and use of both material (land, technology, water, etc.) and social/cultural resources (such as education, technical knowledge, and political power). Although the concept was used, defined, and challenged (at Sussex, as elsewhere, a more recent emphasis has been on "poverty reduction") in somewhat different ways over the years, it has continued to percolate through development debates, especially in the literature on pastoralists and rangeland ecology.[3] The most common response that I received from Maasai activists to my constant query, "what do you mean by livelihoods?" echoed the Chambers-influenced definition: "It refers to the entire way of life of people."

In Tanzania, the alternative discourse of "pastoralist livelihoods" emerged in 2003 from the convergence of a series of meetings and workshops among pastoralist activists and policy discussions about Tanzania's second poverty reduction strategy (PRS) proposal. To qualify for forgiveness of their international debts, Tanzania, like many other countries, was required to produce a PRS. The first strategy, formulated in 2000, was generally recognized as a top-down, cookie-cutter template that took little account of the realities and desires of everyday Tanzanians. Moreover, the strategy made no direct mention of "pastoralists" or "pastoralism," only "livestock"—specifically the need for destocking to prevent environmental destruction. In 2003, the Tanzanian government, under pressure from civil society organizations, launched a national, "participative" process to solicit input and feedback from a diverse range of citizens and organizations for a revised PRS, which became known as MKUKUTA in Swahili. The president's office advertised in national newspapers for organizations to submit proposals to organize workshops and seminars to discuss the revised strategy. Both PINGOs and TAPHGO, the two umbrella groups, applied, and PINGOs succeeded in getting funds.

PINGOs held a series of workshops, then wrote a report that they presented in several local and national venues that detailed specific recommendations for the inclusion of and attention to "rangeland livelihoods" in the MKUKUTA (PINGOs 2003b, 2004). "Rangeland livelihoods" was defined as "encompass[ing] all communities that live on the rangelands including livestock keepers, hunter gatherers and farming/livestock keeping based methods" (PINGOs 2003b). But some pastoralist activists argued that "rangeland livelihoods" seemed to focus attention on the specific needs of the land and ecology, rather than the people living on the land. As a result, in the course of the meetings, debates and workshops, they revised the phrase to "pastoralist livelihoods," which emphasized the people, but only certain people. Participants paid little attention to "hunter-gatherer livelihoods," in part because pastoralists were better organized to shape the discussions to focus on their own concerns, to the exclusion of hunter-gatherers.

For example, in 2003, PINGOs, with donor support, held a Roundtable Discussion on Pastoralism to bring together "stakeholders" to discuss the "fate of pastoralism and pastoralists in Tanzania" (PINGOs 2003a). Among other things, participants called for the "recognition of pastoralism as a viable livelihood option" and argued that "[l]and alienation is the most fundamental problem affecting pastoralism in Tanzania." Participants, who included several MPs, reviewed the characterizations of pastoralists and pastoralism in various government policies, including the 1983 National Livestock Policy, the 1990/91 Tanzania Forest Action Plan, and the 1995 National Land Policy. They described the problems facing pastoralists, such as lack of formal education, inadequate representation in parliament and other policy-making processes, cultural survival, and marginalization.

They were also wary of aligning themselves with agropastoralists because of their very different livestock production strategies, especially in terms of herd mobility. According to one 2004 PINGOs workshop report, "Fundamental to pastoralism as a livelihood is the issue of mobility and the ability of pastoralists to access, use, and own land, water and natural resources which support this form of livestock husbandry."4 Although participants briefly discussed the plight of hunter-gatherers, most of the workshop focused on pastoralist livelihoods. They heard comparative reports about the experiences of pastoralists in the poverty reduction strategy processes in Uganda and Kenya, then debated, discussed and prioritized their own recommendations for the strategy review in Tanzania. Their final recommendations

> centered on the need to recognize pastoralism as a viable livelihood strategy and form of land use in the next PRS, including support for pastoralist claims to the land and resource base that supports their land use practices. Other means of supporting pastoralist livelihoods and alleviating poverty in rangelands include . . . improving education and health services, improving access to water, reviewing investment policies to ensure they benefit local people such a pastoralists, and improving marketing opportunities for livestock. (PINGOs 2004:1)

The first draft of MKUKUTA ignored the recommendations of PINGOs. In response, PINGOs and other groups petitioned the government, complained to donors, and lobbied MPs and local government officials. Eventually, their advocacy activities succeeded in the addition of two key sections to the final version of the MKUKUTA; section 2.5.1, "to promote efficient utilization of rangelands and empowerment of pastoralist institutions for improved livelihoods," and, more importantly, section 2.5.3, "to promote pastoralism as a sustainable livelihood" (URT 2005b).

Engaging the Neoliberal State: Reforming Livestock Policy

Pastoralist activists were understandably pleased that the promotion of pastoralism as a sustainable livelihood was now enshrined in the MKU-KUTA, one of the guiding documents for national policy. But they quickly faced a new challenge—a proposed new National Livestock Policy. The following brief overview of the activities, events, and discussions surrounding the engagement of pastoralist activists with the proposed new policy suggest some of the creative strategies deployed by pastoralists as well as formidable challenges that they face in their current advocacy efforts in the name of "pastoralist livelihoods" (cf. Tenga et al. 2008).

In contrast to the widespread consultations for MKUKUTA, the Ministry of Livestock and Water Development (which was divided into two separate ministries following the October 2005 elections) held no consultations with pastoralist communities or organizations before it produced a "final draft" of the new National Livestock Policy in April 2005. According to the vision statement, "By year 2025, there should be a livestock sector, which to a large extent shall be commercially run, modern and sustainable, using improved and highly productive livestock to ensure food security, improved income for the household and nation while conserving the environment" (URT 2005a:iv). Eager to have the new National Livestock Policy approved by Parliament before the upcoming national election in October 2005, the ministry circumvented and condensed the regular procedures for policy consultations. Although it held a National Consultative Workshop on the policy in March 2005, it invited only representatives from the private sector, not civil society. Nonetheless, news of the workshop was leaked, and several pastoralist activists sped to Dar es Salaam to "crash" the meeting. These activists organized a meeting of pastoralist CSOs in May 2005, who agreed to mobilize and lobby for revisions to the policy, although they all recognized that they were entering the policy process at a very late stage. Nonetheless, they decided that the most effective and efficient way to move forward was to form a Livestock Policy Task Force (LP Task Force) comprising a representative from each of the two umbrella groups, the Tanzania Natural Resource Forum (TNRF), Vet-Aid Tanzania, the Sand County Foundation, and Reconcile/IIED. The LP Task Force was tasked to review the draft policy in detail, develop recommendations for its improvement, and coordinate advocacy to have its outputs incorporated into the final draft by the ministry. In June 2005, the LP Task Force met with the minister of livestock and water development, Edward Lowassa, to ask if he would be willing to consider recommendations for the policy from pastoralist CSOs. He agreed, and the LP Task Force set to work.

In August 2005, I attended a workshop sponsored by TAPHGO where the LP Task Force presented their recommendations for discussion and amendment to over sixty representatives from pastoralist organizations and donors, as well as the ministry official responsible for developing the new policy and an official from the Ministry of Range Management (although invited, no MPs were able attend because they had to pick up their election forms) (TAPHGO 2005). Prior to discussing the LP Task Force recommendations, TAPHGO presented the results of two studies that it had commissioned to survey livestock production models in Botswana and Kenya, analyze their advantages and disadvantages, and use the results to inform advocacy for livestock policy in Tanzania (TAPHGO 2004a, 2004b; cf. TAPHGO 2004c). These studies were in response to rumors that had been circulating among pastoralist activists for the past few years that the Tanzanian government was considering imposing the "Botswana model" of livestock production (fenced ranches geared to commercial production for the export market) in Tanzania. Debate then ensued about the consequences of these policies, especially for poor people in Kenya and Botswana, and the lessons to be learned for Tanzania. Some participants raised parallels between the negative characterizations of pastoralists and false assumptions about pastoralism in the $20 million, ten-year Masai Range and Livestock Development Project that USAID had financed in Tanzania from 1969 to 1979 (Hodgson 1999b, 2001a) and the proposed new National Livestock Policy. Several older pastoralists (as well as the official from the Ministry of Livestock and Water Development), who had been educated and trained by USAID as part of the Masai Range Project, were sensitive to criticism of the project goals and assumptions by younger activists, attributing its failure instead to the difficult political economic climate at the time. One activist reminded everyone that it was important to consider the global context of the policy; the new policy was produced in a time of "neoliberalism," in contrast to the 1983 National Livestock Policy (which has since been replaced by the 1997 National Agricultural and Livestock Policy), which was produced in a time of "central planning and government control," "when Nyerere was fighting the World Bank." He claimed that the bad policy was not necessarily the result of bad intentions, but poor assumptions premised on "deeply rooted mindsets."

The Livestock Ministry official listened attentively to the presentations and debates, and responded occasionally. He claimed that the ministry had wanted more participation in the policy design process, but did not have enough money. Moreover, "this is just a policy, it is very general and broad. What matters are the strategies for implementation." In response, a prominent pastoralist leader strongly refuted his claims. First, "I don't think that I agree that the government has good intentions with regards to pastoralists. If that was true, then they wouldn't be trying to 'phase out' pastoralism as a livelihood." Second, "if the government had a good intention, they would have informed us about the policy process, but we were never informed." Third, "if we have a bad policy, we can't have a good implementation." And finally, "we have rights as pastoralists and as citizens to participate in these policy processes."

Toward the end of the third and final day, after a series of breakout groups and reports, the official from the Range Management Ministry finally spoke (as far as I could see, he had slept, read his newspaper, or talked/texted on his cell phone through most of the workshop). He angrily chastised participants for their ignorance and lectured them about the scientific value of such concepts as "carrying capacity" and "livestock unit," the evils of setting fires, and the need for pastoralists to "sell useless cattle to help improve their lives, to go to school, to go to the hospital, to buy clothes, and to have a respectable place to live!" Many participants raised their hands eagerly to respond; others just rolled their eyes at the familiar negative stereotyped and pejorative diatribes.

At the end of the meeting, the Ministry of Livestock official said that he supported many of the recommendations, and promised that they would be handed over to the next minister (since there was likely to be a shuffling of ministers after the national election in October 2005) for careful consideration. Participants agreed to support the LP Task Force recommendations, with some minor revisions, and asked the LP Task Force to continue to work together to monitor the livestock policy, develop a set of implementation strategies, and review and propose recommendations for other related policy "reforms" that were underway, including range management, wildlife, and local government reform. Almost everyone present signed a petition supporting the recommendations. Finally, they thanked the Ministry of Livestock official and asked him if he would be willing to serve on the LP Task Force "to help us draft strategies that will not be rejected." He agreed, proclaiming, "I am a servant of the government, a servant of the people. If I am asked to work, then that is my job." Participants thumped their tables in approval.

In September 2005, the LP Task Force presented its recommendations to the minister and the minister's policy development team. The submission, in the form of a PowerPoint presentation, consisted of a brief overview of the key issues, a detailed list of proposed amendments to the livestock policy, and the signatures of 130 supporters. According to the LP Task Force (2005), there were five key problems with the proposed version of the policy. First, the policy "does not have a sufficient focus on livelihoods and poverty reduction. It is too production orientated and not sufficiently cognizant of the NSGRP/ MKUKUTA." Instead, the policy should develop ways to help "poor livestock keepers to attain sustainable levels of production and to better access markets for their livelihoods and poverty reduction." Second, the policy "displays a lack of understanding of the functioning of agro-pastoral and pastoral production systems and their significance for local livelihoods and the national economy." The LP Task Force recommended that the policy acknowledge that "mobility. . . . [is] key for sustainable livelihoods and livestock production in the rangelands." They urged the government to support the development of "1) participatory and adaptive management approaches at local level based on managed mobility for well-managed rangelands, healthy herds and improved livelihoods; 2) participatory and traditional regulations governing mobile rangeland management systems to regulate movement and manage diseases rather than stopping pastoral mobility and movement altogether." Third, they exhorted the government to better understand the "costs and benefits" of rangeland mobility in terms of "disease and land use conflict." They argued that "these issues are surmountable with appropriate support and conflict management processes. The benefits of mobility (reliable and sustainable livelihoods) should be judged against the costs (disease and land-use conflict). *We argue that the overall benefits of mobility-based rangeland use systems will continue to be much greater than the costs*" (emphasis in original). Fourth, they claimed that the policy gave "insufficient consideration" to "supporting pastoralist and agro-pastoralist-based land-use planning and conflict resolution." Given the increased pressure on pastoralist management systems produced by competing land uses and land alienation such as agriculture and protected areas, "the government needs to empower pastoralists together with other communities to address these problems by supporting: 1) the development of local level conflict management /resolution processes that are equitable, accessible and sustainable; 2) the development and implementation of participatory and equitable land-use planning and range management by-laws driven by local needs." Finally, the LP Task Force argued that the policy "under-estimates the realistic potential of pastoralist-based livestock production to contribute to the national growth targets planned for the livestock sector." As they explained, "without the participation of pastoralists, it will not be possible to generate the revenue from these areas needed to reach the goal of a 10% increase in the input of livestock to GDP and a 9% growth in livestock exports by 2010 as laid out in the MKUKUTA/NSGRP and Livestock Policy." Thus, they recommended that "a priority should be to work with NGOs and the private sector to develop systems that equitably include pastoralists and agropastoralists in national and international marketing and trade."

The ensuing recommendations suggested deletions, additions, and revisions to specific sections of the policy, from the broadly negative characterization of pastoralism in the overview, to particular recommendations, to language choices. For example, the original overview stated :

> On the other hand, the extensive system which is mostly agro-pastoralism and pastoralism is a livestock production system which is based on seasonal availability of forage and water thus requiring mobility. *This system is constrained by poor animal husbandry, lack of modernization, accumulation of stock beyond the carrying capacity and lack of market orientation.* In order to develop and achieve its goals, the industry requires a comprehensive livestock policy to guide all stakeholders. (URT 2005a:1, emphasis in original)

The LP Task Force recommended replacing that language with the following more positive characterization:

> On the other hand, the extensive system, which is mostly agro-pastoralism and pastoralism *generates roughly 80% of the livestock produced in Tanzania and supports the majority of livestock based livelihoods in Tanzania. In order to develop and*

achieve sector goals in relation to production and sustainable livelihoods, the sector requires a comprehensive livestock policy to guide all stakeholders. (LPTF 2005: slide 21, emphasis in original)

Despite these pointed recommendations, the LP Task Force made strategic compromises in its recommendations, such as condoning the use of the government's preferred phrase, "livestock farmers," to refer to pastoralists, even though most angrily rejected such a classification as overly economistic and demeaning. As one activist noted in the 2005 TAPHGO workshop, after complaining about the government's preference for the phrases "livestock producer" and "livestock farmer" rather than "pastoralist," "the government focuses on economic indicators, but they have little meaning for pastoralists . . . we need to distinguish the 'development of the economy' from the 'development of people.'" As he later told me, "the government wants to change us from pastoralists to 'livestock farmers,' to change our system of livestock keeping. These are not accidental but calculated phrases." Nonetheless, the LP Task Force acquiesced to the government's preference to use "livestock farmer" in accordance with "FAO guidelines."

As of September 2005, there were mixed signals from the Ministry of Livestock about whether or not it would take into consideration the LP Task Force recommendations. As a result of the national elections in October 2005, Jakaya Kikwete, a strong proponent of neoliberal reform, was elected president. One of President Kikwete's first actions was to appoint his long-time friend and supporter, Edward Lowassa (who had served formerly as the minister of water and livestock development) as prime minister. Lowassa had been reelected for a third term as MP for Monduli District, one of the so-called pastoralist districts in Arusha Region. (Although he claimed to be a Maasai, few Maasai recognized him as such, noting that although he was raised in Monduli, his mother was Meru and his father was Chagga.) Soon thereafter, President Kikwete created a separate Ministry of Livestock and appointed a new minister to replace Lowassa. Finally, he quickly joined forces with Lowassa to launch an aggressive media campaign to denounce the "destructive" and "outdated" practices of nomadic pastoralists, demand that they be settled, and make plans to "ensure that livestock keepers are turned into skilled farmers."[5] As Kikwete wondered, echoing long-standing stereotypes, "How do we change the mindset of a nomadic livestock keeper from considering large herds for prestige to that of an important economic resource?"[6]

Pastoralist activists (and sympathetic donors) scrambled to respond through the media (newspaper editorials, television spots), sponsored research on the livestock trade and contributions of pastoralists to the national economy (TAPHGO 2006), met with MPs from pastoralist districts to educate them about the issues and encourage them to lobby, and strategized with each other through further discussions and workshops (e.g., PINGOs 2006) about how to respond.

Rumors about the status of the LP Task Force recommendations were rampant. At a meeting on pastoralism and HIV/AIDS a few months later, another ministry official claimed that he was now the formal liaison for pastoralist organizations and that the LP Task Force recommendations were under serious review. Some pastoralist activists believed that the recommendations had been ignored and that the final policy would look much like the April 2005 draft under discussion. Everyone thought that the final policy would be released at any time. Many claimed success in just having stalled the policy.

In December 2006, the government at last released the final version of the National Livestock Policy (URT 2006a). Although the final policy incorporated almost none of the specific recommendations made by the LP Task Force, it reflected a few of the more conceptual suggestions in some key paragraphs and phrases, especially a modest effort to focus the policy on improving the livelihoods of livestock farmers, not just their contributions to the national economy. Most notably, many (but not all) references to "increase incomes" of livestock farmers were replaced by "to support the livelihoods" of livestock farmers, thereby recognizing that more income alone did not necessarily translate into enhanced economic security or well-being. In addition, "water supply in rangelands" was replaced with "water supply in pastoral and agro-pastoral areas" (URT 2006a:18), and some of the more disparaging characterizations of "livestock farmers" were muted. Finally, new language in several sections of the policy now called for the government to make "efforts . . . to promote and support pastoral and agro-pastoral organizations" (URT 2006a:16). But one of the main recommendations of the LP Task Force, which was to revise the policy to recognize the value, even necessity, of seasonal mobility, extensive livestock production systems, and communal grazing, was ignored. Instead, the policy was replete with references to the "uncontrolled movement of livestock" and/or the "uncontrolled movement of pastoralists" as a major cause of poor rangeland use, overstocking, the spread of livestock disease, social conflict, environmental degradation, and pollution.

And so, notwithstanding these small concessions to the recognition and support of pastoralist livelihoods in the policy, President Kikwete and Prime Minister Lowassa (until he resigned in February 2008 over allegations of corruption) continued their public campaign to settle pastoralists, restrict their movements, and convert them into "livestock farmers." Allegedly, according to a memo issued by the minister of livestock, after a visit in 2007 to pastoralist districts in northern Tanzania, President Kikwete stated that "the livestock keeping using mobility as its key strategy has no future for pastoralists in the country. The president insisted that after 10 years from now livestock will no longer be able to sustain the livelihoods of communities such as the Maasai and Barbaig pastoralists. He suggested that the only way forward is modernisation of this sector" (Diallo 2007). The harassment and victimization of pastoralists continued, including their forced eviction from Kilosa (described in chapter 2), disputes over prime grazing land in Soit Sambu that was leased to an American tourism company, and, most recently, the razing of Maasai homes to evict pastoralists from a hunting block owned by the controversial Ortello Business Company in July 2009.[7] At times the accusations against pastoralists (and, more specifically, their livestock) have bordered on the ludicrous as they served as scapegoats for many of the problems confronting Tanzanian society. They (and their cattle) have been blamed for causing droughts (instead of a large, mismanaged hydroelectric dam) and even global warming.[8]

Advocacy and Adversaries

Despite these ongoing accusations and tensions, the efforts of pastoralist organizations to shape the proposed national livestock policy and their modest success shows how, in contrast to even a decade ago, they have developed a sophisticated array of advocacy strategies to engage and influence the state. Perhaps most importantly, they recognize that the Tanzanian "state" is composed of many different sectors, ministries, offices, officials, and staff members, who do not necessarily share a common interest or approach to pastoralist issues. According to my interviews and observations, many government officials think of Maasai and other pastoralists as "pests," that is, as persistent, annoying troublemakers who stand in the way of government plans (although their characterization as "pests" speaks to their success in getting themselves heard). But other officials, including the few Maasai and Tanzanians with a pastoralist heritage who work in the government, are more sympathetic to the plight of pastoralists. Savvy Maasai leaders have cultivated relationships with these allies, who in turn have provided them with copies of draft policies, confidential reports, and information about important policy meetings. Moreover, now that some of the Maasai leaders are themselves lawyers, bureaucrats, and college graduates, they face less discrimination in their interactions with "Swahili," given their shared elite status. As one expatriate who has worked with pastoralists for years told me, "You can't walk into a government office in Dar [the de facto capital of Tanzania] with holes in your ears and expect to be listened to."

One faction of the Tanzanian state that pastoralists have aggressively tried to organize and work with is the MPs from pastoralist areas. Several years ago, they created the Tanzania Pastoralist Parliamentary Group (Pastoralist Parliamentary Group), which was modeled on a similar, successful version in Ethiopia. The purpose of the Pastoralist Parliamentary Group was to encourage pastoralist MPs to better coordinate themselves and represent pastoralist issues in Parliament. Pastoralist leaders, especially the heads of TAPHGO and PINGOs, invited the MPs to their workshops and conferences, tried to meet regularly with them in Dodoma (the official capital of Tanzania and site of Parliament) or Dar es Salaam, and sent them research reports, policy recommendations, and other information to inform their deliberations and decisions.

Unfortunately, the Pastoralist Parliamentary Group in Tanzania has been only moderately successful, for several reasons. Most policies and laws are actually drafted and revised in the ministries, so that there is little, if any, room for revision once they are tabled (i.e., proposed for a vote) in Parliament. Secondly, according to one Maasai NGO leader, a key difference between Ethiopia (and also Kenya, where the model has been successfully adopted) is that there are many pastoralists in political office in those countries and pastoralists as a constituency are politically powerful. In contrast, "we have only a few pastoralist MPs in Tanzania. So the idea needs contextualization, we need to think about how to initiate, strengthen, and build alliances. Politics is numbers." Third, the MPs themselves are always changing, so the pastoralist activists have to start from the beginning every five years in terms of building alliances, educating them about issues, and so forth. And finally, as pastoralist leaders have found out all too often (especially with their experiences with former Prime Minister Lowassa, who is still the

MP for Monduli District), just because an MP is from a pastoralist background or represents a primarily pastoralist district does not mean that he (and, rarely, she) necessarily shares their perspectives about (or concerns for) what policies are in the "best interests" of pastoralists.

Pastoralists have often found more support and success cultivating and lobbying sympathetic donors to leverage the government. In 2005, for example, they successfully worked with select donors to stall approval of a huge livestock development project sponsored by the International Fund for Agricultural Development (IFAD, a UN agency) until project sponsors (which included several government officials) revised the proposal to address several of their serious concerns. These concerns included the lack of sufficient (if any) consultation with pastoralists themselves, a focus on a "production" perspective rather than a "livelihoods" perspective, and a lack of clearly defined implementation goals that addressed pastoralist livelihood concerns. Although IFAD and the government claimed to have carried out several "consultations" with relevant constituencies, the pastoralist leaders learned about the proposal only when a concerned donor on the IFAD advisory board sent them a copy. Pastoralist leaders prepared a response to IFAD through the LP Task Force; worked with donors from Denmark, Ireland, Japan, and the United Kingdom to develop their own (similar) "donor" response; and lobbied government officials, the IFAD program officer, and others to address their concerns before moving forward (several pastoralist leaders and their allies shared some of this correspondence with me). Much to the deep displeasure of senior Tanzanian government officials, approval of the project (which included a US$20.6 million loan from IFAD) by the IFAD executive board in Rome was delayed pending revisions.[9] In contrast to the final version of the National Livestock Policy, the final version of the IFAD project addressed many of the pastoralists' concerns, including their dependence on mobility. IFAD donated an additional $100,000 to pay for "additional stakeholder consultations," and agreed that "based on the outcomes, detailed implementation approaches will be developed with relevant performance indicators from a livelihood perspective, including pastoralist and agro-pastoralists needs, taking into consideration their traditional way of living and mobility, and recognizing their contributions to productive and economic systems."[10]

The experience with IFAD highlights another key strategy employed by pastoralists, which has been to develop access to information through informal circuits of communication with sympathetic donors and government officials. In addition to leaked reports, proposals, and other documents, pastoralists have learned to effectively use e-mail, cell phones, and the Internet to share information among themselves and advocate for their causes. The availability of cell phones has enabled them to organize themselves to respond immediately to news of "secret" meetings, undisclosed reports, and sudden visits by foreign donors, politicians, and other possible allies. Through e-mail, they have been able to circulate and revise draft policy statements and other documents without having to meet face-to-face. Finally, although TAPHGO and PINGOs both have Web sites (and occasional newsletters), so do many of their membership organizations. Moreover, one key coalition in which they are involved, the Tanzania Natural Resource Forum (TNRF), has developed a remarkable e-library from which activists, policy makers, and others can download copies of government laws and policies (which, until recently, were notoriously difficult to get copies of), draft proposals, public policy statements, and other useful information.[11]

The involvement of key pastoralist leaders with TNRF is part of another strategy, which has been to strengthen their alliances with prominent, respected national civil society groups in Tanzania, such as Hakikazi Catalyst, Haki Ardhi, and Policy Forum. Such alliances protect vulnerable organizations from attacks, enable the coordination of campaigns to lobby the government, and encourage pastoralists to consider and frame their political struggles in terms of broader economic and political justice agendas. Hakikazi Catalyst, for example, has an excellent reputation as a civil society organization committed to working for social justice by empowering poor and uneducated people in Tanzania to better understand and shape government policies that affect their lives. They are perhaps best known for developing a series of "plain language guides" in Swahili and English, replete with often pointed and hilarious cartoons, to explain and critique different government policies. Among other efforts, they worked with several pastoralist organizations to develop a series of guides about "Pastoralism in Tanzania's Policy Framework," featured pastoralist issues in their monthly newsletter, and assisted in facilitating various workshops on advocacy and policy issues organized by the pastoralist CSOs.[12]

Like these national CSOs, pastoralist organizations have expanded their use of the independent media (newspapers, radio, TV, and the Internet) to counter government critiques and present their own perspectives. They regularly invite journalists to their workshops and conferences in hopes of some (positive) coverage, alert the media to attacks on pastoralists and possibly illegal land deals, appear on Tanzanian talk shows and news broadcasts, and circulate news releases highlighting recent research studies, project agreements, and other accomplishments. Headlines such as "Pastoralists demand more benefits from wildlife"[13] and "Herders decry oppressive polices"[14] appear regularly in independent newspapers such as the *Arusha Times*, describing the purpose and conclusions of TAPHGO and PINGOs workshops and detailing the arguments and viewpoints of pastoralist activists about proposed government policies and actual government practices.

Pastoralist activists have also learned the value of research to inform their policy recommendations and advocacy. TAPHGO, PINGOs, and others commissioned various research projects to support their recommendations for the national livestock policy, as well as research on such topics as pastoralist attitudes toward HIV/AIDS; a survey of educational access, attainment, and infrastructure; and the extent of land alienation. For most, however, the priority has been to design and support research that describes and quantifies the contributions of pastoralists to the national economy. These contributions include not just the sale of livestock and livestock products, but the indirect support that pastoralists provide to wildlife and therefore wildlife tourism by maintaining landscapes and ecosystems. One challenge to such research is the lack of disaggregated, reliable data. A second is that research can be a slow process. As one Maasai NGO leader commented about one of TAPHGO's research efforts, "So TAPHGO sponsored two research trips to Kenya and Botswana to investigate ranching models and policy, but didn't act quickly on them. So perhaps it was too late. If they had done something just after the visits, it would have been more effective." Moreover, by focusing on economic contributions, the activists neglect cultural and social issues and the very histories of dispossession and displacement that have produced the present conflicts.

Finally, TAPHGO and PINGOs have both tried to broaden and deepen their base of support by sponsoring workshops for their member organizations about how to conduct advocacy generally and how to respond to certain policies (on livestock and land) specifically. They (and some of their member organizations) have also offered smaller training workshops for rural Maasai about their legal, political, and economic rights as citizens, especially in terms of the new village land law and other relevant laws and policies. I attended several of these workshops, and found them clear, engaging, and especially helpful in understanding the complicated (and sometimes contradictory) laws about rights to land and resources. Most of these workshops included men and women, followed a participatory "workshop" format, and took place in Maa. One of the biggest challenges was that of language—translating concepts such as "gender" and "livelihoods" from English and Swahili into Maa in ways that clarified (rather than further confused) the issues at hand. Moreover, given widespread illiteracy, the workshops had to rely primarily on oral rather than written presentations, summaries, and conclusions.

Despite these achievements, the ability of pastoralist organizations such as TAPHGO and PINGOs to advocate effectively for pastoralists (and, occasionally, for hunter-gatherers) is hampered by several daunting challenges. The first challenge is structural, that is, the presence of not just one but two "umbrella organizations" charged with coordinating pastoralist advocacy initiatives. Although this dilemma is a product of earlier historical and political decisions, it has produced what donors (among others) have variously described to me as a "complicated political landscape" and a "political mine-field." Donors were confused about which organization to support (which one "really" represents pastoralist interests?), member organizations worried about repercussions if they joined just one (or even both) umbrella groups, and the enduring undercurrent of jealousy and competition between the two organizations undermined, at times, the ability of pastoralists to present a united response to government critiques and conflicts.

I worked with and studied both organizations during my year of research in 2005 and 2006, and found them both engaged in meaningful, important work. At the time, TAPHGO was led by a former Catholic priest, Moses Sangale, a respected Maasai elder (of the Makaa age set) who had run parishes throughout Maasai areas and received a diploma in development studies from Kimmage (Ireland). I knew Moses well from my three years of community development work in the mid-1980s for the Catholic diocese, which included several projects in his parishes. Moreover, since he was as an age mate of my husband's, by Maasai protocol we shared a close, joking relationship as peers. Moses reported to a board of directors comprised of prominent, educated Maasai and chaired by Israel ole Karyongi, a top administrator in the Lutheran Diocese of Arusha. In addition to Moses as coordinator, TAPHGO's staff consisted of several secretaries, a financial officer, and two program officers, only some of whom were Maasai.

The coordinator of PINGOs Forum, Edward Porokwa, was Maasai junior elder (of the Landiss age set) from a well-known family in Simanjiro that encouraged all of their children, girls and boys, to pursue not just secondary school education but college degrees as well.[15] After completing secondary school (where I taught him English literature for a term in the mid-1980s), Edward received a law degree from the University of Dar es Salaam, and practiced law briefly before becoming involved in the indigenous rights movement and pastoralist advocacy. Because of our age difference and our previous relationship as teacher and student, our relationship and conversations, while friendly and engaging, were always a bit more formal and constrained by Maasai protocols of respect. In contrast to TAPHGO, Edward reported to a board that included both elite and non-elite Maasai, as well as Barabaig and Hadzabe representatives. Moreover, his large staff (a secretary, accountant, and four program officers) intentionally included Maasai and non-Maasai.

Not surprisingly, almost everyone I spoke to (including donors, allies, Maasai leaders, and community members) had an opinion about the relative efficacy of TAPHGO versus PINGOs and whether they should continue as two separate organizations. A commonly shared characterization of TAPHGO was that of "wise elder" and PINGOs as "energetic warrior." As one expatriate very familiar with both organizations commented to me, "I've always said it would be great if you could merge the energy of PINGOS with the wisdom of TAPHGO." Many Maasai and donors shared his opinion, which was an assessment of their different approaches and programs, as well as the age difference in their leadership and the composition of their boards. As a senior Maasai leader explained, "I think the TAPHGO Board is strong, but not the PINGOs Board. There is nothing. You need to consider the level of the people who are elected—they need to have some kind of education. You can't just put in village people." He argued that the PINGOs board was in fact "not a board, but just a gathering of people." In other words, in his opinion, they exerted little oversight on the activities of the coordinator or the organization. Nonetheless, he believed that "PINGOS overshadows TAPHGO on advocacy by far—in all aspects, even the personalities." Another Maasai leader summed it up somewhat differently. In his perspective, "PINGOs is very active and dynamic right now, although TAPHGO has potential."

Everyone recognized the dilemmas for advocacy and coordination posed by the existence of two umbrella groups. Most people whom I spoke to thought that the two organizations should figure out a way either to merge into one or to more clearly distinguish their missions, with one organization (PINGOs) coordinating advocacy efforts and the other (TAPHGO) coordinating service-delivery programs among member organizations. Although well aware of everyone's concerns, by the time I last visited Tanzania in October 2006, neither organization was yet willing to consider merging or dividing up their missions.

A second major challenge is geographical; most pastoralist organizations are located on the periphery, far from the political center of Dar es Salaam. Both TAPHGO and PINGOs, and most of their member organizations, have offices in Arusha (a regional capital in northern Tanzania) or in the surrounding pastoralist districts. Arusha is approximately four hundred miles by road from Dar, which takes a full day by car or bus or a brief (but expensive) plane ride. Although technological improvements, in the form of cell phones and the Internet, have helped to overcome the spatial distance, pastoralist leaders struggle to maintain an active political presence in Dar, where most government ministries and offices and donor organizations are located. As one Maasai leader confided to me, "We have no presence in Dar as pastoralists. Thus we are always overtaken by events." I replied that it was not always the fault of pastoralists that they were overtaken by events, since, for example, the government had tried to suppress circulation of the draft livestock policy. "But that just proves our isolation," he responded. "We need someone to be there, to pedal information from ministry to ministry and then back to us." One strategy they developed to counter the political distance and provide a way for quick, coordinated response, was the creation of the Livestock Policy Task Force (which has since been renamed twice, after much debate, first the Rangeland Livelihoods Task Force and, more recently, the Pastoralism and Livelihoods Task Force). They have also sought ways to make themselves more visible in Dar es Salaam and Dodoma, such as participating in the annual exhibit of civil society organizations in Dodoma and attending meetings organized for member organizations, donors, and others of national CSOs such as the "breakfast debates" of the Policy Forum. They have also repeatedly discussed the idea of hiring a permanent pastoralist "lobbyist" to work in Dar es Salaam or setting up a small satellite office in Dar.

In conclusion, despite their reframing of their struggles from the language of "indigenous rights" to that of "pastoralist livelihoods," their expanded array of advocacy strategies, and their moderate successes, Maasai and other pastoralists face ongoing challenges in finding ways to effectively inform and shape state policy. They have been hampered by problems of structural disunity and geographical distance, but also by the ongoing reluctance of many government officials to take Maasai/pastoralist concerns, much less Maasai leaders, seriously. Their spatial marginalization mirrors their continued political marginalization in national policy debates, a marginalization exacerbated by the government's push, under international pressure, to "reform" its land policies, improve livestock production for national gains, and spread its increasingly thin resources among increasingly destitute citizens.

5

"IF WE HAD OUR COWS"

Community Perspectives on
the Challenge of Change

> We all work very hard, no one is sleeping. Everyone
> is trying very hard to do everything they can to sur-
> vive, to make a living. Especially the Kurianga and
> Landiss [younger male age sets]. Many go to town to
> work, usually as guards. But then they use the money
> to build houses, buy cattle, and build better lives. No
> one is just sitting there with their arms folded [he
> folds his arms] waiting for it to rain. Some work
> from morning to night.

—OLD MAASAI MAN IN EMAIRETE

So, more than twenty years later, what has the development of nongovernmental organizations (NGOs), community-based organizations (CBOs)
and, now, civil society organizations (CSOs) meant for the everyday lives of
pastoralists, especially Maasai men and women? Has the decision of Maasai
organizations to reposition their struggles from discourses of indigenous
rights to pastoralist livelihoods, from international to national advocacy, and
from calling themselves NGOs to CSOs changed their relationships with
their constituents? How are these organizations perceived by the people they
are supposed to be representing, helping, empowering, and advocating for?

To explore these and related questions, this chapter draws on a broad
survey of Maasai areas that I conducted in 2005 and 2006, opportunistic
individual and group interviews with Maasai men and women of all ages
and backgrounds, and available statistical data to compare the current situation of Maasai with their lives, experiences, and perspectives in the mid-

1980s. Although data is never collected by ethnicity or principal livelihood in Tanzania, and what data exists is still fairly unreliable, comparing selected data from the districts inhabited primarily by pastoralists ("the pastoralist districts," which include those in Arusha Region, Monduli, Ngorongoro, and Longido, and those in the new Manyara Region, Kiteto and Simanjiro) with national data suggests some disturbing disparities and trends (URT 2005c). Together, the interviews, observations, and statistical data present a complicated portrait of a resilient people struggling to survive in difficult times, frustrated by their inability to secure a better life for their children, and ambivalent about the assistance (and lack of assistance) they have received from the government, religious organizations, and NGOs. Although clearly neither stark improvements nor significant declines in their situation can be directly attributed to the interventions of NGOs, the evidence suggests that the presence of these organizations has, in general, helped some community members diversify, secure, and improve their livelihoods in modest ways, but done little to help them address the structural inequalities (such as lack of sufficient quality schools and healthcare facilities) impeding their collective progress.

Pastoralists Today

Like many states in the Global South, Tanzania has fiercely embraced the Millennium Development Goals (MDGs), a broad set of country-specific statistical goals (such as infant mortality and gender ratios in education) designed in consultation with the United Nations to improve the well-being of people in the Global South.[1] Moreover, the state has proposed an even more ambitious set of social and economic goals in two key policy documents: Tanzania Vision 2025 (which outlines a "new economic and social vision for Tanzania," including good, quality lives for all; good governance; and a competitive, neoliberal economy) (URT 1997); and MKUKUTA (the latest poverty reduction strategy proposal, discussed in the previous chapter) (URT 2005b). Although both discuss the need to direct resources and thought toward overcoming pervasive economic inequalities among Tanzanians, neither addresses the specific social, cultural, or economic needs of pastoralists (except, as noted in chapter 4, for a brief mention in the MKUKUTA of the need to strengthen "pastoralist livelihoods"). More troubling, both documents reflect the strong neoliberal assumptions and goals of the Tanzanian state, which is intent on "reforming" economic and political sectors to meet global demnds for increased competition. To date, the government has privatized key industries, revised land regulations to encourage the sale and alienation of land, promoted large-scale commercial agriculture, expanded the highly profitable wildlife tourism and big-game hunting sectors, instituted service fees for healthcare (primary school fees were instituted then revoked), withdrawn support for education and other social services, and encouraged pastoralists to replace transhumant pastoralism with more "productive" and less "environmentally harmful" modes of livestock "farming" (as opposed to "herding"), such as ranches. As a result, there has been increased alienation of pastoralist lands (especially drought and dry-season grazing land), competition for water sources and other livestock-related resources, decline in the use of health facilities, and increased impoverishment.

"No One Is Sleeping"

In 2005 and 2006, I conducted semi-structured interviews and focus groups in three of the four "pastoralist" districts (Longido District was not yet formally subdivided from Monduli Distict)—Monduli, Ngorongoro, and Kiteto.[2] I interviewed women and men, young and old, educated and uneducated, either individually or in groups, in Swahili or Maa, depending on their preference. In addition, I traveled through these districts and Simanjiro District to compare their situation with that I had observed twenty years before (1985–87, and, for much of Monduli District, during repeated research trips since 1990), participate in workshops and meetings, and hold informal conversations with a range of men and women about the changes that had occurred in their lives, their needs and priorities, their perspectives about and relationships with NGOs, the Tanzanian government, and religious organizations, and their aspirations for their future and that of their children.

The Maasai men and women I spoke with were very articulate about all of these topics. My experience in Engarenaibor, a community in northern Tanzania near the Kenyan border, was typical of many of my visits. Twenty years ago, when I first visited Engarenaibor, it was a dusty, desolate village serving dispersed homesteads across the plains. Like many Maasai villages at the time, the village "center" housed a small primary school, a dilapidated shack that served as the village office, and a few small shops selling sugar, flour, cooking oil, rice, matches, and other household sundries. Finding the village was itself a challenge, as we navigated a barely visible dirt track through the acacia trees, trying not to get diverted onto cattle trails or dumped into the ruts and furrows of the plains. We saw very few people around the village, until, alerted by the sound of our car, they began to slowly walk in from surrounding homesteads (some many miles away) to gather for our meeting to discuss their development priorities and plans.

When I returned in October 2006 for the first time in twenty years, I was shocked at the transformation. Instead of an inscrutable dirt track, we followed a smooth, graded, murram road complete with drainage channels, signposts, and bridges. Engarenaibor was now a bustling town with several main streets, over twenty shops, restaurants, bars, and guest houses built from cement block and corrugated iron roofs; a nursery school and large primary school; several churches; and a constant traffic of cars, motorcycles, and bicycles. The town was full of men and women, mostly Maasai, pursuing work and pleasure. Women sat in groups on porches, under shade trees, and along the road selling small piles of foodstuffs, household items, and other goods. Men talked together on the streets or in the bars and shops, buying goods and making deals. Young men hung out by the bars, playing on the tattered foosball and pool tables, or dashed through town on their bikes. The few young women present were helping their mothers sell goods or running quick errands. As we reached the center of town, we drove through an elaborate painted metal gate into the courtyard of our guesthouse, which consisted of five guest rooms (with beds, chairs, and nightstands) on two sides of the courtyard; a communal washroom, latrine, and urinal at the back, and the owner's store and personal quarters at the front. The rooms were clean, the sheets crisp, and the furniture comfortable.

My companion was a remarkable Maasai woman named "Nanyore" who lived in the town of Kimokowa, on a major road near the border between Tanzanian and Kenya. Nanyore was the fifth of six wives of an older Maasai man and mother of four children. Several years ago, she decided that she was finished having children and that she wanted to pursue further education to learn what she perceived as relevant (and marketable) skills such as English, computers, and leadership training. At the time, she had only a primary school education. But she discussed her ambitions with her husband, a respected leader who had become quite wealthy through herding, farming, and key purchases of land. He agreed to let her study in Nairobi for several months at a time, her co-wives agreed to care for her children while she was away, and the Maasai

Women's Development Organization (MWEDO, see chapter 3) agreed to help pay her tuition and other costs as part of their program to support the education of pastoralist girls and women. In time, Nanyore decided to apply her new skills to local politics; she campaigned for one of the designated "women's seats" on the district council and won. In addition, she has worked with MWEDO over the years as a community leader, board member, and avid volunteer.

We had become friends over the past year or so, and she accepted my offer to accompany me on some of my survey trips throughout Maasai areas near her village. As a well-known and well-respected leader, she was able to introduce me to the women and men we met and interviewed during our travels. Moreover, as a longtime community member, she offered insights, suggestions, and background information about many of the places and people that we encountered along the way. And finally, Nanyore was good company, always ready with a laugh, eager to hear people's opinions, and respectful of everyone, no matter how poor, bedraggled, or desperate.

After settling ourselves in our room and arranging for dinner, we joined a group of eight women selling goods in the shade of a nearby porch. They were all from Ngosuak, a village about a two hours' walk from Engarenaibor. Except for a very old woman who was resting under a large tree, each woman had several small, identical piles in front of her—of salt, sugar, onions, powdered washing detergent and/or snuff—that she was trying to sell. They chatted together about their children, gossip about people they saw walking along the road, and other matters. After we introduced ourselves (they knew Nanyore) and shared the extended greetings that are expected among Maasai, they agreed to answer my questions. When I asked about the changes they had experienced in their lives, individual women took turns listing certain changes, with other women shaking their heads and muttering in vigorous agreement.

As with all of the interviews that I conducted, many women noted that a major change was their attitude to education. As one woman told me, "Before we were ignorant [Maa: *merdai*], we didn't value education. But now we want all of our children to be educated." They echoed the comments that residents of Emairete, Mti Mmoja, and Embopong' had shared with me in the early 1990s (Hodgson 2001a:182–88) about their desperate desire to educate their children so that they would not be "blind" and "ignorant" like their parents. As a Maasai man from Emairete told me in 2006, "My father was ignorant and did not send me to school, so now I am blind. But my children will be educated so that they can function in the world."

The problem, as they discussed later, was that there were still too few schools in Maasai areas, and the existing ones had too few teachers, too many students, and not enough books, blackboards, or other resources. At this point, the very old woman under the tree, who had been listening quietly to the discussion, spoke: "They [the government] started one school, but it meets outside in the dirt. The children write in the dirt. But if a wind comes then whew! All the writing is blown away! And they have no water." (I later learned that the primary school had two classes; one met in a small hut built by the parents, and the other met outside under a tree.) I had heard similar complaints about the poor quality of the village school a few months earlier from women in Embopong', a remote community in the Rift Valley. They all agreed that the primary school in Embopong' was terrible, so they drew on kinship and friendship networks to try to send their children to the primary school in a nearby town. As one angry mother told me, "They don't learn anything at the . . . school. Today they are taking their Standard 7 exams, and few of the students can hardly write their names. No one will pass. It is a waste—what kind of education is that?" A few women from Ngosuak complained not just about the poor quality of the few primary schools, but also about the limited opportunities for Maasai children to attend secondary school. As a woman from Mairowa told me later that day, "A smart child may finish Standard 7, but then his or her parents cannot afford to finance any further education, so they cannot continue."

As these women and men suggest, disparities in the infrastructure and quality of education between pastoralist and non-pastoralist districts is evident in the lack of classrooms, ratio of teachers to students, and availability of textbooks and other resources, despite some recent government programs to provide money to pastoralist and other districts to build classrooms and teachers' houses, purchase textbooks and school supplies, and provide teacher training. Some parents who want their children to succeed (and can afford it) pay several thousand shillings a month for "tuition"—extra lessons after school with their teachers that cover what should have been taught during the school day and provide additional income for poorly paid teachers.

For example, although 78 percent of children in Tanzania were enrolled in primary school in 2000, gross enrollment in the pastoralist districts ranged from 77 percent in Simanjiro District in 2003 to only 8 percent in Monduli

District in 1999.[3] The discrepancy is even greater if attendance and completion data is considered. In 2000, 70 percent of the national cohort completed primary school. But in Simanjiro District in 2003, there were a total of 2,759 boys and 2,115 girls enrolled in Standard 1, as compared to only 729 boys and 527 girls in Standard 7—a dramatic decline suggesting a completion rate of approximately 26 percent (Simanjiro District Report 2005: table 38). Similarly, in Monduli District, 2,272 (51%) of the original 4,470 boys and 1,620 (41%) of the 3,426 girls enrolled in Standard 1 in 2002 had left school by Standard 4 in 2005 (MWEDO 2006:7).

Mothers were especially adamant that they wanted their daughters, not just their sons, to attend school for as long as possible. As an old woman in Kimokowa told me, "I really want girls to study. Before they were married/ sold off [Swahili: *kuozwa*], and some returned because their husband had no property. Then they became burdens to their fathers. Now, with education, they can support themselves." Several women I spoke to in other places said that not only would educated girls be able to support themselves, but they would support their parents as well: "A girl will help her parents, she won't forget her parents. But once a boy marries, he forgets his parents, saying 'I have my own kids!'" "A girl loves her parents until the end," noted another woman. These comments suggest fairly radical changes in gender and generational relationships, since historically, elderly men and women depended on their sons for support.

Despite their desires to educate their girls, the gender ratios for primary school enrollment in pastoralist districts are still deeply skewed in favor of boys. Nationally, the ratio in 2005 was 98 girls for every 100 boys who attended primary school (URT 2006b). But the ratio was 222 boys to 100 girls in Monduli District in 2005 (MWEDO 2006:7) and 132 to 100 for Simanjiro in 2003 (Simanjiro District Report 2005). The disproportionately higher enrollment of boys than girls among pastoralists points to enduring cultural and social barriers to the education of pastoralist girls such as the value of their household labor, parental fears over early pregnancy, the persistence of arranged marriage and bridewealth, and parental doubts about the value and "return on investment" of female education (Hodgson 2001a; Pratt 2003). When I asked a village chairperson why he did not enforce the government's mandatory education law, he replied, "But what is the point? If they [parents] are forced to send their children to school, then they won't buy them uniforms, notebooks, or anything and the children will be miserable. I see it as my job to encourage them to send their children to school, but I can't force them. People need to decide on their own, and for some it takes time to see the value of education."

Secondary school data is more mixed. Although the pass rate in Simanjiro District for the secondary school exam in recent years was approximately the same as the national average of 22 percent, anecdotal and partial data suggests much lower pass rates in the other pastoralist districts (e.g., MWEDO 2006). Moreover, the stark lack of secondary schools within pastoralist districts (in 2005 there were two in Simanjiro, two in Kiteto, four in Monduli, and four in Ngorongoro, as compared to twenty-two in neighboring Arumeru District), means that the few pastoralist children who pass the exam and obtain secondary school placements must attend boarding schools far from home. Recent initiatives by organizations to promote, provide, and fund secondary education for pastoralist girls have done much to rectify the former gender imbalance in secondary school attendance by pastoralist girls as compared to pastoralist boys. In 2004, for example, 129 of the 175 girls (74%) from Simanjiro District who passed the exam were selected for secondary schools, in addition to the 132 boys (out of 186 who passed—71%) (Simanjiro District Report 2005). Nonetheless, the total number of pastoralist boys and girls who complete primary school, successfully pass the exam, and attend secondary school is still a trickle as compared to other children. And without significant supplementary funding, year-long pre–Form I training programs, and consistent efforts to uphold the rights of girls to attend school despite sometimes severe parental refusal, the trickle of girls would be even smaller.

Another key change that they identified was the tremendous loss of cattle holdings, and subsequent expansion of farming by Maasai: "In the past we had more cattle, but now they are gone. And so we farm." When I asked another group of women whether they farmed, they all replied "Yes!" in unison. "Just a few of us were farming before," said one woman, "but now many more farm because of the droughts." They were frustrated, however, with the government's lack of support for their farming. As one woman explained, "We need ox plows for our farms. We told the government, 'We are farmers now and we need ox plows.'" Another woman, who also ran a small dry goods shop in Engarenaibor, told me, "I have lots of land, but I could only farm four acres because I didn't get the tractor. There is a list of people for the tractor to visit, and I was low on the list. So by the time it got to me . . . it was too late." Like this woman, many people I spoke to were eager to farm more acreage, but complained about lack of farming tools, ox plows, tractors, expertise, and more.

Third, almost all the women whom I interviewed told me that they were now actively trying to make money by selling and trading food, livestock, milk, hides, beadwork, and other goods. The reason for this change, they explained, was "because of the problem of hunger and desire for development. Before we used to stay home, but now we go out." Moreover, many women, such as those from Ngosuak and others that we spoke to in Engarenaibor, had organized themselves into groups to help one another through rotating credit, loans, advice, and support. The sizes of the groups ranged from about ten to fifteen members, and membership was based on residential proximity, not necessarily clan or kin relations. The women from Ngosuak explained to us that that each of them had contributed one goat and 20,000 TZ shillings, and took turns taking 200,000 TZ shillings from the group to use as capital to purchase goats, sugar, and other goods for resale, then return the money to the group for another member to use. Later in the day, when we interviewed a similar group of women from Mairowa village, they described a similar process: "Our group name is 'Lenkishon.' We each contribute money, and then someone gets it in turn. She then goes to Gilai to buy goats, brings them back, and sells them. The government helped us to start some groups, but then they did nothing. So we decided to start them ourselves and the government agreed to help." When I asked whether they thought that having such groups had helped them, all the women enthusiastically agreed. They especially appreciated the financial incentives and support provided by the groups. As a woman from Ngosuak told me, "we are not in *groups*, but in *business*." Another woman elaborated: "Before, women stayed home. Now they have decided to support themselves. Some women are doing 'big big' business like men." Some women noted that the groups not only were an important source of capital, but provided assistance in times of need: "If someone has a problem, other members of the group will help her." For others, working in groups served as a way to learn new things, despite their illiteracy and lack of schooling: "The group helps us to build our capacity and to learn. You see an educated person doing certain kinds of work that you would like to do, but you can't because you are not educated, but you want to be able to do it." Several women mentioned learning new skills such as how to stand in front of a meeting to talk. But one old woman was less positive about learning how to participate in meetings: "Before we were never told to go to meetings, but now we go to meetings all the time." "Do you think the meetings help?" I asked. "Not really," she replied. "They are run by young people who talk very fast, so we old people cannot understand and participate."

When I asked what their husbands thought about their trading, many women responded with sharp retorts about lazy husbands and shifting workloads. "They just wait at home for me to bring them food!" exclaimed one woman from Ngosuak, to gales of laughter from the group. Other women were less jovial about their new responsibilities as the primary food-providers for their households. "One day I am just going to quit bringing food home," complained a thin, older woman. As a woman from Mairowa explained to me, sitting under a tree selling goods with her daughter, "before we stayed home and were brought things, now we depend on ourselves." Her comments were echoed by others: "I trade in order to do something rather than just sit at home. And to support myself. Our husbands do not support us anymore. But some women do not even have the means to buy small things to sell and their husbands don't see the point." Several women told me that they had little choice but to try to earn some money through trading because they were widowed, they were separated from their husbands, or their husbands were too sick, old, or disabled to help. Nonetheless, those women with husbands still had to ask for permission to travel and trade: "We need their permission for everything!"

The problem with trading, as was visibly evident from the many groups of women trying to sell the same goods in Engarenaibor, was the lack of markets and distinct products. "Another change," explained a young woman trader, "is that we have started to trade. But now we are all doing it, so often no one sells anything. We go home just as we came." According to another Maasai woman, who served on her village council, "There is a problem [with the women in groups]. The money goes around to each member, then every member uses it to buy the same things to sell, like sugar and flour, so the money just stays there." Most women I spoke to were very aware of the dilemma, but unsure about how to address it, besides seeking and asking for help in finding "new markets." But their mobility and types of trade goods were clearly limited by their other household obligations, lack of transportation, and distance from market centers. As one woman explained, "We don't come every day. Once we have gotten water [for our households], we arrive with these things [in Engarenaibor] at 1 p.m. But it is too late. If people need things, they have already bought from others. So we return with what we came with." When I asked one group how they used the profits from their sales, they just laughed, "We don't make profits!" Or as a woman from Ngo-suak commented wistfully, "I am not sure why we are trading. There is no profit. In fact, we probably lose money . . . we have to buy tea and small things to eat [when in town selling]." The few women who sold goods had different strategies for using the money. One woman replied, "If I earn 100 shillings, I eat it that day, but it is still worth it because I get to keep what-ever I earn." Another woman was more pragmatic: "I use half of my profits for food and keep the other half to buy more things to sell." Several women said they used their profits to pay for the costs of primary school for their children, suggesting that this new category of expenses was increasingly identified as the obligation of women.

Women experienced the consequences of the oversaturation of the mar-ket differently, depending on whether they relied on selling goods as the primary income to support their households, a source of supplementary funds to provide additional basic and perhaps even prestige goods, or as a means of earning independent income that they controlled completely. As a young woman in Emairete told me, while her husband lay on his bed quietly listening to our conversation: "One of the big problems is that men did noth-ing. Women now did all the work. Once a woman had a child, men expected women to do everything. Since there are no livestock anymore, men have given up hope; they have left it up to women to take care of everyone."

Several men who I spoke to echoed the sense of futility expressed by some women over the meager profits they earned from their additional la-bors. According to a male junior elder from Ngosuak, "There is no profit, but there is also no loss [in women's trading]. They just sit there all day and use the money to buy little things." Others, such as a local Maasai school teacher in Kimokowa, were more optimistic, and actively helped the women to or-ganize themselves, learn basic accounting, and search for marketing outlets. According to a middle-aged man from Mti Mmoja, "Before, women didn't go out and make money, but now we see that women can make even more money than men." One older man from Mti Mmoja, whom I have known for many years, told me that he supported women's trading, but worried about the losses they experienced because of their illiteracy and inexperience with budgets. He allowed his wives to pursue only one of two projects, both of which he thought actually made profits: buying "skinny" goats or cattle to fatten and sell or working on a cooperative farm together, where they shared the responsibility of buying seed and laboring on the farm.

Besides trading small foodstuffs, many Maasai women tried to earn money by making and selling to tourists and others the elaborate beaded jewelry, belts, and other goods for which they were renowned, an activity they had pursued for decades (Hodgson 2001a). Beadwork as a source of cash appealed to women because it was a portable, flexible task that they could pick up and put down throughout the day between other work; they often sewed together in groups while they talked and watched their children; the craft drew on skills they had learned as children; and beadwork was a visible source of cultural pride, prestige, and expression for women (cf. Kratz and Pido 2000). Numerous NGOs, such as MWEDO, had long encouraged and helped women to produce beadwork for sale by providing ideas for new designs and items (such as Christmas ornaments or Christian crosses), assisting in setting up small tourist stalls, and seeking new markets for their products (see p. 152). But the marketing of beadwork was difficult, given a glut of beadwork on the local market, the precarious nature of tourist preferences and tastes, and the challenges of producing uniform and high-quality items for international orders from fair trade stores and other global buyers.

In February 2006, I met with a group of women in Longido who, with the help of MWEDO, had organized themselves to produce and sell beadwork to tourists from a small stand along the main highway between Nairobi and Arusha. When I arrived (with Nanyore), about fifteen women were milling about a line of rough tables made from sticks and dried grass, on top of which they were arranging their beadwork, then covering it with plastic sacks to protect the items from dust. After greetings, we sat down to talk. They told me that the tables were only temporary. They had sold their beadwork in a covered stall, but they had taken it apart because one of MWEDO's donors had promised to build them a permanent structure in which to display and sell their wares. (While we sat on the ground talking, two men were building a structure with metal poles and wooden boards.) After a discussion about changes in their lives, the problems they were facing, and other issues, we talked about their beadwork project. An old woman told me that their biggest problems were hunger, poverty, and lack of cattle: "The women who come here to sell are the very poorest; they have no other way to earn money." They started the bead project in 2002 with the help of MWEDO, which provided them a grant of 500,000 TZ shillings (approximately US$400) to start their business. MWEDO's program officer met with them to advise them and brought other Maasai women to talk to them as well. Every woman had her own table to sell her beadwork and agreed to contribute 10 percent of her revenue to the group account to support their annual dues to MWEDO, travel by their leaders, and other group expenses.

But the project, according to the women, faced many challenges. Tourism in Tanzania was seasonal, "so sometimes we go three months without having a tourist stop." "We are busier during the high season, but now there is nothing." Longido hosted a cultural tourism project, which brought the tourists to visit the stalls, but those visitors were sporadic and few. Otherwise, the women depended on people in cars and tour buses seeing them and stopping or on visiting donor delegations brought by MWEDO. But when I visited, they were difficult to find, as their sign had been destroyed by a road improvement project (presumably the new building will also be more visible from the road and have a sign). Moreover, there are many such beadwork stands (and bigger tourist shops selling not only beadwork but other crafts and souvenirs) along the main tourist routes, providing substantial competition. The Longido women, however, had ideas for how to attract more tourists such as erecting a new sign, providing toilets, and selling snacks and soft drinks. In addition, they were very interested in possible new markets for their goods in Tanzania or internationally. But they claimed that they lacked the capital or expertise to implement these ideas, and needed the help of MWEDO and other NGOs. (And even me: "Can you help us find a market?" they asked me at the end of our talk.)

As my friend from Mti Mmoja argued, the more lucrative income-generating projects for women seemed to be those in which they bought and sold livestock for a profit. But these projects were possible only for select women who could receive permission from men to participate (which was sometimes difficult since livestock trading, especially of cattle, had long been an activity dominated by men), accumulate enough capital to purchase the animals, rely on other women to fulfill their household obligations (including childcare) during their absence traveling to and from livestock markets, and ensure that they retained control over the animals and profits during the course of the transactions. Despite these challenges, many women I spoke to were eager to enter into the livestock trade and were discussing ways (such as the rotating credit groups) to realize their plans.

One of the most successful women's livestock projects that I saw in 2005–2006 was coordinated by the Pastoralist Women's Council (PWC), a Maasai women's NGO based in Soit Sambu village, in northern Tanzania (see chapter 3). With the financial support of a British donor, PWC created the Women's Solidarity Boma (*boma* is Swahili for homestead or cattle kraal). Over the past few years, PWC, with help from some women members, bought young bulls, fed them, and sold them to support the education of young girls. Between 2006 and 2008, they sold sixty bulls to generate 9 million TZ shillings (approximately $8,000) to pay school and college fees for nine girls. In addition, several of the small groups of women organized by PWC had invested their profits from selling foodstuffs, running a grinding machine, and marketing beadwork into livestock (see p. 153). One group had also purchased ox plows, which they used to plow their own farms and the farms of "poor people" and rented to others to use. Individual women had also used their profits to buy livestock of their own, especially sheep and goats (animals that were easier to manage and to protect their rights of ownership in). The women I interviewed were very proud of their accomplishments, and attributed their improved social status vis-à-vis men to their demonstrated capacity to make money:

> Now we can support ourselves as women. We can do business and buy rice and vegetables for our families. Men like these things, but they don't want to pay for them. So it has decreased the "I want, I want, I want" [Swahili: *naomba, naomba, naomba*]. Now we can buy these things for ourselves. This helps us get respect from men; now they respect us more.

Like the women I interviewed in Engarenaibor, they spoke of their new abilities to attend meetings, speak in front of men and women, and refuse to agree to proposals they did not support. When I asked what their husbands thought, one woman claimed that

> men see PWC as good. They serve the community so men see the value. In this area, if a wife is not a member, sometimes a man will even pay the [annual membership] fee for his wife to join! They see that women have profited, that they give gifts to each other, that they are self-supporting. So men are happy.

"Every man wants his wife to belong!" interjected another woman, to the approval of the others in the room. "Maasai women here are like *wazungu* [Swahili: whites or Euro-Americans]," concluded one very old woman in Mti Mmoja. "They take care of the kids, buy the things they need, and don't depend on their husbands."

Men on the Move

Although some women characterized their husbands and other Maasai men as "lazy" and "without hope" in the face of the contemporary challenges, many Maasai men, especially younger men, were actively seeking ways to earn money to support themselves and their families. Farming was their primary strategy to diversify their sources of income and supplement the food and income earned from livestock husbandry. According to an older man in Engarenaibor, Maasai started farming for three reasons: it was a way to cope with their increasing impoverishment; because, with some education, they finally recognized the value of farming; and, finally, "we began to see new things when we traveled. We visited other places and saw that farming was a good thing." "We realize that farming is more secure than cattle," explained an older man from Emairete. "Cattle may die, but we will always have land." Most Maasai cultivated maize and beans to feed their families, selling any surplus for cash. A few men (and women), however, cultivated cash crops such as flower seeds and barley (for the breweries) on a contract basis for large corporations.

One day I met "Letipap," I man I had known for years in Emairete, as he was riding his shiny new bicycle across the crater floor. We talked about his successful work as a subcontractor for a multinational flower seed company based in the Netherlands. He told me that he had made over one million Tanzanian shillings in profit in his last sale, and compared the pros and cons of the two main seed companies that sought contract farmers in the area. Although happy with his profits, he took the opportunity to ask me what *wazungu* (white people) did with the flower seed. I explained that either people bought the seeds to plant flowers around their houses to make them look prettier, or companies bought the seeds to plant and sell cut flowers. "Really?" he said, shaking his head in disbelief. "I thought the seeds were used for fuel." Another man whom I knew in Mti Mmoja explained that he had started farming flower seeds the year before—he planted one kilo of seeds on a quarter of an acre, which produced forty kilos of seeds that he was able to sell for 3,000 TZ shillings per kilo. "They were much more profitable than any other crop. I plan to plant one acre next year."

In addition to farming, young men (*ilmurran*, often glossed as "warriors") traveled to Arusha, Dar es Salaam, and other towns to seek work as night watchmen, security guards, casual laborers, and other positions in the informal economy. The Maasai men interviewed by Ann May in 1999 and 2001 for her study of Maasai migrants in Arusha and Dar es Salaam (May 2002; May and McCabe 2004; May and Ikayo 2007), explained that they had migrated because of the dramatic losses in livestock. As one man put it bluntly, "If we had our cows, do you think we would have come to guard these non-Maasais?" (May and Ikayo 2007:279). The "typical" Maasai migrant that she interviewed "was a 32.6 year old male with no formal education . . . married to 1.2 wives, with 2.14 children" (May and McCabe 2004:11–12). They came from all of the pastoralist districts, and circulated back and forth between the city and their homestead:

> This "average" migrant began around 1997 to seek work in cities as a mlinzi [Swahili: guard] and traveled home every few months, taking money, food, and/or animals from his earnings. Before going home, a Maasai man often sought out a relative or agnate to take over his job, which he then reclaimed when he returned to the city in a nonseasonal pattern of "oscillation and job exchange" to and from town (May 2002). (May and McCabe 2004:12)

Most of the men sent regular remittances back to their homesteads and invested any remaining funds into livestock.

Other young men sought to establish themselves as brokers in the expanding tanzanite mining industry, buying rough gems directly from the artisanal miners in Mererani (the only place where tanzanite is found) and selling them to a network of brokers and stonecutters. Many were inspired by the extraordinary success of a few Maasai such as Lengai ole Mako, a poor, barely literate man from Simanjiro who became a multimillionaire "mining baron" by expanding his small brokerage trade into Mako Mining Ltd., a huge, vertically integrated mining enterprise that includes "deep shaft Tanzanite mines, a brokerage firm and cutting and polishing facilities in Arusha" (Homewood et al. 2009:257–58). But the Maasai tanzanite brokers whom I met and heard about had more modest (and uneven) success. One young man had used his profits to build himself a "modern" home (a rectangular house with mud brick walls, corrugated iron roof, and wooden furniture inside), purchase a used four-wheel-drive truck, and buy more livestock as an investment toward future ventures. Other successful brokers dazzled children at home when they sped through the plains on their shiny new motorbikes. And a few gave up and returned home poorer than before, unable to make the necessary connections with miners, brokers, and cutters to succeed. According to Sachedina and Trench (2009:292), Maasai brokers from Emboreet, a town on the Simanjiro plains, maintain strong links with their communities and usually are resident labor in Mererani for a season before returning to Emboreet to assist with core livelihood strategies of farming and livestock husbandry. . . . The goal of the brokers was to grow their initial investment of cash into funds to be used in Emboreet to support livestock and diversification into farming. Few individuals interviewed indicated a desire to stay in Mererani long term. But it represents a strategy for diversification that enables Maasai to return to their villages with profits faster than if they were to seek waged employment in Arusha or on the Karatu coffee estates.

Moreover, they suggest, one aspect of working as brokers that appeals to young Maasai men "is that brokers maintain a level of independence; they are self-employed, work largely in groups of their own age-sets, while trading is, broadly speaking, a familiar activity for many Maasai" (Sachedina and Trench 2009:292).

Although very few Maasai men have worked as miners of tanzanite, I met a number of men (and boys) mining rubies near Mundarara village near Engarenaibor in 2006. The two mines were now owned by a Chagga man, but were worked primarily by Maasai from Tanzania and Kenya. The main mine is just a huge, deep hole into which the men cast buckets on ropes to bring rocks to the top, then use garden clippers and other tools to separate the ruby slag from the green stone in which it is embedded. When I drove up, men of all ages, from young boys to elderly men, were sitting in small groups all over a hilltop near some small restaurants and shops, chipping and cutting away at the slag (see p. 154). According to the men, there was not a lot of profit in ruby mining, in part because they lacked the right equipment to retrieve the larger, higher-quality stones. Brokers from Arusha visited occasionally, buying the piles of ruby slag to sell in Arusha and Nairobi. I held up a small handful of the ruby slag and asked how much it would sell for. "About 2,500 TZ shillings," replied one man (less than US$2 at the time). By my estimate, from watching the men work while we spoke, it took between three to five hours to produce that handful, depending on the quality of the stones.

In the past, some men pursued economic diversification through polygyny, assigning one wife to take charge of the herds, another the fields, and perhaps another to run a small store (Hodgson 2001a:180). My evidence and that of others (e.g., Homewood et al. 2009) suggests that in addition to women's efforts to earn additional income through petty trade and others means, children are becoming increasingly key to successful diversification, with resources channeled to support the education of some children so that they can seek salaried employment and serve as mediators with the "Swahili" world of politicians, bureaucrats, doctors, and development workers, while other children are trained to manage the herds, farm the land, or work as temporary, casual laborers. For example, Katherine Homewood and her co-authors (Homewood et al. 2009:259–61) describe the case of Mohono ole Sarika, a Maasai elder from Emboreet village, who has five wives and twenty-nine children. Of those children, he sent only nine of his sons to school (only one of whom completed Standard 7), and none of his daughters ("on the basis that a boy returns his investment to the boma whereas a girl is expected to marry and leave home" Homewood et al. 2009:261). After moving his family thirteen times over the past twenty-five years in search of better water and pastures for his livestock, he finally settled in his current location in 1997, and had no plans to move. His family decided to start farming in 1999 after they lost three hundred cattle in an epidemic of East Coast Fever in 1998 and then the drought of 1998–2000. In 2004, the family farmed twenty-four acres of maize by hiring tractors to till the land and non-Maasai laborers to weed, guard the fields at night, and harvest. Like most other Maasai, the family relied on livestock for food (in the form of milk, meat, and blood), cash to meet other expenses, and ritual and kin obligations such as bridewealth. Women in the family also sold the hides and skins for additional cash. A family member who lives in his homestead also earned some money from a small honey-harvesting business. But the key source of income for the family is the remittances they received from two sons who worked as tanzanite brokers. Comparative evidence from Maasai areas in Tanzania (and Kenya) suggest that the kind of diversification pursued by Mohono and his family, especially the reliance on livestock, cultivation, and some form of remittances (including from community wildlife conservation projects), has increasingly become the norm for Maasai families of all economic levels (Homewood et al. 2009).

Finally, those Maasai men (and, increasingly, women) with more formal education were qualified to pursue other employment opportunities as teachers, government workers, health practitioners, and, of course, staff members and program officers with NGOs. Many of them lived in Arusha during the week, and visited their rural homesteads on the weekends to bring food and supplies for their extended family, survey their herds, consult with elders and age mates about local affairs, expose their educated, urban children to rural life, and otherwise cultivate and maintain connections with their rural communities. Elite men typically built a "modern" house in or near their family homestead to mark their presence and continuing involvement in homestead affairs, but also to avail themselves of conveniences such as running water and electricity that they have become accustomed to in the city. Similarly, elite women often used some of their income to construct modern homes near their natal or marital homesteads, in part to mark their presence and connections, but also to protect their profits from the requests and demands of their husbands. As Nanyore explained one day as we were walking together in Kimokowa, when she had put her money in a bank account, her husband was constantly asking her to take money out for one thing or another, and she could not refuse him. "So I decided that rather than put my money in a bank, I would slowly buy building materials and hope that my husband would give me permission to build a house." She pointed to a stack of corrugated iron sheets lying near her present house: "I bought them twenty at a time, and now I have sixty."

We Need Everything

In my numerous interviews with Maasai men, they mentioned many of the same changes identified by women: severe losses in livestock, widespread adoption of agriculture, and a fierce embrace of the value of education and biomedical healthcare. Other changes were more tangible—"modern" houses, new schools, and cars ("Who would ever have thought a Maasai would have a car?" wondered one old man, only half-jokingly.) They also agreed with the women about the top problems confronting Maasai: lack of clean, accessible water (both potable water for household use and water sources for cattle and farming), lack of adequate, quality healthcare and education, and deep economic insecurity. These problems were often condensed into two words: poverty (Maa: *enkaisinani*) and hunger (Maa: *esumash*). "We need everything," said a woman from Ngosuak. "We have been told that everything will be brought, but nothing has ever come."

Women, who are primarily responsible for hauling water for household use, complained bitterly about how far they had to walk to find water, often rising in the middle of the night so that they could return in time to feed their children. "Water is a huge problem," explained a woman from Ngosuak. "It is very far away. You can have food at home, but you can't cook it because you don't have any water." Another woman from Ngosuak claimed that she had to walk eight hours round trip to get water for her household. "We have to spend so much time getting water that we can't do other things to help ourselves get ahead," grumbled a woman from Mairowa. The limited water supplies often provoked conflict and tension between men and women, as men tried to meet the water needs of their herds and women of their households. As a woman from Longido explained, "There is one water source near Longido mountain that everyone depends on, livestock and people. But the men insist on watering the livestock first, so we have to wait . . . and then maybe we get no water or very dirty water." Even those communities such as Emairete with nearby water sources confronted problems of availability—the water pipe at the school dried up during the dry season; cattle came from all over to drink from their dam ("they drink it all up"), and pipes and dips were continually broken and in need of repair. Moreover, the difficulties and time constraints to get water have transformed it into a commodity in many areas. Outside of Engarenaibor, we met women with donkeys loading them up with water containers to sell for 30 TZ shillings a liter, while an entrepreneurial man with a tractor and trailer sold water for 300 TZ shillings a bucket in Emairete.

Similarly, women from remote communities such as Ngosuak complained about the distance they had to travel for medical attention: "If someone is hurt, they have to wait for someone to walk here [to Engarenaibor], hire a car, and then return to pick them up." "Our huge need is a hospital," said on older woman in Emairete; "we need someplace for sick and pregnant women to go. It seems that people, especially children, having been dying more in the past few years. We had six children die from measles in just one week last year!" Several of the communities that I visited had recently helped to build new dispensaries—but the buildings stood closed and empty, lacking personnel, equipment, and medicines. And yet, in almost every community, I heard sad stories about the recent deaths of pregnant women, children, and babies, and sensed a feeling of hopelessness and helplessness among residents about how to prevent such needless deaths in the future. Moreover, in the few communities I visited with functioning dispensaries, women and men complained about the cost of a doctor's visit, the expensive medicines, and the sometimes inadequate care. "Healthcare is so expensive!" lamented a woman from Embopong'. "It costs 1,000 TZ shillings just to see the doctor and then if he prescribes a shot or medicine, it could cost another 1,000 to 3,000 TZ shillings or more. And then it is often not the right medicine anyways!" Another woman from

Embopong' decried the expense and inconvenience of healthcare: "A person is very sick, so you send someone over there [to the dispensary] to bring the doctor, but he won't come because he has no money or means to travel. And we have no way to bring the sick person to him. It is really a problem. And he often doesn't even have the right medicine."[4]

As these comments suggest, pastoralists suffer from disparities in healthcare in comparison with national averages, resulting in limited progress in reducing child mortality, improving maternal health, and reversing the spread of HIV/AIDS, malaria, and other major diseases. The limited economic opportunities and political rights of pastoralist women make them, and their children, particularly vulnerable to health problems.

Health indicators in pastoralist districts are notoriously underreported, in part because they do not include deaths outside health facilities; traditional birth attendants assist about 90 percent of deliveries, and few report maternal or infant deaths to health centers (Simanjiro District Report 2005). Moreover, Mother-Child Health (MCH) clinics are not offered at all health facilities, decreasing the likelihood of referrals and routine data collection. The recent introduction of fees for health services (except for MCH clinics, which are supposed to be free) and escalating costs of medicines have created further barriers to healthcare for poor pastoralist women, who must often ask their husbands for money, and their children. Even those who try to use the health system in pastoralist districts face innumerable challenges and frustrations, including absent doctors, cancelled clinics, and lack of medicines. In 2005, as I was interviewing a man in Emairete in his modest house, with his wife sitting quietly on the bed nursing her three-month-old baby, he told me of their discouraging experiences with the government health system. She tried to visit the local MCH clinic three times when she was pregnant and three times after her baby was born, for a check-up. "But," he said, shaking his head, "she went to the clinic in Enguiki [about a five-mile walk] and was told that it was cancelled. Then she walked to Eluwai [another three miles further], but the doctor wasn't there. So then she went to the Monduli hospital [twelve miles away], and she was told to return another time. It was all very frustrating and tiring." Many women must still travel long distances for more than rudimentary healthcare, such as in difficult pregnancies and deliveries, further contributing to maternal and infant mortality. Fortunately, this woman had a successful pregnancy and healthy child. A young woman from the same community had died just the night before in childbirth because she could not reach the hospital in time once she started having complications.

The top causes of morbidity and mortality in pastoralist districts are malaria, pneumonia, diarrhea, and tuberculosis.[5] While the national average in 2004 for age-under-five mortality and maternal mortality was 126 children per 1,000 births and 1,500 per 100,000 respectively, these figures are substantially higher (but seriously underreported) in pastoralist districts.[6] Although the distribution of dispensaries by population in pastoralist districts seems equitable when compared to other districts, even the government acknowledges that "when viewed in terms of land area per dispensary then it is quite obvious that it is the districts of Ngorongoro, Kiteto/Simanjiro [then one district] and Monduli which are underprivileged" (Arusha Regional Commissioner's Office 1998:139). In other words, pastoralists are at a significant disadvantage because of their remote, dispersed locations. For example, table 5.1 compares the number of health facilities in 1997 and 2007 in two pastoralist districts in Arusha Region (Monduli and Ngorongoro), with Arumeru District, another primarily rural district in Arusha Region with few Maasai residents. Not only does the table reflect the huge disparity in the number of health facilities per square kilometer between the pastoralist districts and Arumeru, but it shows that little progress has been made to redress these inequities—while an additional thirty-seven health facilities (which includes dispensaries, health centers, and hospitals) were opened in Arumeru district between 1997 and 2007, only two new facilities were opened in Monduli, and none in Ngorongoro. Moreover, the two hospitals that do exist in Ngorongoro are operated by the Catholic Church, not the government (the Church also supports the Flying Medical Service, which provides regular clinics and emergency care to remote communities). These difficulties are further magnified by the poor roads and lack of viable transportation within pastoralist districts.

The health situation of pastoralists, especially pastoralist women and children, is further complicated by the lurking menace of HIV/AIDS. Between 1992 and 1996, there were a total of 126 cases (50 male and 76 female) of HIV/AIDS diagnosed in the four pastoralist districts (Arusha Regional Commissioner's Office 1998:162). But in 2004, 213 people (18.36% of those tested; 95 male and 118 female) tested positive for HIV/AIDS in Simanjiro District alone (Simanjiro District Report 2005:18). Similarly, at Endulen Hospital in Ngorongoro District, the recorded cases of HIV-positive patients rose from 7 in 1998 to 21 in 2002 (Coast 2002). Despite a lack of systematic testing, the adult (15–49

Table 5.1.
Comparison of Number of Health Facilities in Relationship to Land Area
by District, Arusha Region, 1997 and 2007

District	Total Land Area (sq. km.)	1997		2007	
		Total No. Health Facilities	Av. Land Area per sq. km. per health facility	Total No. Health Facilities	Av. Land Area per sq. km. per health facility
Arumeru	2,896.0	58	49.9	95	30.5
Monduli / Longido	14, 201.0	41	346.4	44	322.8
Ngorongoro	14,036.0	18	779.8	18	779.8

Source: Adapted from "Health," Arusha Regional Commissioner's Office (2009)

years) prevalence rate of HIV/AIDS is estimated to range between 15 percent and 18 percent among pastoralists (as compared to the national average of 8.8%), with slightly higher rates among adult women.[7]

Numerous factors contribute to almost unanimous agreement that the prevalence rate of HIV/AIDS among pastoralists will only increase in coming years. Since the primary mode of transmission for pastoralists is heterosexual sex, relevant factors include the practice of polygyny, the tolerance if not encouragement of prepubescent sexual activity for girls, high levels of sexual networking inside and outside of marriage, low levels of condom knowledge and use, strong cultural resistance to condom use, and high levels of untreated STDs among all age groups and both sexes.[8] Moreover, most experts agree that mother-to-child transmission (MTCT) is on the rise because of high fertility and prolonged breastfeeding. Finally, Coast (2001) suggests that Maasai girls will have a substantially lower age of infection than girls from other ethnic groups, in part because of their early sexual activity, with consequent reductions in fertility levels.

The vulnerability of pastoralists to HIV/AIDS is further exacerbated by the lack of health services and infrastructure described above (including very few voluntary counseling and testing centers [VCTs] in pastoralist districts), the increasing reliance by men on migration and women on sex as livelihood strategies, and low levels of education and literacy. For example, although antiretrovirals (ARVs) are now free in Tanzania, there is substantial inequality in access. Since there are no facilities in Simanjiro and Kiteto for referral and distribution, patients are referred to hospitals in Arusha town. Thus, in addition to the normal difficulties of following a complicated medical regimen, pastoralists from these districts must cope with the costs of travel and lodging in Arusha and repeated absences from work and family. Finally, although the Tanzanian government has launched a widespread HIV/AIDS education and awareness initiative through the Tanzanian Commission for AIDS, most of the materials and workshops are conducted in Swahili and designed for literate audiences, and therefore unsuitable for pastoralists.

There Is No Government? And as for NGOs . . .

When asked what the government had done to help them with their problems, most men and women just scoffed in response, "What government?" "There is no government! [Maa: *meata*]," complained an old woman. "Their government has done nothing for us!" said an old woman from Emairete, shaking her head sadly, "They don't care." "You can't know what the government does," responded a younger woman from Kimokowa. A Maasai schoolteacher shared their disillusionment: "They don't really work with Maasai; they haven't done much. Most development projects have been sponsored by religious organizations. . . . The government really doesn't think about Maasai as people." A few people listed discrete projects—a water tank here, a school there—but most decried the lack of government involvement and interest in their lives. According to one woman, "the government surveyed for water in the 1980s, but still hasn't done anything [as of 2006]." Despite their frustrations, some villagers still hoped that the government might help their communities. "We told the government about our problems," explained a woman from Ngosuak, "including the need for a school and teachers' housing . . . now we hope they will do something." Finally, a woman from Embopong' mentioned another problem with the government that points to ongoing issues of corruption and women's alienation from the "democratic" process (cf. Hodgson 2001a:188–95): "[The government] only cares for men," she claimed. "The elections are coming, and only the men will be paid to vote."

When asked if religious organizations had provided assistance to their community, most people said no. A few people, however, noted that some religious organizations (primarily Christian churches) had assisted them materially by providing nursery schools and food relief. Many women praised the spiritual assistance of the churches in the form of bringing the Gospel (Maa/Swahili: *injili*) and "teaching us to get along."[9] Others mentioned how the Christian churches had helped to cure *orpeko*, a form of spirit possession that had spread among Maasai women in the 1980s and 1990s, but was now on the decline (Hodgson 1997, 2001a).

Finally, despite the extensive outreach efforts of many pastoralist and Maasai NGOs, Maasai community members were often unaware of their existence. After first asking if they knew of any NGOs working in their area, we then named organizations that claimed to be active in the area to see if people had heard of them (or if they knew of their work). Often people identified specific NGOs by the person running them or by the program officer. "What is the NGO that Moses is running?" asked one young man. "TAPHGO," I replied. "Right. And then there is the NGO that Parkipuny was involved in." Similarly, several women in Engarenaibor said they had never heard of MWEDO, but readily mentioned the work of Nina Sokoine, a MWEDO program officer, who had conducted some training sessions on rotating credit, adult education, and HIV/AIDS in the area. Most were understandably more aware of local CBOs based in their communities, although they often knew very little about their actual projects. Some men in Engarenaibor were blunt about the gendered dynamics of NGO involvement in their community: "[We] only know about those [NGOs] which are helping women."

The ability to recall the names and activities of NGOs varied by communities, individuals, and, not surprisingly, how recently a representative from an NGO had visited and how active the NGO was in the community. For example, when I visited Engarenaibor in October 2006, many women mentioned Wordstar, an NGO that promotes adult education, because they were actively trying to form adult education groups at the time. Other people named CORDS, which had recently brought grinding machines to several villages (including Engarenaibor) and opened a store for veterinary medicines in Engarenaibor, among other projects (see discussion in chapter 3). Similarly, PWC was well established and recognized by both women and men, yet also identified with its charismatic founder, Maanda Ngoitiko. But most people responded like one older woman from Ngosuak: "We get a lot of groups who come to talk to us, but I can't remember their names!" "A group came last month," said an old man in Engarenaibor. "They said 'we are pastoralists, we have come to help you.' Not just Maasai but all pastoralists. I can't remember their name now . . . "

Most people described the following pattern—an NGO would organize a community meeting, seek support for a project, make promises, then never follow up or return. Most villagers were tired of the endless stream of organizations (and government officials) that visited, called meetings, promised assistance, then never delivered. As an older woman in Emairete wondered:

> I am glad you asked [about these NGOs]. I have been worrying
> about the same thing myself. Some of these groups come, they take
> all of our names, and then what happens—nothing!! I have heard of
> such organizations, and I wonder about them. Who do they help?
> Where does the money go? I think they just take the money and it
> stays there. It [the money] never reaches the village.

"Letinga," an Arusha man I have known for decades who lives in Emairete, shared his concerns. He told me a story about walking through the town of Monduli with a friend and seeing a large new house. He asked his friend who lived there. His friend told him it was a man with an NGO. When Saruni suggested they ask the NGO for help, his friend said not to bother, as the NGO "did its own thing." "But he had a huge house, a big car and clearly lots of money," said Letinga. "Where does all of this money come from?" he wondered. He thought that donors should just give money directly to villages and skip NGOs as intermediaries. "There is just too much corruption. A donor thinks they are giving money to help Emairete, but it goes to Emboreet—how do the donors know?" As a Maasai school teacher from Emairete commented, "Many [NGOs] seem to have an outward open face [Swahili: *sura ya wasi*] that hides a poor foundation or secret objectives."

Moreover, villagers claimed that those NGOs that did return focused their attention only on certain villages (such as Engarenaibor) and ignored others (such as Ngosuak). As a result, the remote communities that often most needed assistance in terms of health services, schools, water sources, or farming technology were usually the least likely to be selected for help, since they were difficult for busy program officers with finite resources, limited time, and scarce vehicles to visit. "I have heard about [the NGOs]," said one male Maasai teacher, "but they have not yet worked in our area." "There are lots of them in Simanjiro," said a young man from Emairete; "I am not sure why they aren't working here."

The uneven presence and absence of NGOs between and even within communities sometimes prompted feelings of jealousy and ill will by communities and community members who felt spurned (cf. Igoe 2000). The almost obsessive focus of many NGOs on Maasai people, as opposed to others, prompted this vehement diatribe from Letinga. One afternoon, as we sat on stools outside his house, he told me a story about a Maasai man we both knew who had offered to help send one of Letinga's daughters to a nearby secondary school with the support of a scholarship for Maasai girls (Letinga had helped the man attend school years before over the protests of his parents). But, the man advised, Letinga had to change his daughter's name to sound "more Maasai" and "less Arusha" so that she would be accepted.

> But what is wrong with helping an Arusha girl? I was born here in 1941 and have lived here all my life. Why should I be treated any differently than my Maasai neighbor? The problem with these NGOs is that they only want to help "pure, pure Maasai," not the rest of us. They thereby bring discrimination and problems to the village. We already have some problems between Maasai and Arusha in the village; we don't need to intensify them with these NGOs. It is just discrimination.

He then told me a story about another one of his daughters, who had studied successfully at a secondary school for Maasai girls and was a finalist for a scholarship to study at college in the United States. Even though she placed second in the exam, and there were two scholarships, the Lutheran bishop picked another girl to go in her place, presumably, according to Letinga, because she was Maasai and not Arusha like his daughter.

As this and previous comments suggest, the presence and proliferation of NGOs produced cautious optimism at best and cynicism and bitterness at worst, especially if people had contributed money to subsidize a project (such as constructing a school or borehole) that never transpired. Clearly, as my description of Engarenaibor suggests, changes had occurred, but many of these were due to the liberalization of the economy—which, as elsewhere in Tanzania and the world, enabled those with capital and connections to prosper, encouraged a few entrepreneurs (such as the tanzanite brokers) to succeed, and impoverished many by undermining their resource base (land and livestock), health, and access to quality education (a key means of achieving economic mobility and security).

The Strength of the Poor

I was deeply moved by my sojourns and surveys in these Maasai communities. Despite a palpable undercurrent of despair and even fear for the future, most of the people I met and spoke to, especially the women, were creatively and relentlessly trying to do everything possible to support their families. As one very old women told me, shaking her head sadly, "We [Maasai] are like an old ripped cloth, it keep getting tattered and torn, and soon there will be nothing left. Do you see all the ilmurran in town? At every gate is a murran working as a guard. Do you think they go there because they want to or because they have to?" Given the dramatic decline in livestock holdings, diminishing resource base, uncertain land tenure, and formidable obstacles to successful transhumant livestock production, women and men were trying to find work and make money, however small the amount. According to a Maasai school teacher in Emairete, "People are working hard to move ahead, especially the women. Many women are the sole supporters of their families and households, while their 'no-good' husbands just drink and waste time." Moreover, he continued:

> There is a change in people themselves. No one wants to waste time anymore. If they are willing to talk to you, it is because they think they can get something out of you. Even the young people. *Esoto* [culturally sanctioned occasions for flirting, dancing, and sexual play between ilmurran and young, uncircumcised girls] is still practiced, but it is no longer important. The Kurianga [the name of the ilmurran age group at the time] realize that it is a waste of time, and they have other things to do like farming. . . . The Kurianga work very hard—they don't care about cultural taboos anymore. One of them started selling peanuts. He didn't care if people laughed at him for carrying peanuts. But now he has a nice store and has done well for himself.

As his comments suggest, the drive to make money has reshaped cultural practices and attitudes. Unhurried banter has been replaced by short, strategic conversations, *Esoto* and moonlight dancing between *ilmurran* and *ntoyie* (young, uncircumcised girls) by endless work. Women no longer gather in the afternoon under the shade trees in their homesteads to rest and visit, but walk long miles to sit in small groups in towns such as Engarenaibor to sell their wares. Young men travel further in search of work—to the tanzanite mines and the cities of Arusha and Dar es Salaam. Even the elderly, who should be resting at home cared for by their children and surrounded by their grandchildren, are working in the fields, traveling to towns, and doing what they can to help. My Maasai friend Lengilassie, an uneducated but always thoughtful senior elder, summed up the situation well one day, as we talked about these changes: "[Despite our problems], we keep doing what we have done so far; 'the strength of the poor themselves' [Swahili: *nguvu ya maskini mwenyewe*]. If we don't study, if we don't learn, then we can't feed ourselves. You need your own strength to survive."

CONCLUSION

What Do You Want?

One day in 2006 a prominent Maasai activist told me a story about a re-cent meeting that he had had with the U.S. ambassador to Tanzania. After my friend made a long presentation about the struggles of pastoralist orga-nizations and activists to retain their land and protect their livelihoods and the anti-pastoralist bias of most government policies and practices, the am-bassador replied, "What do you want?" My friend then described a similar meeting with representatives from IFAD, after the successful intervention of pastoralists to revise the policy. "What do you want?" they asked. He also met with ambassador of Japan. The ambassador asked, "What are these things called pastoralists?" My friend replied "They are people, not things." Although the ambassador did not speak English well, he listened to my friend. And then he asked, "What do you want as pastoralists?" My friend later shared these stories at a workshop convened by PINGOs for pastoralist activists, members of Parliament, and sympathetic partners and donors to debate strategies for more effective advocacy with the Tanzanian state. "We are not prepared for this question," he concluded.

The repetition of this question, "what do you want?" suggests that, over the years, Maasai activists have done a better job of describing what they do not want (such as land alienation and forceful settlement in ranches) than what they do want. One reason is that they were almost always forced to respond to policies and practices that they perceived as harmful in some way, rather than have the time and political space to devise and propose policies of their own for the government to consider. But the dilemma of not being prepared with a positive, coherent plan was also the product of the "precari-ous alliances," "structural predicaments," and social frictions and factions described in this book.

The book has traced the emergence, consolidation, and transformations of Maasai NGOs over a twenty-year period as they positioned and repositioned themselves to advocate for the recognition of pastoralists' economic, political, and cultural rights and their secure access to resources. The struggles of pastoralists to adopt and create new forms of collective belonging and political action have taken place in the context of a specific historical conjuncture of several political-economic processes: the adoption and implementation of neoliberal political and economic "reforms" by the Tanzanian state, the reframing of donor development agendas to target "grassroots" organizations, and the emergence of new opportunities for transnational advocacy and connection through the expansion of the indigenous rights movement. Through the formation of NGOs and their involvement with the indigenous rights movement, Maasai and other pastoralists sought to simultaneously challenge and circumvent the Tanzanian state in order to seek political and economic empowerment in the face of their long history of disenfranchisement and marginalization. In so doing, they confronted a drastically restructured political and economic landscape shaped by democratization, economic liberalization, and decentralization that had transformed their relationship with the government, donors, and their communities.

The structural predicaments faced by these NGOs at this time were numerous, intense, and unrelenting. Of course, translocal and especially transnational organizing of any kind must confront similar problems (Brown and Fox 1998; Edelman 2001; McAdam et al. 1996). As the vast literature on social movements makes clear, building political alliances, or "umbrella organizations," is no easy matter, and sustaining them over time is even more difficult. Members must share a common cause or objective that is sufficiently unifying and inspiring, compromise over differences in their particular agendas, share information and resources, and seek ways to maintain their visibility and momentum. Moreover, all movements confront spatial and temporal challenges to their long-term viability: they must create the necessary mechanisms to reach, engage, and coordinate groups and individuals who are often dispersed in different places, and they must negotiate shifts, both gradual and sudden, in the internal dynamics of their members as well as local, regional, national, and transnational economic and political landscapes over time (cf. Li 2001a; Saugestad 2001).

The structural predicaments of the Maasai NGOs, however, were unique in some ways. The historical conjuncture between the intensified inequalities experienced by marginalized minorities such as Maasai as a result of neoliberal economic interventions; donor fantasies about, and expectations of, the possibilities for NGOs and civil society; and the transnational prominence, appeal, and strength of the indigenous rights movement was no coincidence. For Maasai and other groups, "becoming indigenous" was one of the few politically viable strategies available in a time of radical dislocation. By reframing their long-standing grievances and demands against their states in order to position themselves as indigenous, they gained greater international visibility, increased legitimacy, and enormous resources. But they also introduced a complex cultural politics of inclusion and exclusion that intensified the structural predicaments outlined above. In particular, the ambivalent place in all of these processes of the Tanzanian state—crippled by mandated cutbacks in personnel and resources, struggling to understand and implement democratic "reforms" and the tenets of "decentralization"—made the state even more wary of the collective demands and pressures of indigenous peoples and their organizations. Moreover, the role of donors as brokers and intermediaries with particular, sometimes contradictory, notions of "civil society," "the state," "NGOs," and "indigenous peoples" only further complicated matters.

In time, Maasai activists decided for a range of reasons that they needed to reposition themselves in at least three critical ways. They abandoned their efforts at international advocacy in order to focus almost exclusively on more effective (and less confrontational) advocacy with the Tanzanian state. As part of this change, they reframed their struggles from the language of "indigenous rights" to that of "pastoralist livelihoods," a discourse more acceptable to the state's interests in economic development. Moreover, in recognition of the increasingly negative perceptions of NGOs and the expanding visibility and strength of civil society in Tanzania, they renamed their organizations civil society organizations (CSOs). As the analysis of their efforts to shape the government's proposed new national livestock policy made clear, these changes were somewhat, if only modestly, successful.

Not everyone, however, supported a complete abandonment of involvement in international campaigns for indigenous rights. A few activists have continued to attend the UN Permanent Forum meetings, court indigenous rights advocacy groups, and mourn what they see as a neglect of cultural and social issues in the "pastoralist livelihoods" debates. As one senior activist complained to me, "livelihoods is just a World Bank agenda. . . . When you just say 'pastoralists and hunter-gatherers' you lose your connection with a big global movement. I think this is a weakness. [It] also overlooks the problem of culture." Others argued that Maasai activists could continue their bifurcated strategy of positioning themselves as indigenous peoples internationally and pastoralists at home: "Indigenous is a network—it doesn't prevent you from presenting your case in other ways."

Moreover, as the descriptions of contemporary Maasai communities made clear, the concept of "pastoralist livelihoods," like all such discourses and positionings, raises challenges and concerns of its own. Who, at a time of increasing diversification into agriculture, mining, and wage employment, is really a "pastoralist" anymore? Is there a shared, positive vision of "pastoralist livelihoods" that activists can articulate to government to counter the enduring negative stereotypes that still inform state policies and interventions? Is pastoralism even viable as a secure livelihood any more, given the rapid neoliberal economic transformations currently underway? Maasai activists debated these questions at almost every workshop and conference that I attended and were never able, in my presence, to articulate a clear vision for the future beyond protecting communal land and resources. As one of them declared, "We pastoralists are cheating ourselves, the landscape has changed radically. . . . We are fooling ourselves if we think that we can return to a pastoralist life." Or as another asked, "What kind of pastoralism do you want? The people have increased, the livestock have increased, but the land won't increase."

These debates were further complicated by the increasing differences between the lives of pastoralist activists and the lives of those they claimed to represent. Again, Maasai and other pastoralist activists were acutely aware of these issues. For example, after describing the growing problem of absentee herd owners in Botswana, one male activist joked to the rest of the workshop participants (all NGO leaders), "They are like some people here who go to Simanjiro and Mti Mmoja for the weekend to check on their cattle, then return to work in Arusha." His perceptive comment was greeted with much laughter and some uncomfortable looks. I laughed because I had just finished talking to a Maasai leader about his trip the past weekend to visit his family and cattle in a village in Monduli District.

So what does this overview of shifting Maasai positionings and political strategies tell us about the nature of postcolonial politics in a neoliberal world, especially the relationships among civil society, transnational advocacy, and the nation-state?

First, in contrast to those such as Appadurai (1996) who portend the demise of the nation-state, the Maasai case points to the continuing relevance of the nation-state in shaping political possibilities and positionings in transnational activism. International recognition of the merits of a people's struggle for rights and resources does not necessarily, or even easily, translate into national recognition. It can, on occasion, even backfire, buttressing rather than bridging government hostility. Faced with a series of failed confrontations, the rapid imposition of neoliberal reforms, and the seeming ineffectiveness of international recognition of their plight for their national struggles, pastoralist activists decided to change the terms of political debate. Repositioning themselves from "indigenous peoples" to "pastoralists," from a demand for "rights" to a demand for secure "livelihoods," and from NGOs to CSOs has enabled them to establish a more productive, if still difficult, working relationship with the state.

Second, despite their recent decision to distance themselves from the international indigenous peoples' movement, Maasai and other pastoralist activists benefited in significant ways from their involvement. Many, such as Parkipuny and Samuel, were able to see and learn from the larger patterns of structural similarities between their situation and that of Aborigines, Native Americans, and other indigenous peoples, especially about the possible range of relationships between indigenous peoples and nation-states. As Niezen (2003) argues, adopting the term "indigenous" itself marks a transcendence over the narrow concerns of "ethnicity," at the same time that it is predicated on those same ethnic concerns. By imagining a different kind of community that was at once located within states but connected beyond states, a bifurcated belonging that articulated the local and global, Maasai also learned new ways to belong to and act within the nation.[1] One could argue, in fact, that their success and support from the international indigenous peoples' movement helped them to transform themselves from "subjects" to "citizens" within their state (cf. Mamdani 1996); instead of withdrawing in frustrated anger, they now draw on their "rights" as citizens to demand justice and change. They learned from the comparative experiences of other indigenous peoples how to lobby and advocate the state and how to build strategic alliances among themselves and with other Tanzanians.

Third, this case suggests the value of an ethnographic approach to the study of political organizations, processes, and movements. Ethnography enables us to move beyond grand claims of political scientists, legal debates over definitions of "indigenous," philosophical debates over meanings of "civil society," and so forth to analyze how activists and organizations themselves are defining, using, and shaping the meaning of these terms in their everyday practices and discourses. "Cosmopolitics," according to Bruce Robbins (1998:12), points to a "domain of contested politics" located "both within and beyond the nation . . . that is inhabited by a variety of cosmopolitanisms." Grounding our analysis of "this newly dynamic space of gushingly unrestrained sentiments, pieties, and urgencies" (Robbins 1998:9) in the specific social and historical dynamics of its emergence at a certain time, in a certain place, for certain reasons, helps us to understand its appeal, possible dangers, and consequences.

These lessons affirm the dynamic relationship between transnational political projects such as the indigenous peoples' movement and the nation-states in which participants are inevitably located. Given the enduring centrality of the nation-state (itself a key colonial legacy) to neoliberal economic transformations, which must "reform" the entire state apparatus to make it welcoming for capitalist investment, increased productivity and profit-making, and individual initiative and success, it should come as little surprise that states such as Tanzania forcefully oppose the demands for collective rights and restitution for historical grievances made by indigenous peoples within its borders. The resulting shift to a discourse of "pastoralist livelihoods" could perhaps be understood as a "sell-out" of sorts to government pressure, a concession to neoliberal demands to talk only in the terms of development and economics. Perhaps. But it might be more useful to think about it as a positioning—a politically pragmatic decision made in light of perceived risks and benefits, and only the latest move in an ongoing dynamic of political struggle, of positionings and repositionings, set within complex, shifting fields of power within and beyond, but always including, the nation-state.

Notes

Introduction

1. As David Harvey (2005:2) explains, "neoliberalism is in the first instance a theory of political economic practices that proposes that human well-being can best be advanced by liberating individual entrepreneurial freedoms and skills within an institutional framework characterized by strong private property rights, free markets, and free trade." See also Comaroff and Comaroff (2001).

2. As Saugestad elaborates:

> Central events in this process have been the establishment of representative interest organisations such as the World Council of Indigenous Peoples (WCIP) in Vancouver in 1975; and regional organisations such as the Nordic Saami Council (1956), the Inuit Circumpolar Conference (1973), the Organization of Central American Indigenous Peoples in Panama (1977), the Indian Council of South America (1981), and Working Group of Indigenous Minorities of Southern Africa (WIMSA, 1996). A parallel process has brought out advocacy—and support—NGOs such as the International Work Group for Indigenous Affairs (IWGIA, Scandinavia-based, 1968), Cultural Survival (USA-based, 1972) and Survival International (UK-based, 1972). (Saugestad 2001:47; see also Dahl 2009)

3. Keck and Sikkink (1998) offer an important comparative overview of the forms and networks of transnational advocacy used by activists in each of these movements. Hodgson (2003) describes the impact of similar processes and opportunities in facilitating and promoting the "women's rights are human rights" campaign in Africa.

4. See the special issue of *Cultural Survival Quarterly* (1998) on how the Internet facilitated organizing, strategizing, and lobbying by indigenous organizations.

5. Of course, anthropologists and anthropological knowledge contributed to such transformations in numerous ways: we have been involved as observers, participants, informants, interlocutors, and advocates; our findings have been used to justify or contest the claims of indigenous activists; and our theories and studies have informed local, national, and international debates about the appropriate legal definition of *indigenous*.

6. Some have found the phrase "strategic essentialism" useful to describe and explain this particular deployment of cultural representation in the interests of political objectives. There is a broad literature on identity politics (Calhoun 1994), cultural politics (Alvarez et al. 1998; Friedman 1994; Gupta and Ferguson 1997b; Hale 1997), and social movements (Escobar 1992; Escobar and Alvarez 1992; Gupta 1992; Smith 1994) that informs these studies of indigenous movements.

7. See, e.g., the debate that occurred in the journal *Identities* (Field 1996; Friedman 1996; Mato 1996; Rogers 1996).

8. See, e.g., Hodgson (2001a), Li (2000), Brosius (1999c), Warren (1998), Povinelli (1993, 2002), Ramos (1998).

9. See, e.g., Brosius (1997a, 1997b, 1999a), Conklin and Graham (1995), Li (2000), Hodgson and Schroeder (2002), Howitt (2001), Howitt et al. (1996), Johnston (1997), Turner (1999).

10. For studies of indigenous ideas of "development," see Hodgson (2001a), Gray (1997, 1998), Ramos (1998), Blunt and Warren (1996).

11. For an overview of the issues and positions taken by anthropologists and indigenous activists, see Brown (1998), Posey (1990), Cleveland and Murray (1997), Benthall (1993), Brush (1993, 1996), Greaves (1994), Coombe (1993), Tsosie (1997), Orlove and Brush (1996).

12. There is a vast literature on social movements, collective action, and contentious politics in political science and sociology, and, to a lesser extent, anthropology. Edelman (2001) provides a useful, if somewhat dated, overview of the field.

13. See, e.g., Bornstein (2005), Englund (2006), Jennings (2008).

14. According to Hearn (2007:1098), "The comprador acts as an agent, operating in the interests of international capitalism against the interests of the indigenous popular classes." Comprador theory developed among Marxists in the 1920s as a way to theorize imperialism, and reemerged in the 1960s and 1970s in the context of dependency theory.

15. See the discussion in Hodgson (1999d). Relevant work includes Asad (1973), Berreman (1968), Gough (1968a, 1968b), Huizer and Mannheim (1979), Hymes (1969), Smith (1999).

16. See, e.g., Clifford (1983), Clifford and Marcus (1986).

17. Recent allegations about the actions of anthropologists working with Yanomami in Brazil further oblige us to carefully assess our actions and accountability. Wright (1988) provides an interesting overview of the relationship between anthropological theory and indigenous advocacy, and the article by Field (1999) and ensuing comments offer a provocative case. See also Asad (1973), Gough (1968a).

18. For a more thorough discussion of how I have negotiated the ethical and political dilemmas produced by the contradictory protocols of history and anthropology in terms of naming subjects, places, and so forth in this project and others, see Hodgson (2010).

1. Becoming Indigenous in Africa

1. Although there are increasing numbers of histories of particular movements, to my knowledge there is no published historical overview of the entire movement. Niezen (2003), however, provides a thoughtful and fairly thorough account of how the movement began and key issues and debates, and Dahl (2009) provides an overview of the movement from the perspective of IWGIA's involvement. Cobo's (1986) five-volume report to the UN offers rich historical detail, as do the numerous publications of IWGIA and Cultural Survival (especially Cultural Survival 1997a, 1997b). See also Maiguashca (1994), Maybury-Lewis (2002), van der Fliert (1994), De Costa 2006).

2. These excerpts and all others are based on interviews I conducted with Parkipuny in 2005 and 2006 in Tanzania.

3. He presented a paper at a symposium on the "Anthropology of Human Rights" at the International Congress of Anthropological and Ethnological Sciences in Vancouver, Canada in August 1983 (*IWGIA Newsletter* 35–36:184).

4. One other Tanzanian accompanied him—Richard Baalow (a Hadzabe activist)—but he did not present a formal statement.

5. Interview with Jens Dahl, 2003 UN Permanent Forum, New York City.

6. In 1991, his participation in the UN Working Group was funded by an organization called World's Indigenous People (WIP), based in the Netherlands.

7. IWGIA was founded in 1968 as a network of human rights activists and researchers concerned about the affairs of indigenous peoples, prompted in part by a sudden awareness of the genocide of Amazonian Indians. Although they published a brief report on Eritrea in 1971 (Knutsson 1971), they were primarily involved with activists from the Americas, and later the Arctic, Oceania, and Asia. According to one former board member, IWGIA consciously positions itself as "political organization," not a "development organization," despite pressures from its donors. For more information about IWGIA, see the recent history written by their long-time director, Jens Dahl (2009), and their Web site: http://www.iwgia.org.

8. These workshops included: "Conference on Indigenous Peoples in Eastern, Central and Southern Africa" (Arusha, 1999) and "Conference to Facilitate Active Participation in the United Nations Permanent Forum on the Indigenous Peoples in Eastern Africa" (Nairobi, 2004).

9. The first African organization supported by IWGIA was the San organization, First Peoples of the Kalahari (FPK), in Botswana in 1993. IWGIA began

working with four Kenyan organizations in 1999–2000, and by 2006 was funding seven projects in Kenya and one in Tanzania. At the time, they planned to begin a land-rights project with a Batwa NGO in Burundi and to renew their temporarily suspended support for FPK (IWGIA 2006).

10. Cameron (2001:66–67) has critiqued IWGIA for scheduling the conference according to its institutional timetable and needs rather than that of PINGOs. Whatever the truth of this allegation, the conference was crucial in convincing an array of African activists to participate in the indigenous peoples' movement.

11. For example, IIED was helping Barabaig and Maasai pastoralists in Tanzania organize to protect their land claims in the 1990s. At a 1993 workshop in Tanzania they cosponsored for representatives from eight pastoralist groups (including one from Kenya), the workshop participants agreed, among other things, that "indigenous rights" should be emphasized, "in accordance with the UN Resolution designating 1993 as the year of indigenous people" (Bulengo and Sheffer 1993:11). An IIED program officer working with pastoralists in eastern and western Africa in 2005, however, found the idea that pastoralists were "indigenous peoples" ludicrous (personal communication). For more about IIED, see http://www.iied.org.

12. Instead, events were planned "in all the areas where indigenous people live . . . Latin American countries, North America, Australia, Nordic countries, and Asian and Pacific countries." United Nations E/CN.4/Sub.2/1991/39 p.2. Cited in Pritchard 1998:43.

13. The Pan Africanist Congress of Azania, from South Africa, attended the UN Working Group as a "national liberation movement" for a few years, beginning in 1984. The South West Africa People's Organization (SWAPO) also attended as a national liberation movement in 1987.

14. The Maa Development Association from Kenya (a Maasai NGO) participated in 1993. Data compiled from list of organizations in attendance appended to the final reports for each session of the UN Working Group. For 2002, see United Nations E/CN.4/Sub.2/2002/24.

15. Observers from African states who participated in the UN Working Group, in order of their first year of participation, included: Senegal (1987–92, 2004), Nigeria (1994–97, 2004–2006), South Africa (1995–2000, 2002, 2004–2005), Ethiopia (1996), Kenya (1996–98, 2005), Libya (1996, 1999), Mauritius (1997–2002, 2004–2006), Mauritania (2000), Democratic Republic of Congo (2001, 2004), Morocco (2001–2002, 2005), Angola (2006), Cameroon (2006), Lesotho (2006). Data compiled from list of member states in attendance appended to the final reports for each session of the UN Working Group.

16. In 1971, the UN ECOSOC authorized the Sub-Commission to study the problem of discrimination against indigenous populations and to suggest measures for eliminating such discrimination. The Sub-Commission promptly appointed José Martinez Cobo as a special rapporteur to conduct the study, which is discussed briefly below. But even before Cobo completed his extensive study

(Cobo 1986), the Sub-Commission proposed the establishment of the UN Working Group, which ECOSOC authorized in 1982.

17. ECOSOC Resolution 1982/34, May 7, 1982.

18. Only NGOs with consultative status are allowed to attend public meetings of ECOSOC and its subsidiary organizations, including the Committee for Human Rights and the Sub-Commission, and to submit written or oral statements on specific agenda items. The first indigenous organization to obtain consultative status with ECOSOC was the International Indian Treaty Council in 1977 (Burger 1994:91). By 2002, twelve indigenous organizations, none of which represented African peoples, had obtained consultative status (UNCHR 2002).

19. Figures taken from annex II ("Participation in the Working Group") of Commission on Human Rights 2006.

20. The UN Working Group was eventually dissolved in December 2007 and replaced by an Expert Mechanism on the Rights of Indigenous Peoples, after ratification of the Declaration (HRC Resolution 6/36, December 14, 2007). The Expert Mechanism has a more direct reporting relationship to the Human Rights Council (which replaced the notoriously mismanaged UN Commission on Human Rights in 2006).

21. Interview with "Rita," 2004 UN Working Group, Geneva.

22. One representative from a prominent transnational advocacy group thought the UN Working Group had lost its legitimacy, in part because it "had been hijacked by its Cuban chair [Alfonso Martínez]" (personal communication, 2004).

23. Alfonso Martínez developed his critique of what he called the "indigenous *problematique* in the African and Asian contexts" in his occasional progress reports on the treaty study (e.g., Alfonso Martínez 1992, 1995), culminating in the clear statement in his final report that "in post-colonial Africa and Asia autochthonous groups/minorities/ethnic groups/peoples who seek to exercise rights presumed to be or actually infringed by the existing autochthonous authorities in the States in which they live cannot, in the view of the Special Rapporteur, claim for themselves, unilaterally and exclusively, the 'indigenous' status in the United Nations context" (Alfonso Martínez 1999: para 88).

24. The Indigenous Caucus is a loose network of all indigenous activists that usually meets before and during the UN Working Group and UN Permanent Forum to try to coordinate advocacy efforts and prepare collective statements on behalf of all indigenous delegates through consensus-based decision making.

25. For example, IWGIA used to launch its annual yearbook at a "side event" at the UN Working Group, but as of 2004, began launching the yearbook at the UN Permanent Forum instead.

26. The term *indigenous*, derived from the Latin *indigena*, meaning "born in a country," or "native," has a long history. In the mid-seventeenth century it referred to people or products "born or produced naturally in a land or region; Native or belonging naturally to the soil, region, etc." *(Oxford English Dictionary* 2002: indigenous). Its current social, political, and legal definitions, however, are much

more ambiguous and even controversial, especially as the term has been taken up by a range of disenfranchised groups to define and promote their movements.

27. Studies that examine the complex politics and struggles of the indigenous movement in Asia include Brosius (1997a, 1997b, 1999c), Kingsbury (1998), Li (2000, 2001a, 2001b, 2007). For Africa, they include Veber et al. (1993), Barume (2000), Saugestad (2001), Cultural Survival (2002, 2006), Sylvain (2002), Cameron (2004), Igoe (2006).

28. For a discussion of these debates and use of these terms, see Berge (1993), Kingsbury (1998), Murumbi (1994), Saugestad (2001), Wæhle (1990), and other papers in Veber et al. (1993).

29. According to Article 1 of ILO Convention 169, indigenous people are:

(a) tribal peoples in independent countries whose social, cultural and economic conditions distinguish them from other sections of the national community, and whose status is regulated wholly or partially by their own customs or traditions or by special laws or regulations;

(b) peoples in independent countries who are regarded as indigenous on account of their descent from populations which inhabited the country, or a geographical region to which the country belongs, at the time of conquest or colonisation or the establishment of present state boundaries and who, irrespective of their legal status, retain some or all of their own social, economic, cultural and political institutions. (ILO 1989: article 1.1)

The 1989 Convention replaced the ILO's 1957 Indigenous and Tribal Populations Convention 107 in order to remove "the assimilationist orientation of the earlier standards" (ILO 1989: preamble). The 1957 Convention reflected and expressed the assumptions and objectives of modernization: the social and economic conditions of "tribal and semi-tribal" populations were described as "at a less advanced stage" than that of "other sections of the national community" (ILO 1957: article 1.1 [a]) or even of an earlier time (ILO 1957: article 1.1[b]). The convention distinguished between "tribal" and "semi-tribal" populations, defining *semi-tribal* as those "groups or persons who, although they are in the process of losing their tribal characteristics, are not yet integrated into the national community" (ILO 1957: article 1.2). A key objective of the 1957 Convention was to "facilitate . . . their progressive integration into their respective national communities" (ILO 1957: preamble).

30. Some activists have complained that the convention does not go far enough in explicitly recognizing political self-determination as a right of indigenous peoples (Kingsbury 1998:439). But as Swepston explains, "the opponents of using this term argued that its inclusion would end any possibility that governments would ratify the Convention once adopted" (1989:261).

31. Every year, the principle of self-identification produces some curious participants at the UN Permanent Forum. In 2008, I sat next to a delegation of "indigenous Irish" representing three NGOs ("Retrieve Foundation Indigenous Irish Council," "Indigenous Irish Youth," and "The Grandmothers of Mother

Earth") who presented several statements calling for recognition of their sacred grandmother. Fellow activists responded with polite applause but little interest.

32. The eight members nominated by government are elected by ECOSOC based on the five regional groupings of states commonly used by the UN (Africa, Asia, Eastern Europe, Latin America and the Caribbean, and Western Europe and other states). The eight members nominated by indigenous organizations are appointed by the president of ECOSOC and represent seven regions "determined to give broad representation to the world's indigenous peoples" (Africa, Asia, Central and South America and the Caribbean, the Arctic, North America, the Pacific, and former UUSR and Eastern Europe), with one additional rotating seat among the first three groups. The UN Working Group "expert" members always included a representative from Africa, as well as the other UN regions, but they were members of the UN Commission for Human Rights who were considered experts on human rights, not representatives of or experts on indigenous peoples. For more on the history of the UN Permanent Forum and alternative structures of representation that were considered, see IWGIA (1999), López-Reyes (1995).

33. In the interests of securing Euro-American political recognition of and support for their agendas, African organizations and activists, like indigenous peoples elsewhere, often had to use names, such as "pygmies," that were personally and politically inaccurate, contentious, and distasteful.

34. For more about Mary Simat's life, see Gittelman (2008).

35. Curiously, Maasai and Tuareg were usually the only African groups to wear distinctly "ethnic" or "indigenous" dress at the Permanent Forum. Delegates from other African societies (including Batwa, San, and Amazigh) preferred to wear dresses, skirts, pants, jackets, and jeans. I am not sure whether this decision represented a difference in pride, strategy, historical and contemporary modes of dress (and reception of that dress), or just personal choice.

36. The aluminum dangles are a recent adaptation that distinguishes Maasai visually as well as aurally—the dangles produced a noticeable rhythmic jangle as Maasai men and women walked down the hallway and into the UN chamber.

37. During his trip to Kenya in January 2004, Magga visited Maasai communities, met with Maasai activists, and participated in the Conference to Facilitate Active Participation in the United Nations Permanent Forum on Indigenous Issues sponsored by IWGIA. The conference brought indigenous representatives from Kenya, Uganda, Tanzania, Ethiopia, and the Democratic Republic of Congo together for three days to discuss "contemporary issues, Human rights, UNPF, and UN specialized agencies, National/Regional policies that affected indigenous peoples in Eastern African Region" (United Nations Report E/C.19/2004/CRP.2, March 22, 2004, 3).

38. Interview with Adam ole Mwarabu, 2003 UN Permanent Forum, New York.

39. http://www.ipacc.org.za/eng/about.asp (accessed April 24, 2008).

40. Several activists voiced similar complaints about the African Indigenous Women's Organization (AIWO), representing a pan-African network of indig-

enous women's organizations. When I asked a Maasai woman activist why she did not attend a meeting about indigenous women organized by AIWO in Nairobi, she replied that she did not really consider AIWO relevant: "They are really above us, and haven't done very much."

41. Interview with James Legei, April 26, 2006, Arusha.

42. The African Commission was established in 1987 after the ratification of the African Charter on Human and Peoples' Rights (the Charter) by the Organization of African Unity (OAU, which has since been replaced by the African Union) on October 21, 1986. The Charter was adopted by the OAU after significant pressure from civil society organizations, media, and religious institutions for African states to acknowledge, promote, and protect human rights in Africa. The mandate of the African Commission is to promote and protect human and peoples' rights in Africa and to interpret the African Charter on Human and Peoples' Rights. The Commission, composed of eleven elected commissioners, meets twice a year to review and discuss the human rights situation, state reports, allegations of human rights abuses, and reports by special rapporteurs and working groups. In addition, it has established a Documentation Centre, organized seminars and conferences on human rights, carried out "fact-finding" missions to specific countries, and published several human rights documents. For more information about the African Commission, see their Web site, http://www.achpr.org, and an IWGIA Web site dedicated to their activities, http://www.iwgia.org/sw249.asp.

43. The other members of the first AC Working Group were two commissioners of the African Commission, N. Barney Pityana and Andrew Chigovera, and three "indigenous experts," Naomi Kipuri (a Maasai anthropologist from Kenya), Mohammed Khattali (Mali), and Zephyrin Kalimba (Rwanda). A third commissioner, Kamel Rezag-Bara, was initially part of the AC Working Group, but he had to withdraw after he was elected chair of the African Commission.

44. For a thoughtful analysis of the debates over "peoples" and the "self" in "self-determination" in the indigenous rights movement, see Muehlebach (2003).

45. The case of Maasai in Kenya provides an interesting contrast that I do not have the space to fully explore in this book. They have continued to maintain active involvement with the international indigenous rights movement and to convert that recognition into some national political leverage and gains. But they also lack the strong coalition of pastoralist organizations present in Tanzania. One possible difference is the vastly different history of how ethnicity has been deployed in national politics in Kenya in contrast to Tanzania (see, e.g., Hughes 2005).

46. United Nations HRC Resolution 2006/2.

47. United Nations A/C.3/61/L.57/Rev.1. Some organizations, such as IPACC, accused Namibia of just acting as a proxy for the objections of the United States (IPACC 2006).

48. "Decision on the United Nations Declaration on the Rights of Indigenous Peoples (Doc. Assembly/AU/9 (VIII) Add.6)." African Union Document Assembly/

AU/Dec.141 (VIII). http://www.iwgia.org/graphics/Synkron-Library/Documents/
InternationalProcesses/DraftDeclaration/AUDecisionOnUNDeclarationDec_2006
.doc (accessed April 24, 2008).

49. The seventeen signers of the response included Hassan Id Balkassm, Joseph
ole Simel (a prominent Maasai activist from Kenya), Naomi Kipuri (a Maasai
activist from Kenya who serves as an expert member of the AC Working Group),
and Benedict ole Nangoro (a Maasai from Tanzania who heads a prominent
pastoralist development organization).

50. See, e.g., IPACC 2006 and the IPACC Web site (http://www.ipacc.org.za)
more generally.

51. The African states that voted in favor were: Algeria, Angola, Benin,
Botswana, Burkina Faso, Cameroon, Cape Verde, Central African Republic,
Comoros, Congo, Democratic Republic of Congo, Djibouti, Egypt, Gabon,
Ghana, Guinea, Lesotho, Liberia, Libya, Madagascar, Malawi, Mali, Mauritius,
Mozambique, Namibia, Niger, Senegal, Sierra Leone, South Africa, Sudan,
Swaziland, United Republic of Tanzania, Zambia, Zimbabwe.

2. Maasai NGOs, the Tanzanian State, and the Politics of Indigeneity

1. In Tanzania, the number of registered NGOs expanded from 17 in 1978, to
813 in 1994, to over 2,000 by 2000 (REPOA 2007:1).

2. Notable (or notorious?) examples include commercials by American
Express and Nike, photographic spreads of Maasai in *Vogue* and *Cosmopolitan*, and
popular movies such as *Out of Africa*.

3. Where possible I use the preferred spelling "Maasai," although I have retained
"Masai" when it is used by others in writing, titles, letters, and other quotations.

4. One of the most famous exceptions was Edward Moringe Sokoine, an
educated Maasai with a modernist agenda who rose through the political ranks of
CCM to eventually serve as prime minister of Tanzania until his sudden death in a
suspicious car accident in 1984. For a profile of Sokoine, see Hodgson
(2001a:196–201).

5. For a detailed discussion of the socialist economy, the transition to
neoliberalism, and the initial impact on Maasai, see Hodgson (2001a). For
discussions of the implementation and impact of neoliberal policies in Tanzania
more generally, see, inter alia, Gibbon (1995), Chachage and Mbilinyi (2003),
Shivji (2006), Pallotti (2008).

6. Since by 2009, Arusha Region had been split into Arusha Region and
Manyara Region, the national parks claimed by the Arusha Regional Commis-
sioner's Office included Arusha National Park (552 sq. km), Manyara National
Park (329 sq. km.), and part of the Serengeti Park and Ngorongoro Conservation
Area (Arusha Regional Commissioner 2009).

7. *Guardian*, February 10, 2006, 6.

8. *Daily News*, January 19, 2006, 1.

9. *Sunday Citizen*, May 28, 2009, 9.

10. Rodgers Luhwago, "The Horrifying Killings in Kilosa District," *Sunday Observer*, November 16, 2008.

11. Musa Juma, "Government Suspends Action on Herders Relocation," *Arusha Times*, May 9–15, 2009.

12. For a historical overview of poverty among Maasai pastoralists, and their institutions for recovery and redistribution, see Waller (1999).

13. By "livestock unit," Ndagala referred to calculations then in use by the Arusha Livestock Officer, where the following types of livestock were equivalent to LUs in the parentheses: 1 bull (1), 1 steer or mature cow (0.7), 1 heifer or immature bull (0.5), and 1 calf, goat, or sheep (0.2) (Ndagala 1990:67).

14. The combination of democratic liberalism and economic liberalization is also known as the "New Policy Agenda" (e.g., Hulme and Edwards 1997).

15. Although I occasionally refer to these NGOs as "pastoralist NGOs" or even "pastoralist and hunter-gatherer NGOs," I usually use "Maasai NGOs" to signal the dominance of Maasai activists and concerns in the agendas and practices of these organizations.

16. Much of this paragraph is drawn verbatim from Hodgson (2001a:232).

17. The first two donors were Humanistic Institute for Cooperation with Developing Countries (HIVOS) and the Netherlands Development Organization (SNV).

18. As he explained, "Two elected members of the Maasai served on the Commission. For one who is the member of Parliament for the district [i.e., Parkipuny], it was the fifth Commission in Ngorongoro he got involved in, in the span of 10 years, between 1980 and 1990. So far nothing has been done on any of the reports submitted by the five Commissions." "A submission made by the Maasai representative of KIPOC organization based in Northern Tanzania." WGIP 91/AFR/3. Also available as DOCIP 970167.

19. The DELTA model refers to a "problem-posing" approach to development developed by the Christian churches that focuses on facilitating the active, reflective, critical engagement of people in their own development, in contrast to the "banking approach" of top-down development. A key training manual was called *Training for Transformation* (Hope and Timmel 1992).

20. Interview with Parkipuny, September 19, 2005, Arusha, Tanzania.

21. For detailed explorations of the Barabaig case and the dynamics of KIPOC-Barabaig, see Lane (1996) and Igoe (2005).

22. This huge amount reflects the extraordinary costs of obtaining building materials at the time, most of which had to be imported, and the artificial constraints of the fixed exchange rate (which was soon lifted).

23. Interview with Parkipuny, September 20, 2005, Arusha, Tanzania.

24. Conversation with Parkipuny, September 19, 2005, Arusha, Tanzania.

25. Letter from ole Ngulay to author, October 16, 1990.

26. The *oloiboni* (plural: *iloibonok*) is a prophet and ritual leader. See Hodgson (2005) for more details.

27. I discuss Father Hillman's life and perspectives as the first Catholic missionary to pursue sustained evangelization efforts among Maasai in Hodgson 2005.

28. In 1983, the Tanzanian government allocated 268,000 acres of Maasai grazing lands in Kiteto District (now Simanjiro District) to Tanzania Cattle Products, a joint venture between the Tanzanian government and an Italian company. The deal seems to have been made with the approval of the village chairs and district council, but without the knowledge or consent of area residents. In addition to losing a large area of prime grazing land, residents were upset that the allocated area encompassed a series of water boreholes that they had developed and financed over the years. Eventually, a group of Maasai mobilized, and the land was returned to the District. But Tanzania Cattle Products then sought land in another area inhabited predominantly by Maasai—Ngorongoro District (Inyuat e Maa 1994a:17–19).

29. I discuss this incident in Hodgson 2001a:235.

30. According to Saruni, between 1991 and May 1994, Inyuat e Maa received the following grants, totaling 48.5 million Tanzanian shillings: Finnish International Development Agency (FINNIDA, 2.7 m shs), Norwegian Agency for Development Cooperation (NORAD, 12.7 m shs), Swedish International Development Authority (SIDA, 5.8 m shs), Danish International Development Agency (DANIDA, 2.0 m shs), Humanistic Institute for Cooperation with Developing Countries (HIVOS, 5.0 m shs), International Institute for Environment and Development (IIED, 20.0 m shs), Canadian University Services Organization (CUSO, .3 m shs), Forest, Trees and People Programme (FTPP, training in participatory research analysis) (Inyuat e Maa 1994b:8).

31. Letter from ole Ngulay to author, August 24, 1991.

32. Recommendation of the Conference Voices of the Earth (Van der Vlist 1994:286–92). Also available as electronic document http://www.idrc.ca/en/ev-30147-201-1-DO-TOPIC.html (accessed June 19, 2008).

33. He visited IIED for three months in 1993 as "Pastoral Land Tenure Fellow" to read and write about pastoralist land tenure issues, visited McGill University in 1993, presented a paper in Sussex England in 1994, spent a week in Florence, Italy, in 1995 as part of an international task force preparing a casebook on community social development for the Copenhagen Social Summit (Ngulay 1995), visited the United States in 1995 for two months on a USAID International Training Program scholarship (he studied project management in Atlanta), and presented a paper at the Sixth Annual Conference of the International Association for the Study of Common Property in Berkeley, California, in 1996 (Ngulay 1996).

34. Interview with Francis ole Ikayo, May 26, 1995, Arusha, Tanzania.

35. The online version of the article (Taylor and Johansson 1996) no longer includes the video excerpts or pictures of the interviewees, just English translations of residents' comments. I viewed the original in the late 1990s at http://www.trees.slu.se/ngorongoro/ngfront.html.

36. Interview with Francis ole Ikayo, December 30, 1996, Arusha, Tanzania.

37. Interview with Francis ole Ikayo and Peter Toima, January 7, 1997, Simanjiro, Tanzania.

38. AWF's influence was quite direct: Patrick Bergin, then the director of AWF's East African office sat on the board of trustees of Inyuat e Maa.

39. According to AWF's Web site, "Partnership Options for Resource-Use Innovation (PORI), a project supported by the U.S. Agency for International Development (USAID) [is] designed to help develop community-based wildlife enterprises in northern Tanzania. . . . Through PORI, AWF works with landowners, park officials and other stakeholders to ensure that wildlife and human communities alike thrive." http://www.awf.org/section/about/history#1990 (accessed June 18, 2008).

40. Inyuat e Maa also requested funds from the U.S.-based McKnight Foundation to develop several women's cooperative bead projects, but it is unclear if funding was ever received.

41. See also Friedman (1994).

42. Interview with "Christopher," May 18, 2006, Arusha, Tanzania.

3. Precarious Alliances

1. Hugo Slim, director, Pilotlight UK, "Africa/Australia Exchange." n.d. Photocopied overview in possession of author.

2. The African visitors from Tanzania were Martin Saning'o (Maasai NGO leader), Ben Lobulu (lawyer and chair of Human Rights Monitoring Group), Daniel Murumbi (Barabaig NGO leader), Matei ole Timan (Maasai MP), and Dr. Ringo Tenga (lawyer); and from Kenya they were Dr. Naomi Kipuri (Maasai anthropologist), Joseph ole Simel (Maasai NGO leader), Keriako Toboko (Maasai lawyer), Justice M. ole Keiwua (Maasai judge), http://www.whoseland.com/people.html (accessed September 12, 2001).

3. Email to author, April 3, 1998.

4. From the perspective of the NGO workers with access to vehicles, it was difficult to resist helping family members and others (including anthropologists) when driving from Arusha to remote rural communities, given the poor public transportation infrastructure and concentration of processed goods and products in towns. For example, one evening I was invited at the last minute to accompany two Maasai leaders on a trip to Simanjiro so that I could see the area after a few years' absence and greet some old friends. After they picked up my husband and the wife of one of the men, we stopped for dinner at a local restaurant. Then we picked up the man's brother-in-law and father-in-law at another restaurant (which entailed a rearrangement of our seating, since the father-in-law could not sit near his daughter). We stopped at a pharmacy on the edge of town so that the father-in-law could pick up some medicines, and then at the local market so that the wife

could buy some fresh loaves of bread (she had already bought some washing detergent and bananas). Finally, along the way we gave a ride to a couple and their child who were walking to their homestead at dusk.

5. As discussed in Hodgson (1999c, 2001a), the first generation of Maasai men in Tanzania to be educated and/or convert to Christianity were disparaged as *ormeek*, a derogatory term used by Maasai to describe "Swahilis." Over time, however, as more men were educated, they were accepted, and use of the term declined.

6. PINGOs Pastoralist Strategy Workshop, February 16, 2006, Arusha, Tanzania.

7. Examples of articles about MWEDO and Ndinini include "Maasai Women's Leader on Study Tour in the United States," *Arusha Times*, April 8–14, 2006, 6; Violet Tillya, "Maasai Traditions Discriminate Women," *Citizen*, February 4, 2006, 6; and Adam Ihucha, "Global Financial Crunch Worries Gender NGO in Maasailand," *Guardian*, December 16, 2008.

8. See, e.g., Mary Mwabukusi, "One Little Girl's Legacy to her Community," *Citizen*, October 3, 2006, 14–15.

9. For example, a photocopied, Swahili-language brochure about Ilaramatak that I picked up in 1999 mentioned *wachungaji waasili* and stated several times that "human rights" was a key objective of the organization (Ilaramatak ca. 1999).

10. *Azimio la Uhai.* "Declaration of NGOs and Interested Persons on Land." Issued by National Land Forum. May 15, 1997, http://www.oxfam.org.uk/resources/Learning/downloads/tanazim.rtf (accessed July 5, 2008).

11. Interview with Benedict ole Nangoro, September 26, 2005, Arusha, Tanzania.

12. The other researchers were Naomi Kipuri, a Maasai anthropologist and indigenous rights activist; Mary Vertucci, an American Catholic sister with a background in education; John ole Kuluo, a Maasai livestock specialist; and James Mollel, a health expert (Kipuri et al. 1997:10).

13. CORDS, http://www.cordstz.org/mission_vision.html (accessed July 17, 2008).

14. CORDS, http://www.cordstz.org/about.html (accessed July 17, 2008).

15. Interview with Benedict ole Nangoro, September 26, 2005, Arusha, Tanzania.

16. They included "Multiculturalism in Africa: Peaceful and Constructive Group Accommodation in Situations Involving Minorities and Indigenous Peoples," sponsored by the UN in Arusha in 2000 (Kipuri 2000); the Conference of the Parties on the Framework Convention on Climate Change sponsored by the UN Environment Program (UNEP) in the Hague in 2000; the "African Regional Experts Working Group on Indicators of Wellbeing and Indigenous Peoples," sponsored, in part, by the UN Permanent Forum in 2006; and an "International Expert Seminar on Indicators Relevant to Indigenous Peoples, the Convention on Biological Diversity and the Millennium Development Goals" in 2007 in the Philippines.

17. Interview with Benedict ole Nangoro, September 26, 2005, Arusha, Tanzania.

18. Interview with Benedict ole Nangoro, September 26, 2005, Arusha, Tanzania.

19. Francis Ikayo served as the coordinator of the Pastoral Caucus Secretariat. The workshop was sponsored by Forest, Trees and People Programme (FTPP) and IIED.

20. Donors included the Food and Agriculture Organization (FAO), DANIDA, Embassy of the Netherlands, and IIED.

21. Interview with Benedict ole Nangoro, September 26, 2005, Arusha, Tanzania.

22. By 1996, PINGOs had nine member organizations: Inyuat e Moipo, KIPOC, BULGADA (a Barabaig NGO), Ilaramatak Lolkonerei, Mongo Wamono (Hadzabe), Ilaramatak Mkomazi, LADO, Oseremi, and UWAMA (Mwau and Reynders 1996:45).

23. For more on PINGOs, see Cameron (2001), Igoe (2000, 2003, 2004, 2006), PINGOs (1999), and their Web site: http://pingosforum.org/.

24. Interview with Francis ole Ikayo, January 6, 1997, Arusha, Tanzania.

25. The workshop was sponsored by OXFAM and VETAID.

26. The proposed names for the new umbrella organization reflected similar debates and tensions over identity and representation: MABAWA (Maasai, Barabaig, Wahadzabe); Tanzania Pastoralist Forum (TPF); Tanzania Pastoral Hunter-Gatherer Forum; Union of Pastoralists and Hunter Gatherer Organizations (UMWATA); and Tanzania Association of Pastoralists, Indigenous Hunters and Gatherers.

27. Cameron argues that "a judicious mix of tactical approaches to the state should have been given pride of place by PINGOs. This should have included court cases (legalism), lobbying government leaders (interest group politics), constitutionalism, and support for sympathetic party officials (parliamentarianism)" (2001:68; cf. Bratton 1990).

28. Although it may be easier to mobilize at the national level over land rights, struggles over land and resources on the land continue to divide residents within communities and pit communities against each other (cf. Hodgson 2001a; Hodgson and Schroeder 2002). As Saugestad (e-mail to author, March 25, 2002) reminds us, land, unlike donor funds, is a zero-sum game.

4. Repositionings

1. "Workshop on Livestock Policy," sponsored by TAPHGO, August 5, 2005.

2. These excerpts are based on interviews that I conducted with "Samuel" in 2005 and 2006.

3. For a succinct overview of the approach, see the introduction to McCabe (2004) and Fratkin and Mearns (2003).

4. The "Consultative Workshop on Rangeland Livelihoods and the Poverty Reduction Strategy (PRS) Review" was organized by PINGOs in March 2004 in collaboration with HakiKazi Catalyst, Sand County Foundation, Organisation for Orkonerei Pastoralists Advancement, and Ujamaa Community Resource Trust. In addition to the workshop report (PINGOs 2004), see Odhiambo 2006 for a

comparative analysis of the participation of pastoralists from Kenya, Uganda, and Tanzania in the poverty reduction strategy proposal process.

5. "Call to Modernise Livestock Keeping," *Daily News*, January 19, 2006, 1.

6. "Leaders Call for 'Special Zones' to Spur Economy," *Guardian*, March 17, 2006, 2.

7. For details on Mkomazi, see Brockington (2002); for Soit Sambu, see Ndaskoi (2009b); and for the Ortello Business Company, see Mvungi (2009), MERC (2002).

8. "Pray for Rain, Preserve Water Sources—Premier," *Citizen*, January 12, 2006, 4; Ramadhani Kupaza, "Maasai Cattle Cause Global Warming," *Arusha Times*, February 7–13, 2009, http://www.arushatimes.co.tz/2009/5/society_1.htm (accessed February 15, 2009).

9. See "Report and Recommendation of the President to the Executive Board on a Proposed Loan to the United Republic of Tanzania for the Agricultural Sector Development Programme—Livestock: Support for Pastoral and Agro-Pastoral Development," IFAD EB 2005/85/R.21/Rev.1, http://www.ifad.org/gbdocs/eb/85/e/EB-2005-85-R-21-REV-1.pdf (accessed July 14, 2009).

10. See "Agricultural Sector Development Programme—Livestock: Support for Pastoral and Agro-Pastoral Development of the United Republic of Tanzania. Report on Actions and Milestones," IFAD EB 2005/86/R.20, http://www.ifad.org/gbdocs/eb/86/e/EB-2005-86-R-20.pdf (accessed July 14, 2009).

11. See http://www.tnrf.org for more information.

12. For more about Hakikazi Catalyst, see http://www.hakikazi.org.

13. Edward Selasini, "Pastoralists Demand More Benefits from Wildlife," *Arusha Times*, September 9–15, 2006.

14. Happy Lazaro, "Herders Decry Oppressive Polices," *Arusha Times*, March 14–20, 2009.

15. I describe the life and perspectives of his late father, Thomas Porokwa, in Hodgson 2001a:139–47.

5. "If We Had Our Cows"

1. For more information on the Millennium Development Goals, see http://www.un.org/millenniumgoals.

2. I conducted interviews and focus groups in Monduli District (Emairete, Mti Mmoja, Embopong', Kimekowa, Longido, Engarenaibor [including women from Ngosuak, Mairowa, and Naribil], Mundarara), Ngorongoro District (Soit Sambu, Loliondo), and Kiteto District (Kijungu, Namolog).

3. The figure was computed by dividing the total population for ages 7–13 in 2002 (Tanzania Population and Housing Census 2002) by the gross enrollment data from the stated year from the 2005 Simanjiro District Report and a report from the Monduli District education officer.

4. Of course, not all communities had the same problems. A woman from Namanga (a large town that straddles the Kenyan-Tanzanian border), who was listening to women from Ngosuak discuss the problems of water and health interjected, "I am from Namanga—we have everything!"

5. Arusha Regional Commissioner (1998, 2009), Simanjiro District Report (2005).

6. "At a Glance: Tanzania, United Republic of," UNICEF table of statistics, http://www.unicef.org/infobycountry/Tanzania_statistics.html (accessed January 19, 2006).

7. Estimations of HIV/AIDS prevalence among Maasai vary widely, from 30–40% (ACE Africa 2008) to 18–30% (Simanjiro District Report 2005)

8. These factors, among others, are listed in Dr. Ernestina Coast's 2002 report on HIV/AIDs in Ngorongoro for ERETO-NPP, one of the most detailed and thorough reports available, http://personal.lse.ac.uk/coast/Coast%20-20%20 HIVAIDS%20in%20Ngorongoro%20District.pdf. Other recent reports and research confirm most of her findings for other pastoralist districts.

9. For more about the appeal of Christianity, especially Catholicism, to Maasai women, see Hodgson (2005).

Conclusion

1. Similar in some ways to the "cosmopolitan ethnicity" described by Werbner (2002) for Kalanga elites in Botswana.

Bibliography

ACE Africa. 2008. Tanzania Baseline Survey in Kimnyaki and Mateves villages, Arusha District. http://www.ace-africa.org/index.php?page=arusha-district (accessed May 14, 2009).

African Commission on Human and Peoples' Rights (African Commission). 2000. "Resolution on the Rights of Indigenous Populations/Communities in Africa." November 6, 2000. http://www.iwgia.org/graphics/Synkron-Library/ Documents/InternationalProcesses/ACHR/ResolutionsDeclarations/ Resolution2000E.htm (accessed April 24, 2008).

———. 2003. Resolution on the Adoption of the "Report of the African Commission's Working Group on Indigenous Populations/Communities." November 20, 2003. http://www.iwgia.org/graphics/Synkron-Library/Documents/ InternationalProcesses/ACHR/ResolutionsDeclarations/Resolution34 sessionE.htm (accessed April 24, 2008).

———. 2005. *Report of the African Commission's Working Group of Experts on Indigenous Populations/Communities.* Copenhagen: ACHPR and IWGIA.

———. 2007. Advisory Opinion of the African Commission on Human and Peoples' Rights on the United Nations Declaration on the Rights of Indigenous Peoples. Adopted by the African Commission on Human and Peoples' Rights at its 41st Ordinary Session held in May 2007 in Accra, Ghana. http:// www.iwgia.org/graphics/Synkron-Library/Documents/International Processes/DraftDeclaration/07-08-08AdvisoryOpinionENG.pdf (accessed April 24, 2008).

African Group [of States]. 2006. "Draft Aide Memoire. African Group. United Nations Declaration on the Rights of Indigenous Peoples." New York, November 9, 2006. http://www.iwgia.org/graphics/Synkron-Library/Documents/ InternationalProcesses/DraftDeclaration/AfricanGroupAideMemoireOn Declaration.pdf (accessed April 24, 2008).

African Group of Experts. 2007. "Response Note to 'The Draft Aide Memoire of the African Group on the UN Declaration on the Rights of Indigenous

Peoples.'" 21 March 2007. http://www.iwgia.org/graphics/Synkron-Library/
Documents/InternationalProcesses/DraftDeclaration/ResponseNoteToAide-
Memoire_EN.pdf (accessed April 24, 2008).

Albert, Bruce. 1997. "'Ethnographic Situation' and Ethnic Movements: Notes on
Post-Malinowskian Fieldwork." *Critique of Anthropology* 17, no. 1: 53–65.

Alfonso Martínez, Miguel. 1992. "First Progress Report. Study on Treaties,
Agreements and Other Constructive Arrangements between States and
Indigenous Populations." United Nations E/CN.4/Sub.2/1992/32.

———. 1995. "Second Progress Report. Study on Treaties, Agreements and Other
Constructive Arrangements between States and Indigenous Populations."
United Nations E/CN.4/Sub.2/1995/27.

———. 1999. "Final Report. Human Rights of Indigenous Peoples. Study on
Treaties, Agreements and Other Constructive Arrangements between States
and Indigenous Populations." United Nations E/CN.4/Sub.2/1999/20.

Alonso, Ana Maria. 1994. "The Politics of Space, Time and Substance: State
Formation, Nationalism and Ethnicity." *Annual Review of Anthropology* 23:
379–405.

Alvarez, Sonia E., Evelina Dagnino, and Arturo Escobar, eds. 1998. *Cultures of
Politics, Politics of Cultures: Re-visioning Latin American Social Movements.*
Boulder, Colo.: Westview.

American Anthropological Association. 2009. Code of Ethics of the American
Anthropological Association. http://www.aaanet.org/issues/policy-advocacy/
upload/AAA-Ethics-Code-2009.pdf (accessed December 1, 2010).

An-Na'im, Abdullahi A., ed. 2002. *Cultural Transformation and Human Rights in
Africa.* London: Zed Books.

Anonymous. 2000. "Comments on Briefing Paper for Pastoralist Workshop."
Paper distributed to participants of workshop on "The Future of Pastoralist
NGOs in Tanzania," June 5.

Appadurai, Arjun. 1996. *Modernity at Large: Cultural Dimensions of Globalization.*
Minneapolis: University of Minnesota Press.

Århem, Kaj. 1985a. *The Maasai and the State: The Impact of Rural Development Policies
on a Pastoral People in Tanzania.* IWGIA Document 52. Copenhagen: IWGIA.

———. 1985b. *Pastoralist Man in the Garden of Eden: The Maasai of the Ngorongoro
Conservation Area, Tanzania.* Uppsala: Scandinavian Institute of African
Studies.

Arusha Regional Commissioner's Office. 1998. "Arusha Region Socio-Economic
Profile." Joint Publication with the Planning Commission, Dar es Salaam.
Photocopy in author's possession.

———. 2009. Online source for data on health, education, and other areas. http://
www.arusha.go.tz (accessed May 14, 2009).

"Arusha Resolutions." 1999. *Indigenous Affairs* 2: 50–55. Also available as an
electronic document, http://www.iwgia.org/sw579.asp (accessed April 24,
2008).

Asad, Talal, ed. 1973. *Anthropology and the Colonial Encounter*. Atlantic Highlands, N.J.: Humanities Press.

Askew, Kelly. 2002. *Performing the Nation: Swahili Music and Cultural Politics in Tanzania*. Chicago: University of Chicago Press.

Barume, Albert Kwokwo. 2000. *Heading toward Extinction? Indigenous Rights in Africa: The Case of the Twa of the Kahuzi-Biega National Park, Democratic Republic of Congo*. IWGIA Document 101. Copenhagen: IWGIA.

Bayart, Jean-François. 1993. *The State in Africa: The Politics of the Belly*. New York: Addison-Wesley.

Bebbington, Anthony, and Roger Riddell. 1997. "Heavy Hands, Hidden Hands, Holding Hands? Donors, Intermediary NGOs and Civil Society Organisations." In *NGOs, States and Donors: Too Close for Comfort?* ed. David Hulme and Michael Edwards. New York: St. Martin's Press.

Benthall, Jonathan. 1993. "Rights to Ethnobiology." *Anthropology Today* 9, no. 3: 1–2.

Berge, Gunnvor. 1993. "Reflections on the Concept of Indigenous Peoples in Africa: The Case of the Tuareg." In *"Never Drink from the Same Cup": Proceedings of the Conference on Indigenous Peoples in Africa (Tune, Denmark, 1993)*, ed. Hannes Veber, Jens Dahl, Fiona Wilson, and Espen Wæhle. IWGIA Document 74. Copenhagen: IWGIA.

Bernsten, John. 1980. "The Enemy Is Us: Eponymy in the Historiography of the Maasai." *History in Africa* 7: 1–21.

Berreman, Gerald. 1968. "Is Anthropology Alive? Social Responsibility in Social Anthropology." *Current Anthropology* 9, no. 5: 391–96.

Blunt, Peter, and D. Michael Warren, eds. 1996. *Indigenous Organizations and Development*. London: Intermediate Technology Publications.

Börjeson, Lowe, Dorothy L. Hodgson, and Pius Z. Yanda. 2008. "Northeast Tanzania's Disappearing Rangelands: Historical Perspectives on Recent Land Use Change." *International Journal of African Historical Studies* 41, no. 3: 523–56.

Bornstein, Erica. 2005. *The Spirit of Development: Protestant NGOs, Morality, and Economics in Zimbabwe*. Palo Alto: Stanford University Press.

Bowen, John. 2000. "Should We Have a Universal Concept of 'Indigenous Peoples' Rights?" Ethnicity and Essentialism in the Twenty-First Century." *Anthropology Today* 16, no. 4: 12–16.

Bradbury, Mark, Simon Fisher, and Charles Lane. 1995. "Working with Pastoralist NGOs and Land Conflicts in Tanzania: A Report on a Workshop in Terrat, Tanzania, 11th-15th December, 1994." Pastoral Land Tenure Series 7. London: International Institute for Environment and Development.

Bratton, Michael. 1989. "The Politics of Government-NGO Relations in Africa." *World Development* 17, no. 4: 569–87.

———. 1990. "Non-Governmental Organizations in Africa: Can They Influence Public Policy?" *Development and Change* 21, no. 1: 87–118.

Brockington, Dan. 2002. *Fortress Conservation: The Preservation of Mkomazi Game Reserve, Tanzania*. Oxford: James Currey.

Brosius, J. Peter. 1997a. "Endangered Forest, Endangered People: Environmentalist Representations of Indigenous Knowledge." *Human Ecology* 25, no. 1: 47–69.

——. 1997b. "Prior Transcripts, Divergent Paths: Resistance and Acquiescence
to Logging in Sarawak, East Malaysia." *Comparative Studies in Society and
History* 39, no. 3: 468–510.

——. 1999a. "Analyses and Interventions: Anthropological Engagements with
Environmentalism." *Current Anthropology* 40, no. 3: 277–309.

——. 1999b. "On the Practice of Transnational Cultural Critique." *Identities* 6,
no. 2–3: 179–200.

——. 1999c. "Locations and Representations: Writing in the Political Present in
Sarawak, East Malaysia." *Identities* 6, no. 2–3: 345–86.

——, ed. 1999d. *Environmentalism, Indigenous Rights and Transnational Cultural
Critique.* Special issue of *Identities* 6, no. 2/3.

Brosius, J. Peter, Anna Lowenhaupt Tsing, and Charles Zerner. 1998. "Representing Communities: Histories and Politics of Community-Based Natural
Resource Management." *Society and Natural Resources* 11, no. 2: 157–69.

Brown, L. David, and Jonathan A. Fox. 1998. "Accountability within Transna-
tional Coalitions." In *The Struggle for Accountability: The World Bank, NGOs and
Grassroots Movements,* ed. Jonathan A. Fox and L. David Brown. Cambridge,
Mass.: MIT Press.

Brown, Michael. 1998. "Can Culture be Copyrighted?" *Cultural Anthropology* 39,
no. 2: 193–222.

Brubaker, Rogers, and Frederick Cooper. 2000. "Beyond 'Identity.'" *Theory and
Society* 29 , no. 1: 1–47.

Brush, Stephen B. 1993. "Indigenous Knowledge of Biological Resources and
Intellectual Property Rights: The Role of Anthropology." *American Anthropologist* 95, no. 3: 653–71.

——. 1996. "Whose Knowledge, Whose Genes, Whose Rights?" In *Valuing
Local Knowledge,* ed. Stephen B. Brush and Doreen Stabinsky. Washington,
D.C.: Island Press.

Bulengo, Martha, and Rudolf Scheffer. 1993. "Proceedings of a NGO/Donor
Workshop on Pastoralism and Development." Unpublished report, Tanzania,
June 1–3.

Burger, Julian. 1994. "United Nations Working Group on Indigenous Populations:
The United Nations and Indigenous People." In *Indigenous Peoples and
International Organizations,* ed. Lydia van der Fliert. Tokyo: U.N. University
Press.

Burke, Timothy. 1996. *Lifebuoy Men, Lux Women: Commodification, Consumption
and Cleanliness in Modern Zimbabwe.* Durham, N.C.: Duke University Press.

Calhoun, Craig, ed. 1994. *Social Theory and the Politics of Identity.* Cambridge,
Mass.: Blackwell.

Cameron, Greg. 2001. "Taking Stock of Pastoralist NGOs in Tanzania." *Review
of African Political Economy* 87: 55–72.

———. 2004. "The Globalization of Indigenous Rights in Tanzanian Pastoralist NGOs." In *Development of Local Knowledge: New Approaches to Issues in Natural Resource Management, Conservation, and Agriculture,* ed. Alan Bicker, Paul Sillitoe, and Johan Pottier. London: Routledge.

Chachage, Chachage S. L., and Marjorie Mbilinyi, eds. 2003. *Against Neo Liberalism: Gender, Democracy and Development.* Dar es Salaam: Tanzania Gender Networking Programme.

Chambers, Robert. 1987. "Sustainable Livelihoods, Environment and Development: Putting Rural Poor People First." IDS Discussion Paper 240. Brighton: University of Sussex Institute of Development Studies.

———. 1999. "In Search of Professionalism, Bureaucracy and Sustainable Livelihoods for the 21st Century." *IDS Bulletin* 22: 5–11.

Chambers, Robert, N. C. Saxena, and Tushaar Shah. 1989. *To the Hands of the Poor: Water and Trees.* London: Intermediate Technology Publications.

Chambers, Robert, and Gordon Conway. 1992. *Sustainable Rural Livelihoods: Practical Concepts for the 21st Century.* Brighton: Institute for Development Studies.

Cleveland, David A., and Stephen C. Murray. 1997. "The World's Crop Genetic Resources and the Rights of Indigenous Farmers." *Current Anthropology* 38, no. 4: 477–515.

Clifford, James. 1983. "On Ethnographic Authority." *Representations* 1, no. 2: 118–45.

Clifford, James, and George Marcus, eds. 1986. *Writing Culture: The Poetics and Politics of Ethnography.* Berkeley: University of California Press.

Coast, Ernestine. 2001. "Maasai Demography." PhD thesis, Department of Anthropology, University of London. http://eprints.lse.ac.uk/archive/00000264/ (accessed December 12, 2008).

———. 2002. "HIV AIDS in Ngorongoro District. Report for ERETO-NPP." Photocopy in author's possession.

Cobo, José Martinez. 1986. *The Study of the Problem of Discrimination against Indigenous Populations.* Vols. 1–5. United Nations Document E/CN.4/Sub.2/1986/7.

Coe, Cati. 2005. *Dilemmas of Culture in African Schools: Youth, Nationalism and the Transformation of Knowledge.* Chicago: University of Chicago Press.

Comaroff, Jean, and John L. Comaroff, eds. 1993. *Modernity and Its Malcontents: Ritual and Power in Postcolonial Africa.* Chicago: University of Chicago Press.

———. 2001. *Millennial Capitalism and the Culture of Neoliberalism.* Durham, N.C.: Duke University Press.

Comaroff, John L., and Jean Comaroff, eds. 1999. *Civil Society and the Political Imagination in Africa: Critical Perspectives.* Chicago: University of Chicago Press.

Conklin, Beth A. 1997. "Body Paint, Feathers and VCRs: Aesthetics and Authenticity in Amazonian Activism." *American Ethnologist* 24, no. 4: 711–37.

———. 2002. "Shamans versus Pirates in the Amazonian Treasure Chest." *American Anthropologist* 104, no. 4: 1050–61.

Conklin, Beth A., and Laura R. Graham. 1995. "The Shifting Middle Ground: Amazonian Indians and Eco-Politics." *American Anthropologist* 97, no. 4: 695–710.

Coombe, Rosemary J. 1993. "The Properties of Culture and the Politics of Possessing Identity: Native Claims in the Cultural Appropriation Controversy." *Canadian Journal of Law and Jurisprudence* 6: 249–85.

Cooper, Frederick. 2005. *Colonialism in Question: Theory, Knowledge, History.* Berkeley: University of California Press.

Cultural Survival . 1997a. "25 Years of the Indigenous Movement: The Americas and Australia." Special issue, *Cultural Survival Quarterly* 21, no. 2.

———. 1997b. "25 Years of the Indigenous Movement: Africa and Asia." Special issue, *Cultural Survival Quarterly* 21, no. 3.

———. 1998. "The Internet and Indigenous Groups." Special issue, *Cultural Survival Quarterly* 21, no. 4.

———. 2002. "The Kalahari San: Self-Determination in the Desert." Special issue, *Cultural Survival Quarterly* 26, no. 1.

———. 2006. "Indigeneity in Africa." Special issue, *Cultural Survival Quarterly* 30, no. 2.

Daborn, Chris. 2000. "Pastoralist Development in Tanzania: A Plan for the Way Forward." Paper distributed to a workshop on "The Future of Pastoralist NGOs in Tanzania," June 5.

Dahl, Jens. 2009. *IWGIA: A History.* Copenhagen: IWGIA.

Das, Veena, and Deborah Poole, eds. 2004. *Anthropology in the Margins of the State.* Santa Fe: School of American Research Press.

Dean, Bartholomew, and Jerome M. Levi, eds. 2003. *At the Risk of Being Heard: Identity, Indigenous Rights and Postcolonial States.* Ann Arbor: University of Michigan Press.

De Costa, Ravi. 2006. "Identity, Authority, and the Moral Worlds of Indigenous Petitions." *Comparative Studies in Society and History* 48, no. 3: 669–98.

De la Peña, Guillermo. 2005. "Social and Cultural Policies toward Indigenous Peoples: Perspectives from Latin America." *Annual Review of Anthropology* 34: 717–39.

Diallo, A. M. 2007. "Memo: Visit of Honourable President Jakaya Kikwete to Arusha Region." English translation of Swahili original. In author's possession.

Dove, Michael. 2006. "Indigenous People and Environmental Politics." *Annual Review of Anthropology* 35: 191–208.

Edelman, Marc. 2001. "Social Movements: Changing Paradigms and Forms of Politics." *Annual Review of Anthropology* 30: 285–317.

Edwards, Michael, and David Hulme. 1992. *Making a Difference: NGOs and Development in a Changing World.* London: Earthscan.

———. eds. 1995. *NGO Performance and Accountability: Beyond the Magic Bullet.* London: Earthscan.

Englund, Harri. 2006. *Prisoners of Freedom: Human Rights and the African Poor.*
Berkeley: University of California Press.

Englund, Harri, and Francis Nyamnjoh, eds. 2004. *Rights and the Politics of
Recognition in Africa.* London: Zed Books.

Escobar, Arturo. 1992. "Imagining a Post-Development Era? Critical Thought,
Development and Social Movements." *Social Text* 10, no. 2–3: 20–56.

———. 1995. *Encountering Development: The Making and Unmaking of the Third
World.* Princeton, N. J.: Princeton University Press.

Escobar, Arturo, and Sonia Alvarez, eds. 1992. *The Making of Social Movements in
Latin America: Identity, Strategy and Democracy.* Boulder, Colo.: Westview Press.

Ferguson, James. 1990. *The Anti-Politics Machine: "Development," Depoliticization
and Bureaucratic Power in Lesotho.* New York: Cambridge University Press.

———. 1999. *Expectations of Modernity: Myths and Meanings of Urban Life on the
Zambian Copperbelt.* Berkeley: University of California.

———. 2006. *Global Shadows: Africa in the Neoliberal World Order.* Durham, N.C.:
Duke University Press.

Ferguson, James, and Akhil Gupta. 2002. "Spatializing States: Toward an Ethnography of Neoliberal Governmentality." *American Ethnologist* 29, no. 4: 981–1002.

Field, Les. 1996. "Mired Positions: Moving beyond Metropolitan Authority and
Indigenous Authenticity." *Identities* 3, no. 1–2: 137–54.

———. 1999. "Complicities and Collaborations: Anthropologists and the 'Unac-
knowledged Tribes' of California." *Current Anthropology* 40, no. 2: 193–209.

Fisher, William F. 1997. "Doing Good? The Politics and Antipolitics of NGO
Practices." *Annual Review of Anthropology* 26: 439–64.

Fowler, Alan. 1995. "NGOs and the Globalization of Social Welfare: Perspectives
from East Africa." In *Service Provision under Stress in East Africa,* ed. Joseph
Semboja and Ole Therkildsen. Copenhagen: Centre for Development
Research.

Fratkin, Elliot, and Robin Mearns. 2003. "Sustainability and Pastoral Livelihoods: Lessons from East African Maasai and Mongolia." *Human Organization* 62, no. 2: 112–22.

Friedman, Jonathan. 1994. *Cultural Identity and Global Process.* London: Sage.

———. 1996. "The Politics of De-Authentification: Escaping from Identity, a
Response to 'Beyond Authenticity' by Mark Rogers." *Identities* 3, no. 1–2:
127–36.

Galaty, John. 1993. "Maasai Expansion and the New East Africa Pastoralism." In
Being Maasai, ed. Thomas Spear and Richard Waller. London: James Currey.

Gibbon, Peter, ed. 1995. *Liberalised Development in Tanzania: Studies in Accumulation Processes and Local Institutions.* Uppsala: Nordiska Afrikainstitutet.

———. 2001. "Civil Society, Locality and Globalization in Rural Tanzania: A
Forty-Year Perspective." *Development and Change* 32: 819–44.

Gittelman, Melissa. 2008. "Against the Odds." *Cultural Survival Quarterly* 32, no.
1: 16–17.

Gledhill, John. 2004. "Neoliberalism." In *A Companion to the Anthropology of Politics*, ed. David Nugent and Joan Vincent. Oxford: Oxford University Press.

Gough, Kathleen. 1968a. "Anthropology and Imperialism." *Monthly Review* 19, no. 11: 12–27.

———. 1968b. "New Proposals for Anthropologists." *Current Anthropology* 9, no. 5: 403–407.

Gray, Andrew. 1997. *Indigenous Rights and Development: Self-Determination in an Amazonian Community.* Oxford: Bergahn Books.

Greaves, Tom, ed. 1994. *IPR for Indigenous Peoples: A Sourcebook.* Oklahoma City: Society for Applied Anthropology.

Gupta, Akhil. 1992. "The Song of the Non-Aligned World: Transnational Identities and the Reinscription of Space in Late Capitalism." *Cultural Anthropology* 7, no. 1: 6–23.

———. 1998. *Postcolonial Developments: Agriculture in the Making of Modern India.* Durham, N.C.: Duke University Press.

Gupta, Akhil, and James Ferguson. 1997a. "Discipline and Practice: 'The Field' as Site, Method, and Location in Anthropology." In *Anthropological Locations: Boundaries and Grounds of a Field Science*, ed. Akhil Gupta and James Ferguson. Berkeley: University of California Press.

———, eds. 1997b. *Culture, Power, Place: Explorations in Critical Anthropology.* Durham, N.C.: Duke University Press.

Gupta, Akhil, and Aradhana Sharma. 2006. "Globalization and Postcolonial States." *Current Anthropology* 47, no. 2: 277–307.

Hale, Charles. 1997. "Cultural Politics of Identity in Latin America." *Annual Review of Anthropology* 26: 567–90.

Hannerz, Ulf. 1996. *Transnational Connections: Culture, People, Places.* New York: Routledge.

Harvey, David. 2005. *A Brief History of Neoliberalism.* Oxford: Oxford University Press.

Hatfield, Colby. 1977. "End of Tour Report of C. R. Hatfield, Jr., Sociologist, Masai Range Development Project (1975–1977)." Prepared for USAID. In author's possession.

Hearn, Julie. 2007. "African NGOs: The New Compradors?" *Development and Change* 38, no. 6: 1095–110.

Hobsbawm, Eric, and Terence Ranger, eds. 1983. *The Invention of Tradition.* Cambridge: Cambridge University Press.

Hodgson, Dorothy L. 1997. "Embodying the Contradictions of Modernity: Gender and Spirit Possession among Maasai in Tanzania." In *Gendered Encounters: Challenging Cultural Boundaries and Social Hierarchies in Africa*, ed. Maria Grosz-Ngate and Omari Kokole. New York: Routledge.

———. 1999a. "Pastoralism, Patriarchy and History: Changing Gender Relations among Maasai in Tanganyika, 1890–1940." *Journal of African History* 40, no. 1: 41–65.

———. 1999b. "Images and Interventions: The 'Problems' of 'Pastoralist' Development." In *The Poor Are Not Us: Poverty and Pastoralism in Eastern Africa,* ed. David Anderson and Vigdis Broch-Due. London: James Currey.

———. 1999c. "'Once Intrepid Warriors': Modernity and the Production of Maasai Masculinities." *Ethnology* 38, no. 2: 121–50.

———. 1999d. "Critical Interventions: Dilemmas of Accountability in Contemporary Ethnographic Research." *Identities: Global Studies in Culture and Power* 6, no. 2–3: 201–24.

———. 1999e. "Women as Children: Culture, Political Economy and Gender Inequality among Kisongo Maasai." *Nomadic Peoples,* n.s., 3, no. 2: 115–30.

———, ed. 2000. *Rethinking Pastoralism in Africa: Gender, Culture and the Myth of the Patriarchal Pastoralist.* Oxford: James Currey.

———. 2001a. *Once Intrepid Warriors: Gender, Ethnicity, and the Cultural Politics of Maasai Development.* Bloomington: Indiana University Press.

———, ed. 2001b. *Gendered Modernities: Ethnographic Perspectives.* New York: Palgrave.

———. 2003. "Women's Rights as Human Rights: Women in Law and Development in Africa (WiLDAF)." Special issue of *Africa Today* on *Women, Language and Law* 49, no. 2: 1–26.

———. 2005. *The Church of Women: Gendered Encounters Between Maasai and Missionaries.* Bloomington: Indiana University Press.

———. 2010. "The Politics of Naming: Ethical Dilemmas, Disciplinary Divides in Anthropology and History." In *Anthrohistory: Unsettling Knowledge and the Question of Discipline,* ed. Chandra Bhimull, David William Cohen, Fernando Coronil, Edward L. Murphy, Monica E. Patterson, and Julie Skurski. Ann Arbor: University of Michigan Press.

———. n.d. "Culture Claims: Being Maasai at the United Nations." Paper presented at conference on "Performing Indigeneity," organized by Laura Graham and Glenn Penny at the University of Iowa.

Hodgson, Dorothy L., and Ethel Brooks, eds. *Activisms.* Special issue, *WSQ* [formerly *Women's Studies Quarterly*] 35, no. 3 and 4.

Hodgson, Dorothy L., and Richard Schroeder. 2002. "Dilemmas of Countermapping Community Resources in Tanzania." *Development and Change* 33, no. 1: 79–100.

Homewood, Katherine, Patti Kristjanson, and Pippa Chenevix Trench, eds. 2009. *Staying Maasai? Livelihoods, Conservation and Development in East African Rangelands.* New York: Springer.

Hope, Ann, and Sally Timmel. 1992. *Training for Transformation.* Zimbabwe: Mambo Press.

Howitt, Richard. 2001. *Rethinking Resource Management: Justice, Sustainability and Indigenous Peoples.* London: Routledge.

Howitt, Richard, John Connell, and Philip Hirsch, eds. 1996. *Resources, Nations and Indigenous Peoples: Case Studies from Australia, Melanesia and Southeast Asia.* New York: Oxford University Press.

Hughes, Lotte. 2005. "Malice in Maasailand: The Historical Roots of Current Political Struggles." *African Affairs* 104, no. 415: 207–24.

Huizer, Gerrit, and Bruce Mannheim, eds. 1979. *The Politics of Anthropology: From Colonialism and Sexism toward a View from Below*. The Hague: Mouton.

Hulme, David, and Michael Edwards, eds. 1997. *NGOs, States and Donors: Too Close for Comfort?* New York: St. Martin's Press.

Hymes, Dell, ed. 1969. *Reinventing Anthropology*. New York: Pantheon.

Igoe, Jim. 2000. "Ethnicity, Civil Society, and the Tanzanian Pastoral NGO Movement: The Continuities and Discontinuities of Liberalized Development." PhD thesis, Department of Anthropology, Boston University.

———. 2003. "Scaling Up Civil Society: Donor Money, NGOs and the Pastoralist Land Rights Movement in Tanzania." *Development and Change* 34, no. 5: 863–85.

———. 2004. *Conservation and Globalization: A Study of National Parks and Indigenous Communities from East Africa to South Dakota*. Belmont, Calif.: Thomson Wadsworth.

———. 2005. "Power and Force in Tanzanian Civil Society: The Story of Barabaig NGOs in the Hanang Community Development Project." In *Between a Rock and a Hard Place: African NGOs, Donors and the State*, ed. Jim Igoe and Tim Kelsall. Durham, N.C.: Carolina Academic Press.

———. 2006. "Becoming Indigenous Peoples: Difference, Inequality, and the Globalization of East African Identity Politics." *African Affairs* 105, no. 420: 399–420.

Igoe, Jim, and Tim Kelsall, eds. 2005. *Between a Rock and a Hard Place: African NGOs, Donors and the State*. Durham, N.C.: Carolina Academic Press.

Ilaramatak Lolkonerei. 1997. "Mkomazi Saga." *EcoNews Africa* 6: 2, 6.

———. ca. 1999. "Olkonerei Integrated Pastoralist Survival Programme (Ilaramatak Lolkonerei). Mpango wa Pamoja wa Wachungaji Asili Kujinusuru Kimaisha Orkonerei." Black and white brochure.

Indigenous Peoples of Africa Co-ordinating Committee (IPACC). 2006. "IPACC Statement on the UN General Assembly Decision to Postpone the Vote on the UN Declaration on the Rights of Indigenous Peoples." Press release, December 5, 2006.

International Labour Organization. 1957. Indigenous and Tribal Peoples Convention 107.

———. 1989. Indigenous and Tribal Peoples Convention 169.

International Work Group on Indigenous Affairs (IWGIA). 1983. "Tanzania: Wildlife Have More Rights than Maasai: Interview with Lazaro Parkipuny." *IWGIA Newsletter* 35–36: 182–84.

———. 1993. *The Indigenous World 1992*. Copenhagen: IWGIA.

———. 1996. *The Indigenous World 1995–96*. Copenhagen: IWGIA.

———. 1999. *The Permanent Forum for Indigenous Peoples: The Struggle for a New Partnership*. IWGIA Document 91. Copenhagen: IWGIA.

———. 2006. "IWGIA Structure and Plans 2006–2008." http://www.iwgia.org.

Inyuat e Maa. 1991a. "First Maasai Conference on Culture and Development. Preliminary Report of a Conference (twice cancelled)." Photocopy in author's possession.

———. 1991b. "First Maasai Conference on Culture and Development. Report of a Conference. Arusha, Tanzania." December 1–5, 1991. Photocopy in author's possession.

———. 1991c. "The Constitution and Rules of Inyuat e Maa (Maa Pastoralists Development Organization)." Photocopy in author's possession.

———. 1994a. "The Second Maa Conference on Culture and Development: Environment and Sustainable Pastoral Development." May 30–June 3, 1994. Photocopy in author's possession.

———. 1994b. "Report of the Interim Executive Secretary presented to the Second General Conference of Inyuat e Maa from 30th May to 3rd June, 1994 at New Arusha Hotel, Arusha." Photocopy in author's possession.

———. 1996a. "Maa Pastoralists and Sustainable Development. A Medium-Term Strategy and Plan, 1996–2000." March 1996. Maa-PDO Secretariat. Photocopy in author's possession.

———. 1996b. "First Maa Women's Conference on Culture and Development. The Setting of the Maa Women of Tanzania. Report of a Conference. Arusha, Tanzania. 6–8th February, 1996." Photocopy in author's possession.

———. 1997. "Maa Pastoralists and Sustainable Development: A Revised Programming Strategy." July 1997. Photocopy in author's possession.

———. 1998. "Assessment of Inyuat e Maa." Photocopy in author's possession.

———. 1999a. "Maasai Advancement Association (Inyuat e Maa) Constitution." Photocopy in author's possession.

———. 1999b. "Workshop Report. Maa Strategic Plan. Background Information. Arusha Workshop. 19–21 July 1999." Photocopy in author's possession.

———. 1999c. "Indicative Strategic Plan for 'MAA' (Maasai Advancement Association). Draft July 28th 1999." Photocopy in author's possession.

———. 2000. "Draft Memorandum of Understanding between the African Wildlife Foundation and Maasai Pastoralists Association (Inyuat e Maa). Regarding Collaboration on Conservation, Eco tourism and Community Development." Photocopy in author's possession.

Jackson, Jean E. 1989. "Is There a Way to Talk about Making Culture without Making Enemies?" *Dialectical Anthropology* 14, no. 2: 127–44.

———. 1991. "Being and Becoming an Indian in Vaupés." In *Nation-States and Indians in Latin America,* ed. Greg Urban and Joel Sherzer. Austin: University of Texas Press.

———. 1995. "Culture, Genuine and Spurious: The Politics of Indianness in the Vaupes, Columbia." *American Ethnologist* 22, no. 1: 3–27.

———. 1999. "The Politics of Ethnographic Practice in the Colombian Vaupés." *Identities* 6, no. 2–3: 281–317.

Jackson, Jean E., and Kay B. Warren. 2005. "Indigenous Movements in Latin America, 1992–2004: Controversies, Ironies, New Directions." *Annual Review of Anthropology* 34: 549–73.

Jennings, Michael. 2008. *Surrogates of the State: NGOs, Development, and Ujamaa in Tanzania*. Bloomfield, Conn.: Kumarian Press.

Johnston, Barbara Rose, ed. 1997. *Life and Death Matters: Human Rights and the Environment at the End of the Millennium*. Walnut Creek, Calif.: Altamira Press.

Kaiza, Felix. 1992. "Can't the Barbaig Recover?" *Express*, 19–25 Nov., 8.

Keck, Margaret E., and Kathryn Sikkink, eds. 1998. *Activists beyond Borders: Advocacy Networks in International Politics*. Ithaca, N.Y.: Cornell University Press.

Kingsbury, Benedict. 1998. "'Indigenous Peoples' in International Law: A Constructivist Approach to the Asian Controversy." *American Journal of International Law* 92, no. 3: 414–57.

Kipuri, Naomi. 2000. "Report on the Seminar on 'Multiculturalism in Africa: Peaceful and constructive group accommodation in situations involving minorities and indigenous peoples' held in Arusha, United Republic of Tanzania 13–15 May 2000." United Nations E/CN.4/Sub.2/AC.5/2000/WP.3.

———. 2001. "Seeking Space in Postcolonial Politics: The Case of Indigenous Peoples in East Africa." In *Challenging Politics: Indigenous Peoples' Experiences with Political Parties and Elections*, ed. Kathrin Wessendorf. IWGIA Document 104. Copenhagen: IWGIA.

Kipuri, Naomi, Benedict ole Nangoro, Mary Vertucci, John ole Kuluo, and James Mollel. 1997. "Pastoralists' Perspectives on Development." http://www.cordstz.org/images/Pardep%20Report%201998%20b.pdf (accessed October 10, 2007).

Knutsson, Karl Eric. 1971. *Report from Eritrea*. IWGIA Document 2. Copenhagen: IWGIA.

Korongoro Integrated People Oriented to Conservation (KIPOC). 1990. The Constitution. Document no. 1. Photocopy, Tanzania.

———. 1991. The Foundational Program: Background, Profile of Activities and Budget. Principal Document no.2. Photocopy, Tanzania.

Kratz, Corinne A., and Donna Pido. 2000. "Gender, Ethnicity and Social Aesthetics in Maasai and Okiek Beadwork." In *Rethinking Pastoralism in Africa: Gender, Culture and the Myth of the Patriarchal Pastoralist*, ed. Dorothy L. Hodgson. Oxford: James Currey.

Kuper, Adam. 2003. "The Return of the Native." *Current Anthropology* 44, no. 3: 389–402.

Lane, Charles. R. 1996. *Pastures Lost: Barabaig Economy, Resource Tenure, and the Alienation of Their Land in Tanzania*. Nairobi: Initiatives Publishers.

Li, Tania Murray. 2000. "Articulating Indigenous Identity in Indonesia: Resource Politics and the Tribal Slot." *Comparative Studies in Society and History* 42, no. 1: 149–79.

————. 2001a. "Masyarakat Adat, Difference and the Limits of Recognition in Indonesia's Forest Zone." *Modern Asia Studies* 35, no. 3: 645–76.

————. 2001b. "Relational Histories and the Production of Difference on Sulawesi's Upland Frontier." *Journal of Asian Studies* 60, no. 1: 41–66.

————. 2002. "Ethnic Cleansing, Recursive Knowledge, and the Dilemmas of Sedentarism." *International Social Science Journal* 173: 361–71.

————. 2007. *The Will to Improve: Governmentality, Development, and the Practice of Politics.* Durham, N.C.: Duke University Press.

Lindsay, Lisa A., and Stephan F. Miescher, eds. 2003. *Men and Masculinities in Modern Africa.* Portsmouth, N.H.: Heinemann.

Lister, Sarah. 2004. "The Future of International NGOs: New Challenges in a Changing World Order." Paper presented at the British Overseas NGOs for Development (BOND) Futures Programme, London.

Livestock Policy Task Force. 2005. "Summary Comments and Amendments to the Final Draft of the National Livestock Policy." A submission to the Minister for Livestock and Water Development, September 26, 2005. PowerPoint presentation.

López-Reyes, Ramón. 1995. "The Establishment of a United Nations Permanent Forum of Indigenous Peoples and Autonomous Assembly of Indigenous Peoples." *Indigenous Affairs* 2: 52–56.

Maasai Environmental Resource Coalition (MERC). 2002. *The Killing Fields of Loliondo: The Hunting Operations of the Ortello Business Company and Their Impact on Maasai Rights, Wildlife, and the Environment.* Washington, D.C.: MERC.

Maasai Women Development Organization (MWEDO). 2005. "Five Year Strategic Plan, 2005–2009." Copy in author's possession.

————. 2006. "Baseline Survey on Pastoralists Education in 3 Districts of Monduli, Kiteto and Simanjiro." Prepared by FAIDA BDS Co. Ltd. Photocopy in author's possession.

MacCannell, Dean. 1976. *The Tourist: A New View of the Leisure Class.* New York: Schocken Books.

Madsen, Andrew. 2000. *The Hadzabe of Tanzania: Land and Human Rights for a Hunter-Gatherer Community.* IWGIA Document 98. Copenhagen: IWGIA.

Maganga, Faustin, Rie Odgaard, and Espen Sjaastad. 2008. "Contested Identities and Resource Conflicts in Morogoro Region, Tanzania: Who Is Indigenous?" In *Conflicts over Land and Water in Africa,* ed. Bill Derman, Rie Odgaard, and Espen Sjaastad. Lansing: Michigan State University Press.

Maiguashca, Bice. 1994. "The Transnational Indigenous Movement in a Changing World Order." In *Global Transformation: Challenges to the State System,* ed. Yoshikazu Sakamoto. Tokyo: UN University Press.

Mamdani, Mahmood. 1996. *Citizen and Subject: Contemporary Africa and the Legacy of Late Colonialism.* Princeton, N.J.: Princeton University Press.

————. ed. 2000. *Beyond Rights Talk and Culture Talk.* New York: St. Martin's.

Mato, Daniel. 1996. "On the Theory, Epistemology, and Politics of the Social Construction of 'Cultural Identities' in the Age of Globalization: Introductory Remarks to Ongoing Debates." *Identities* 3, no. 1–2: 61–72.

May, Ann. 2002. "Unexpected Migrations: Urban Labor Migration of Rural Youth and Maasai Pastoralists in Tanzania." PhD thesis, Department of Anthropology, University of Colorado.

May, Ann, and Frances Ndipapa Ole Ikayo. 2007. "Wearing *Ilkarash:* Narratives of Image, Identity and Change among Maasai Labour Migrants in Tanzania." *Development and Change* 38, no. 2: 275–98.

May, Ann, and J. Terrence McCabe. 2004. "City Work in a Time of AIDS: Maasai Labor Migration in Tanzania." *Africa Today* 51, no. 2: 3–32.

Maybury-Lewis, David. 2002. *Indigenous Peoples, Ethnic Groups and the State.* Boston: Allyn and Bacon.

Mbembe, Achille. 1992a. "Provisional Notes on the Postcolony." *Africa* 62, no. 1: 3–37.

———. 1992b. "The Banality of Power and the Aesthetics of Vulgarity." *Public Culture* 4, no. 2: 1–30.

———. 2001. *On the Postcolony.* Berkeley: University of California Press.

Mbilinyi, Marjorie, and Timothy S. Nyoni. 1999. "The Crisis of Rural Food Security: The Case of Pastoralists in Ngorongoro District." Rural Food Security and Development Project, Institute of Development Studies, University of Dar es Salaam. Photocopy in author's possession.

McAdam, Doug, John D. McCarthy, and Mayer N. Zald, eds. 1996. *Comparative Perspectives on Social Movements.* Cambridge: Cambridge University Press.

McCabe, J. Terrence. 2003. "Sustainability and Livelihood Diversification among the Maasai of Northern Tanzania." *Human Organization* 62, no. 2: 100–111.

———. 2004. *Cattle Bring Us to Our Enemies: Turkana Ecology, Politics and Raiding in a Disequilibrium System.* Ann Arbor: University of Michigan Press.

Meitanga, Dismas P. 2000. "Comments on Your [VETAID Tz] Position Paper." Written on behalf of Community Resource Team, Loliondo. Paper distributed to workshop on "The Future of Pastoralist NGOs in Tanzania," 5 June.

Mercer, Claire. 1999. "Reconceptualizing State-Society Relations in Tanzania: Are NGOs 'Making a Difference'?" *Area* 31, no. 30: 247–58.

Merlan, Francesca. 2005. "Indigenous Movements in Australia." *Annual Review of Anthropology* 34: 473–94.

Morindat, Alais ole. 2000. "Mafanikio na Matatizo ya Mashirika ya Hiara ya Maendeleo (NGOS na CBOs) za Wafugaji Tanzania (Achievements and problems of pastoralist NGOs and CBOs in Tanzania)." Paper presented to workshop on "The Future of Pastoralist NGOs in Tanzania," 5 June.

Morindat, Alais, Eamon Brehony, and Alfred Sakafu. 2003. "Study of Pastoralist-Farmer Conflicts in Kilosa District." Copy in author's possession.

Muburi-Muita, Z. D. 2007. "Talking Notes for H. E. Muburi-Muita on the Occasion of the Interactive Dialogue on the Theme: 'Territories, Lands and

Natural Resources.'" Statement to the 2007 UN Permanent Forum. http://
www.docip.org/gsdl/collect/cendocdo/index/assoc/HASH680f/bb530589.dir/
PF07muburi-muita056.pdf (accessed April 24, 2008).

Muehlebach, Andrea. 2001. "'Making Place' at the United Nations: Indigenous
Cultural Politics at the U.N. Working Group on Indigenous Populations."
Cultural Anthropology 16, no. 3: 415–48.

———. 2003. "What Self in Self-Determination? Notes from the Frontiers of
Transnational Indigenous Activism." *Identities* 10, no. 2: 241–68.

Mung'ong'o, Claude, and Davis Mwamfupe. 2003. "Poverty and Changing Livelihoods of Migrant Maasai Pastoralists in Morogoro and Kilosa Districts, Tanzania." REPOA Research Report 03.5. Dar es Salaam: Mkuki na Nyota Publishers.

Muratorio, Blanca. 1998. "Indigenous Women's Identities and the Politics of
Cultural Reproduction in the Ecuadorian Amazon." *American Anthropologist*
100, no. 2: 409–20.

Murumbi, Daniel. 1994. "The Concept of Indigenous." *Indigenous Affairs* 1: 52–57.

Mvungi, Asraj. 2009. Photo. "A Maasai herdsman from Loliondo, Ngorongoro
District weeps after his boma was burnt following an operation to evict
pastoralists from a hunting block owned by the Ortello Business Company."
IPP Media, July 9, 2009. http://www.ippmedia.com/frontend/index.php
(accessed July 9, 2009).

Mwarabu, Adam Kuleit ole. 2000. "Indications of Suggested Amendments and
Additions to the Question Posed." Written on behalf of Imusot e Purka. Paper
distributed to workshop on "The Future of Pastoralist NGOs in Tanzania," 5
June.

Mwau, Adelina Ndeto, and Jan Reynders. 1996. "In Search of Alternatives:
Evaluation of Ilaramatak Lorkonerei Orkonerei Integrated Pastoralist Survival
Programme." Contracted by HIVOS. Photocopy in possession of author.

Nangoro, Benedict ole. 1995. "Branding the Land: Maasai Responses to Pastoral
Land Tenure Insecurity and Social Change." MPhil diss., Institute of Development Studies, University of Sussex.

———. 1999. "The Current Situation in Tanzania Maasailand." *Indigenous Affairs*
2/1999: 25–29.

———. 2003. "Rights to Land: The Case of the Maasai of Tanzania." *Indigenous
Affairs* 4/2003: 38–46.

Nangoro, Benedict ole, and Chris Daborn. 2000. "Initiatives Required to
Co-Ordinate 'The Future Development of Pastoralism in Tanzania—The Way
Forward': A Position Paper Setting the Agenda for a Pastoralist Workshop."
Paper distributed to workshop on "The Future of Pastoralist NGOs in
Tanzania," 5 June.

Ndagala, Daniel. 1982. "Operation Imparnati: The Sedentarization of Pastoral
Maasai in Tanzania." *Nomadic Peoples* 10: 28–39.

———. 1990. "Territory, Pastoralists, and Livestock: Resource Control among the
Kisongo Maasai." PhD diss., Uppsala University.

Ndaskoi, Navaya ole. 2009a. "Are Animals More Important than Human Beings?"
    New African 483: 56–60.
————. 2009b. "Tanzania Tourist Board Honours Thomson Safaris with the 2009
    Tanzania Conservation Award." http://www.safarilands.org/index.php/news/
    more/tanzania_tourist_board_honours_thomson_safaris_with_the_2009
    _tanzania_conse/ (accessed July 14, 2009).
Nelson, Fred, Benjamin Gardner, Jim Igoe, and Andrew Williams. 2009.
    "Community-Based Conservation and Maasai Livelihoods in Tanzania." In
    *Staying Maasai? Livelihoods, Conservation and Development in East African
    Rangelands,* ed. Katherine Homewood, Patti Kristjanson, and Pippa Chenevix
    Trench. New York: Springer.
Neumann, Roderick P. 1995. "Local Challenges to Global Agendas: Conservation,
    Economic Liberalization and the Pastoralists' Rights Movement in Tanzania."
    Antipode 27, no. 4: 363–82.
Ngulay, Saruni ole. 1993a. "Inyuat e Maa Pastoralists Development Organisation: Aims
    and Possibilities." Paper presented to the IWGIA-CDR Conference on the
    "Question of Indigenous Peoples of Africa," held at Greve, Denmark, 1–3 June 1993.
————. 1993b. "Inyuat e Maa Pastoralists Development Organisation: Aims and
    Possibilities." In *"Never Drink from the Same Cup": Proceedings of the Conference
    on Indigenous Peoples in Africa.* IWGIA Document 74. Copenhagen: IWGIA
    and Centre for Development Research.
————. 1994. "New Partners in Development Cooperation." In *Voices of the Earth:
    Indigenous Peoples, New Partners, and the Right to Self-Determination in Practice,*
    ed. Leo van der Vlist. Utrecht: International Books and Netherlands Centre
    for Indigenous Peoples.
————. 1995. "I Know, I Know; Let Me Do It: Social Development and Maasai
    Perspective." In *Partnership for Social Development: A Casebook.* Franklin, W.
    Va.: Future Generations in cooperation with the Department of International
    Health, Johns Hopkins University. http://www.future.org/downloads/
    casebook.pdf (accessed 16 June 2008).
————. 1996. "Let Me Be Me: Pastoralists' Struggle against Resource Scarcity,
    Displacement and Marginalisation in Tanzania." Paper presented as part of
    the "Voices from the Commons" panel at the Sixth Annual Conference of the
    International Association for the Study of Common Property, Berkeley
    California, 5–8 June 1996. (Note that this was the paper title in the program;
    an online abstract has a different title: "Africa's Two Great Evils: 'Soil Erosion
    and Soul Erosion' Pressure on Customary Institutions for Common Property
    Resources Management; East Africa Case Study in Reference to the Maasai."
    http://www.indiana.edu/~iascp/abstracts/431.html (accessed 16 June 2008).
Niezen, Ronald. 2003. *The Origins of Indigenism: Human Rights and the Politics of
    Identity.* Berkeley: University of California Press.
————. 2004. *A World beyond Difference: Cultural Identity in the Age of Globaliza-
    tion.* Oxford: Blackwell.

———. 2009. *The Rediscovered Self: Indigenous Identity and Cultural Justice.* Montreal: McGill-Queen's University Press.

Odhiambo, Michael Ochieng. 2006. "Cause for Celebration or Celebration of a Cause: Pastoralism and Poverty Reduction Strategies in East Africa." *Indigenous Affairs* 1/06: 24–29.

Organization for Indigenous Peoples of Africa (OIPA). 2003. "African Indigenous Peoples Preparatory Meeting to the World Parks Congress, 2003." Workshop report.

Orlove, Benjamin S., and Stephen B. Brush. 1996. "Anthropology and the Conservation of Biodiversity." *Annual Review of Anthropology* 25: 329–52.

Pallotti, Arrigo. 2008. "Tanzania: Decentralising Power or Spreading Poverty?" *Review of African Political Economy* 116: 221–35.

Parkipuny, Moringe ole. 1975. "Maasai Predicament beyond Pastoralism: A Case Study in the Socio-Economic Transformation of Pastoralism." MA thesis, Development Studies, University of Dar es Salaam.

———. 1979. "Some Crucial Aspects of the Maasai Predicament." In *African Socialism in Practice: The Tanzanian Experience,* ed. Andrew Coulson. Nottingham: Spokesman.

———. 1989. "The Human Rights Situation of Indigenous People in Africa." http://www.cwis.org/fwj/22/hra.htm (accessed October 19, 2001). His comments are also quoted in Muehlebach 2001.

Pastoral Caucus. 1995. "Proceedings of the Pastoral Caucus Workshop on the National Land Policy and National Land Tenure Systems." Arusha, Tanzania, 8–9 March 1995. Photocopy in author's possession.

Pastoral Indigenous Non-Governmental Organizations (PINGOs) Forum. 1999. "Indigenous Self-Organisation in Tanzania: The Case of PINGOs Forum." *Indigenous Affairs* 2: 34–37.

———. 2003a. "Report on the Roundtable Discussion on Pastoralism." Arusha, Tanzania, at Impala Hotel, July 28–29, 2003.

———. 2003b. "A Report on the Consultative Workshop on Rangelands Livelihoods and Vulnerability." Peacock Hotel, Dar es Salaam, Tanzania, December 15–16, 2003.

———. 2004. "Inclusion of Rangelands Livelihoods in National Poverty Eradication/Alleviation Strategies." A Consultative Workshop on Rangeland Livelihoods and the Poverty Reduction Strategy (PRS) Review, 25–26 March 2004, Golden Rose Hotel, Arusha.

———. 2006. "Proceedings of the Joint Pastoralist Stakeholders' Workshop on the Policy and Legal Framework Environment for Pastoralism in Tanzania." April 2006.

Posey, Darrell. 1990. "Intellectual Property Rights and Just Compensation for Indigenous Knowledge." *Anthropology Today* 6, no. 4: 13–16.

Povinelli, Elizabeth. 1993. *Labor's Lot: The Power, History and Culture of Aboriginal Action.* Chicago: University of Chicago Press.

————. 2002. *The Cunning of Recognition: Indigenous Alterities and the Making of Australian Multiculturalism*. Durham, N.C.: Duke University Press.

Pratt, Beth Anne. 2003. "Childhood, Space and Children 'Out of Place': Versions of Maasai Childhood in Monduli Juu, Tanzania." PhD thesis, Department of Anthropology, Boston University.

Pritchard, Sarah. 1998. "Working Group on Indigenous Populations: Mandate, Standard-Setting Activities and Future Perspectives." In *Indigenous Peoples, The United Nations and Human Rights*. London: Zed Press.

Ramos, Alcida Rita. 1998. *Indigenism: Ethnic Politics in Brazil. Madison:* University of Wisconsin Press.

Research on Poverty Alleviation (REPOA). 2007. *Tanzanian Non-Governmental Organisations—Their Perceptions of Their Relationships with the Government of Tanzania and Donors, and Their Role in Poverty Reduction*. Special Paper No. 07.21. Dar es Salaam: Mkuki na Nyota Publishers.

Richard, William. 2000. "Views." Written on behalf of Inyuat e Maa. Paper distributed to workshop on "The Future of Pastoralist NGOs in Tanzania," 5 June.

Robbins, Bruce. 1998. "Introduction Part I: Actually Existing Cosmopolitanism." In *Cosmopolitics: Thinking and Feeling beyond the Nation*, ed. Pheng Cheah and Bruce Robbins. Minneapolis: University of Minnesota Press.

Rogers, Mark. 1996. "Beyond Authenticity: Conservation, Tourism, and the Politics of Representation in the Ecuadorian Amazon." *Identities* 3, no. 1–2: 73–125.

Rose, Mandy. 2000. "When Aborigines Met the Maasai." BBC News, September 6, 2000. http://news6.thdo.bbc.co.uk/hi/English/world/Africa/newsid_911000/911809.stm (accessed September 12, 2001).

Roy, Arundhati. 2004. *Public Power in the Age of Empire*. New York: Seven Stories Press.

Sachedina, Hassan. 2006. "Conservation, Land Rights and Livelihoods in the Tarangire Ecosystem of Tanzania." Paper presented to "Pastoralism and Poverty Reduction in East Africa: A Policy Research Conference." http://www.ilri.org/Link/Publications/Publications/Theme%201/Pastoral%20conference/Papers/SachedinaJune16.pdf (accessed 10 June 2008).

————. 2008. "Wildlife Is Our Oil: Conservation, Livelihoods and NGOs in the Tarangire Ecosystem, Tanzania." DPhil thesis, School of Geography and the Environment, University of Oxford.

Sachedina, Hassan, and Piipa Chenevix Trench. 2009. "Cattle and Crops, Tourism and Tanzanite: Poverty, Land-Use Change and Conservation in Simanjiro District, Tanzania." In *Staying Maasai? Livelihoods, Conservation and Development in East African Rangelands*, ed. Katherine Homewood, Patti Kristjanson, and Pippa Chenevix Trench. New York: Springer.

Sangale, Loserian. 2000a. "Report of the Pastoralists NGOs Workshop." TCDC in Arusha, June 5–8.

———. 2000b. "Key Issues and Questions Facing the Development of Pastoralism in Tanzania." Paper presented to workshop on "The Future of Pastoralist NGOs in Tanzania," 5 June.

Saning'o, Martin, and Ann Heidenreich. 1996. "Rare Land Rights Victory Brings New Hope to the Maasai." *EcoNews Africa* 5, no. 7: 1–2.

Sansom, Mike. 2000. "VetAid-Tz's Initiative to Establish a Tanzanian Pastoralist Forum-African Initiatives Response." Paper distributed to workshop on "The Future of Pastoralist NGOs in Tanzania," 5 June.

Saugestad, Sidsel. 2001. *The Inconvenient Indigenous: Remote Area Development in Botswana, Donor Assistance, and the First People of the Kalahari.* Uppsala: Nordic Africa Institute.

Schein, Louisa. 2000. *Minority Rules: The Miao and the Feminine in China's Cultural Politics.* Durham, N.C.: Duke University Press.

Schneider, Leander. 2006. "The Maasai's New Clothes: A Developmentalist Modernity and Its Exclusions." *Africa Today* 53, no. 1: 100–131.

Schroeder, Richard. 1999. *Shady Practices: Agroforestry and Gender Politics in the Gambia.* Berkeley: University of California Press.

Scott, James C. 1985. *Weapons of the Weak: Everyday Forms of Peasant Resistance.* New Haven, Conn.: Yale University Press.

Shivji, Issa G. 2006. *Let the People Speak: Tanzania Down the Road to Neo-Liberalism.* Dakar, Senegal: CODESRIA.

Sikar, Ndinini Kimesera, and Dorothy L. Hodgson. 2006. "In the Shadows of the MDGs: The Situation of Pastoralist Women and Children in Tanzania." *Indigenous Affairs* 1/06: 30–37.

Simanjiro District Report. 2005. Photocopy of sections in author's possession.

Simpson, Andrew, ed. 2008. *Language and National Identity in Africa.* New York: Oxford University Press.

Smith, Linda Tuhiwai. 1999. *Decolonizing Methodologies: Research and Indigenous Peoples.* London: Zed Books.

Smith, Michael Peter. 1994. "Can You Imagine? Transnational Migration and the Globalization of Grassroots Politics." *Social Text* 39 (Summer): 15–33.

Solway, Jacqueline S. 2002. "Navigating the 'Neutral' State: 'Minority' Rights in Botswana." *Journal of Southern African Studies* 28, no. 4: 711–29.

Speed, Shannon, R. Aida Hernández Castillo, and Lynn M. Stephen, eds. 2006. *Dissident Women: Gender and Cultural Politics in Chiapas.* Austin: University of Texas Press.

Spencer, Paul. 1988. *The Maasai of Matapato: A Study of Rituals of Rebellion.* Bloomington: Indiana University Press.

Stephen, Lynn, ed. 1997. *Women and Social Movements in Latin America: Power from Below.* Austin: University of Texas.

———. 2005. *Zapotec Women: Gender, Class and Ethnicity in Globalized Oaxaca.* 2nd ed. Durham, N.C.: Duke University Press.

Sturm, Circe. 1999. "Comment on Les Field, Complicities and Collaborations." *Current Anthropology* 40, no. 2: 205–207.

Sutton, John. 1993. "Becoming Maasailand." In *Being Maasai*, ed. Thomas Spear and Richard Waller. London: James Currey.

Swepston, Lee. 1989. "Indigenous and Tribal Peoples and International Law: Recent Developments." *Current Anthropology* 30, no. 2: 259–64.

Sylvain, Renée. 2002. "'Land, Water and Truth': San Identity and Global Indigenism." *American Anthropologist* 104, no. 4: 1074–85.

Talle, Aud. 1999. "Pastoralists at the Border: Maasai Poverty and the Development Discourse in Tanzania." In *The Poor Are Not Us: Poverty and Pastoralism*, ed. David M. Anderson and Vigdis Broch-Due. Oxford: James Currey.

Tanzania Pastoralists and Hunter-Gatherers Organization (TAPHGO). 2004a. "Livestock Production System in Botswana—The So-Called 'Botswana Model': Privatizing the Commons, a Trade or Trap? Report of a Study Tour to Botswana." January 18–28, 2004.

———. 2004b. "Report of the Study Tour to Kenya." February 1–7, 2004.

———. 2004c. "Land Tenure and Commercialization of Livestock—the Botswana and Kenya Models, Could They Be Replicated in Tanzania?" Workshop held in Arusha, February 23–24, 2004.

———. 2005. "The Making of the New Livestock Policy in Tanzania: Opportunities and Constraints for Pastoralists. The Proceedings of a Multi-Stakeholder Workshop Organized by Tanzania Pastoralists and Hunter-Gatherer Organization (TAPHGO)." Golden Rose Hotel, Arusha, August 1–2, 2005.

———. 2006. "The Livestock Trade System in Tanzania." A report for TAPHGO by John Letai and Moses ole Neselle.

Tanzania Population and Housing Census. 2002. http://www.tanzania.go.tz/census (accessed January 19, 2006).

Taylor, Charles. 1994. "The Politics of Recognition." In *Multiculturalism: Examining the Politics of Recognition*, ed. Amy Gutman. Princeton, N.J.: Princeton University Press.

Taylor, Geoff, and Lars Johansson. 1996. "Our Voices, Our Words, and Our Pictures: Plans, Truths and Videotapes from Ngorongoro Conservation Area." Trans. Francis ole Ikayo. *Forest, Trees and People Newsletter* 30 (March 1996). http://www.fao.org/docrep/x0271e/x0271e.06.htm (accessed July 11, 2008).

Tenga, Ringo, Amon Matee, Ntengua Mdoe, Raymond Mnenwa, Sengondo Mvungi, and Martin Walsh. 2008. "A Study on Options for Pastoralists to Secure Their Livelihoods in Tanzania: Current Policy, Legal and Economic Issues." Vol. 1: "Main Report." http://www.tnrf.org (accessed July 21, 2008).

Trench, Pippa Chenevix, Steven Kiruswa, Fred Nelson, and Katherine Homewood. 2009. "Still 'People of the Cattle'? Livelihoods, Diversification and Community Conservation in Longido District." In *Staying Maasai? Livelihoods, Conservation and Development in East African Rangelands*, ed. Katherine Homewood, Patti Kristjanson, and Pippa Chenevix Trench. New York: Springer.

Tsosie, Rebecca. 1997. "Indigenous People's Claims to Cultural Property: A Legal Perspective." *Museum Anthropology* 21, no. 3: 5–11.

Turner, Terence. 1991. "Representing, Resisting, Rethinking: Historical Transformations of Kayapo Culture and Anthropological Consciousness." In *Colonial Situations: Essays on the Contextualization of Ethnographic Knowledge*, ed. George Stocking. Madison: University of Wisconsin Press.

———. 1999. "The Role of Indigenous Peoples in the Environmental Crisis: The Example of the Kayapo of the Brazilian Amazon." *Perspectives in Biology and Medicine* 36, no. 3: 526–45.

United Nations. 2007. Declaration on the Rights of Indigenous Peoples. United Nations General Assembly Resolution 61/295. September 13, 2007.

United Nations High Commissioner for Human Rights. 2002. "International Decade of the World's Indigenous People, 1995–2004: List of Organizations." Photocopy in author's possession.

United Republic of Tanzania (URT). Ca. 1997. *The Tanzania Development Vision 2025.* http://www.tanzania.go.tz/vision.htm.

———. 2005a. National Livestock Policy (Final Draft). Ministry of Water and Livestock Development (April 2005). Dar es Salaam: Ministry of Water and Livestock Development.

———. 2005b. National Strategy for Growth and Reduction of Poverty (NSGRP). Dar es Salaam: Vice President's Office.

———. 2005c. *Poverty and Human Development Report.* Dar es Salaam: Mkuki na Nyota Publishers.

———. 2006a. National Livestock Policy. Ministry of Livestock (December 2006).

———. 2006b. *Millenium Development Goals, United Republic of Tanzania.* Progress Report 2006. Ministry of Planning, Economy and Empowerment. http://www.tz.undp.org/docs/MDGprogressreport.pdf (accessed February 14, 2007).

Van Achterberg, Angeline, ed. 1998. *Out of the Shadows: The First African Indigenous Women's Conference.* Amsterdam: Netherlands Centre for Indigenous Peoples.

Van der Fliert, Lydia, ed. 1994. *Indigenous Peoples and International Organisations.* Nottingham: Spokesman.

Van der Vlist, Leo, ed. 1994. *Voices of the Earth: Indigenous Peoples, New Partners, and the Right to Self-Determination in Practice.* Utrecht: International Books and Netherlands Centre for Indigenous Peoples.

Veber, Hanne, Jens Dahl, Fiona Wilson, and Espen Wæhle, eds. 1993. *"Never Drink from the Same Cup": Proceedings of the Conference of Indigenous Peoples in Africa (Tune, Denmark, 1993).* IWGIA Document 74. Copenhagen: IWGIA and Centre for Development Research.

Vinding, Diane, ed. 1998. *Indigenous Women: The Right to a Voice.* IWGIA Document 88. Copenhagen: IWGIA.

Waller, Richard D. 1999. "Pastoral Poverty in Historical Perspective." In *The Poor Are Not Us: Poverty and Pastoralism*, ed. David M. Anderson and Vigdis Broch-Due. Oxford: James Currey.

Warren, Kay. B. 1998. *Indigenous Movements and Their Critics: Pan-Maya Activism in Guatemala*. Princeton, N.J.: Princeton University Press.

Warren, Kay, and Jean E. Jackson, eds. 2002. *Indigenous Movements, Self-Representation, and the State in Latin America*. Austin: University of Texas Press.

Watts, Michael. 2000. "Contested Communities, Malignant Markets, and Gilded Governance: Justice, Resource Extraction and Conservation in the Tropics." In *People, Plants and Justice: The Politics of Nature Conservation*, ed. Charles Zerner. New York: Columbia University Press.

Wæhle, Espen. 1990. "Africa and the Concept of Indigenous Peoples." *IWGIA Yearbook* 1990: 144–48.

Weiss, Brad. 2003. *Sacred Trees, Bitter Harvests: Globalizing Coffee in Northwest Tanzania*. Portsmouth, N.H.: Heinemann.

Werbner, Richard. 1996. "Introduction: Multiple Identities, Plural Arenas." In *Postcolonial Identities in Africa*, ed. Richard Werbner and Terence Ranger. London: Zed Books.

———. 2002. "Citizenship and the Politics of Recognition in Botswana." In *Minorities in the Millennium: Perspectives from Botswana*, ed. Isaac N. Mazonde. Gaborone: Lightbooks.

Werbner, Richard, and Terence Ranger, eds. 1996. *Postcolonial Identities in Africa*. London: Zed Books.

West, Paige, James Igoe, and Dan Brockington. 2006. "Parks and People: The Social Impact of Protected Areas." *Annual Review of Anthropology* 35: 251–77.

Wilmsen, Edwin N., and Patrick McAllister, eds. 1996. *The Politics of Difference: Ethnic Premises in a World of Power*. Chicago: University of Chicago Press.

Wright, Robin M. 1988. "Anthropological Presuppositions of Indigenous Advocacy." *Annual Review of Anthropology* 17: 365–90.

Yarrow, Thomas. 2008. "Life/History: Personal Narratives of Development amongst NGO Workers and Activists in Ghana." *Africa* 78, no. 3: 334–50.

Zerner, Charles, ed. 2000. *People, Plants and Justice: The Politics of Nature Conservation*. New York: Columbia University Press.

Index

Dorothy L. Hodgson is Professor and Chair of Anthropology at Rutgers University, where she is also affiliated with the Center for African Studies and the Women's and Gender Studies Department. She is author of *Once Intrepid Warriors* (2001) and *The Church of Women* (2005), both with Indiana University Press.

DATE DU

CPSIA information can be obtained at www.ICGtesting.com
Printed in the USA
LVOW050005170912

298998LV00003B/2/P

9 780253 223050